BUSINESS ANALYSIS
TECHNIQUES
72 Essential Tools

D0120587

BCS THE CHARTERED INSTITUTE FOR IT

BCS, The Chartered Institute for IT, (COMAS) promotes wider social and economic progress through the advancement of information technology, science and practice. We bring together industry, academics, practitioners and government to share knowledge, promote new thinking, inform the design of new curricula, shape public policy and inform the public. As the professional membership and accreditation body for IT, we serve over 70,000 members including practitioners, academics and students, in the UK and internationally. A leading IT qualification body, we offer a range of widely recognised professional and end-user qualifications.

Joining BCS
BCS qualifications, products and services are designed with your career plans in mind.

We not only provide essential recognition through professional qualifications but also offer many other useful benefits to our members at every level.

BCS Membership demonstrates your commitment to professional development.

It helps to set you apart from other IT practitioners and provides industry recognition of your skills and experience. Employers and customers increasingly require proof of professional qualifications and competence. Professional membership confirms your competence and integrity and sets an independent standard that people can trust. Professional Membership (MBCS) is the pathway to Chartered IT Professional (CITP) Status.
www.bcs.org/membership

Further Information
BCS The Chartered Institute for IT, First Floor, Block D, North Star House, North Star Avenue, Swindon, SN2 1FA, United Kingdom.
T +44 (0) 1793 417 424
F +44 (0) 1793 417 444
www.bcs.org/contact

BUSINESS ANALYSIS TECHNIQUES
72 Essential Tools for Success

James Cadle, Debra Paul and Paul Turner

Published by British Informatics Society Limited (BISL), a wholly owned subsidiary of BCS The Chartered Institute for IT, First Floor, Block D, North Star House, North Star Avenue, Swindon, SN2 1FA, UK. www.bcs.org

ISBN 978-1-906124-23-6

British Cataloguing in Publication Data.
A CIP catalogue record for this book is available at the British Library.

Typeset by Lapiz Digital Services, Chennai, India.
Printed and bound by CPI Group (UK) Ltd, Croydon, CRO 4YY

CONTENTS

LIST OF FIGURES AND TABLES

AUTHORS

James Cadle has been involved in the field of business systems for over thirty years, first with London Transport, then with Sema Group and most recently with Assist Knowledge Development, of which he is a director. He has conducted methods studies and business improvement projects, and has led teams developing and maintaining corporate IT systems.

James presents training courses in business analysis, consultancy skills and project management to a variety of public- and private-sector clients, as well as contributing to various publications. He is a Chartered Member of BCS and a member of the Association for Project Management.

Debra Paul is the Managing Director of Assist Knowledge Development. Debra has extensive knowledge and experience of business analysis, business process improvement and business change. She was joint editor and author of the bestselling BCS publication, *Business Analysis*.

Debra is a Chartered Fellow of the BCS. She is a regular speaker at business seminars and organisational forums. Debra is a founder member of the BA Management Forum, a group that has been formed to advance the business analysis profession and develop the BA internal consultant role.

Paul Turner is a director of Business & IS Skills and of Assist Knowledge Development. He specialises in the provision of training and consultancy in the areas of business analysis and business change. He is an SFIA (Skills Framework for the Information Age) accredited consultant, and contributed the skills components related to business analysis in the latest release of this competency framework.

Paul has a particular interest in the way the job role of the business analyst changes in an Agile development environment. He is a Fellow of BCS and has worked extensively with a range of organisations to raise the profile of professionalism within the business analysis discipline.

LIST OF ABBREVIATIONS

BA	business analyst
BAM	Business Activity Model
BATNA	Best Alternative to a Negotiated Agreement
BBS	Balanced Business Scorecard
CASE	computer-aided software engineering
CATWOE	customer, actor, transformation, *Weltanschauung* or world view, owner and environment (analysis)
CBA	cost–benefit analysis
CRUD (matrix)	create, read, update and delete (matrix)
CSF	critical success factor
DCF	discounted cash flow
ERM	entity relationship model
HR	human resources
IRR	internal rate of return
IT	information technology
JAD	Joint Application Development (workshop – IBM)
KPI	key performance indicator
MoSCoW	must have, should have, could have, want to have but won't have this time
MOST (analysis)	mission, objectives, strategy and tactics (analysis)
NPV	net present value
PESTLE (analysis)	political, economic, socio-cultural, technological, legal and environmental (or ecological) (analysis)
PIR	post-implementation review

RASCI	responsible, accountable, supportive, consulted and informed (charts)
ROI	return on investment
SARAH (model)	shock, anger, rejection, acceptance and hope (model)
SSADM	Structured Systems Analysis and Design Method
STROBE	STRuctured Observation of the Business Environment
SWOT (analysis)	strengths, weaknesses, opportunities and threats
UML	Unified Modeling Language

ALPHABETICAL LIST OF TECHNIQUES

Names and numbers of techniques in standard type indicate the main name that has been used in the book. Techniques shown in italics and with suffixes on the numbers (for example, *17c*) indicate an alias or variant on the main name.

PREFACE

The idea for this book came from a talk given to the UK Chapter of the International Institute of Business Analysts in July 2007. The subject was 'Business Analysis Techniques', and, rather than just concentrating on one or two techniques, we decided to survey the whole field of them and suggest where each could be used. Between us we brainstormed some 80-odd techniques and then grouped them according to different aspects of the business analyst's role. The talk was well received, and various people said afterwards how useful they'd found it. So we wondered whether there might not be a niche for a book that surveyed the wide range of techniques that can be used in business analysis work and gave advice on where and how each might be employed.

In many ways we believe that a business analyst (BA) is in a similar position to that of other skilled professionals. Take a surgeon, for example, who will have available a wide array of instruments during a procedure. Some of these (a scalpel, for instance) are used all the time; others have very specific uses. Skilled surgeons (i) have all of the instruments at their disposal, (ii) know how to use each, and (iii) know which one to select at each point in the procedure. Also, since each procedure is different, each will require its own specific combination of instruments to be used in a particular order. The business analyst, similarly, needs a full kit of tools and the skills and knowledge to be able to use each when and where it is needed.

This book is designed to complement *Business Analysis*, edited by Debra Paul and Donald Yeates and first published by BCS in 2006. *Business Analysis* is the first book specifically on this field, and provides an overall treatment of its subject, presenting the lifecycle of an assignment and reviewing the methods that can be used to carry it out. The book covers many techniques, but the limited space available did not permit the authors to go into a lot of detail. The present book therefore starts where *Business Analysis* leaves off, and 'drills down' into more detail on the various techniques that BAs may apply in their work. We have decided to adopt the process model presented in Chapter 4 of *Business Analysis* to provide a framework for this book, and we hope this will make it easier for readers to see how the two publications complement and support each other. So our first six chapters are called 'Business strategy and objectives', 'Investigate situation', 'Consider perspectives', 'Analyse needs', 'Evaluate options' and 'Define requirements'. But we've also added a seventh chapter called 'Manage change', so that we can cover techniques such as benefits management and realisation, and some of the organisational and human issues associated with change management, more fully.

Each chapter of the book therefore represents a stage in the business analysis process. We give an introduction to each stage and then divide each into logical sections. Within these sections are the techniques, and, for each technique, we give the following elements:

Name of the technique: Here we've selected the most commonly used name, at least in the UK.

Variants/ Aliases: One problem in business analysis (as in other fields) is that people use different names for the same thing, so we list the most common alternative names for the technique. Where there don't seem to be any common synonyms, we have omitted this.

Description of the technique: This is a detailed, step-by-step description of the technique and the way it is used. Some techniques – that of workshops (number 14) is a good example – have sub-techniques (such as brainstorming, in the case of workshops) within them, and these are also described.

Using the technique: This part provides practical advice based on our experience, including discussions of the pros and cons of each technique, and where it does and does not work best.

At the end of each stage we provide references and further reading. Here we list the books that we have found useful over the years in our practice of business analysis, and suggest where our readers might like to go for more information.

We have placed each technique in what we consider to be the most appropriate chapter, but we do need to make an important point here: **many techniques can be used at various stages for different purposes**. For example, we have put workshops under 'Investigate situation', but, clearly, workshops are equally useful at many other points in a project. Similarly, we have prototyping under 'Define requirements', but this can also be used within a workshop to help 'Investigate situation'.

Of course, no book of this type can ever hope to be completely comprehensive. This one includes descriptions of 72 separate techniques or, taking the variants and aliases into account, 129. We are sure individual readers will be upset that some favourite technique of theirs has been omitted, but all we can say in our defence is that we have tried to be as inclusive as possible. (If you do feel strongly that a particular technique should be included, let us know – there may be a later edition and it could be considered for inclusion there.) We have included most of the techniques that we – with our combined experience of working in this field – have found to be useful, and we hope that you will find them useful too.

We would like to thank our 'other halves' – Meg Brinton, Alan Paul and Annie Turner – for putting up with our seclusion while we wrote the book; and also Matthew Flynn, of the BCS, for keeping our noses to the grindstone in the nicest way!

James Cadle
Debra Paul
Paul Turner
February 2010

1 BUSINESS STRATEGY AND OBJECTIVES

INTRODUCTION

The development of business analysis as a professional discipline has extended the role and responsibilities of the business analyst (BA). Increasingly, BAs are engaged at an early point. They investigate ideas and problems, formulate options for a way forward and produce business cases setting out their conclusions and recommendations. As a result, the responsibility for advising organisations on effective courses of action lies with BAs, and their work precedes that of the project manager.

The early engagement of BAs also places a critical responsibility upon them – the need to ensure that all business changes are in line with the mission, objectives and strategy of the organisation. This business context is the key foundation for understanding and evaluating all ideas, proposals, issues and problems put forward by managers. While few BAs are involved in analysing and developing strategy, it is vital that they know about the strategy of their organisation so that they can conduct their work with a view to supporting the implementation of the strategy and the achievement of the business objectives. Therefore, it could be argued that BAs have responsibility for the following areas:

- identifying the tactical options that will address a given situation and will support the delivery of the business strategy;
- defining the tactics that will enable the organisation to achieve its strategy;
- supporting the implementation and operation of those tactics;
- redefining the tactics after implementation to take account of business changes and to ensure continuing alignment with business objectives.

Project managers are responsible for delivering the content of the selected options, such as new or enhanced information technology (IT) systems, or improved business processes.

Given the increasing emphasis on early-engagement business analysis, and the need for this work to align with the business strategy and objectives, an understanding of strategic analysis techniques is essential for all BAs. This chapter describes a range of techniques for carrying out strategic analysis and definition, plus techniques to monitor ongoing performance.

The following four areas are covered:

- strategy analysis, including external environment and internal capability;
- strategy definition;
- strategy implementation;
- performance measurement.

Strategy analysis – external business environment (Techniques 1–2)

All organisations have to address the changes that have arisen, or can be predicted to arise, within their operating business environment. Such changes occur constantly, and any organisation that fails to identify and respond to them runs the risk of encountering business problems or even the failure of the entire enterprise. Senior management carries out regular monitoring of the business environment in order to identify any influences that may require action.

There are two techniques that are used to examine the business environment within which an organisation is operating: PESTLE analysis and Porter's Five Forces analysis.

The analysis of the external environment should be an ongoing process for senior management, since the factors identified may provide insights into problems for the future or opportunities for new successes. Using the PESTLE and five forces techniques together helps to provide a detailed picture of the situation facing an organisation. Just using one technique may leave gaps in the knowledge and understanding.

Strategy analysis – internal capability (Techniques 3–5)

Analysing the internal capability of an organisation provides insights into its areas of strength and the inherent weaknesses within it. Business commentators often recommend 'sticking to the knitting' when considering business changes. An analysis of internal capability is essential to understanding where the core skills of the organisation lie, so that relevant courses of action can be identified, and any changes be made in the knowledge that they have a good chance of success. There is little point in adopting strategies that are dependent upon areas of resource where strong capability is lacking.

There are three techniques that may be used to examine the internal capability of an organisation: MOST Analysis, Resource Audit and the Boston Box.

Strategy definition (Techniques 6–7)

During strategy definition, the results of the external and internal environmental analyses are summarised and consolidated in order to examine the situation facing the organisation and identify possible courses of action. When defining the business strategy, the factors outside the management's control are examined within the context of the organisation and its resources.

There are two techniques that may be used to define organisational strategy: SWOT analysis and Ansoff's matrix.

Strategy implementation (Techniques 8–9)

When the strategy has been defined, it is important to consider the range of issues associated with implementing it. One of the key problems here is recognising the range of areas that need to be coordinated if the business changes are to be implemented successfully.

The approaches that support the implementation of strategy are McKinsey's 7-S model and the four-view model.

Performance measurement (Techniques 10–12)

All organisations need to monitor performance. This section explains two techniques used to identify performance measures and carry out the evaluation. These are critical success factors/key performance indicators, and the Balanced Business Scorecard technique.

STRATEGY ANALYSIS – EXTERNAL BUSINESS ENVIRONMENT

Technique 1: PESTLE analysis
Variants/Aliases

There are several similar approaches used to investigate the global business environment within which an organisation operates. The most commonly used approaches to external environment analysis are:

- **PEST** (political, economic, socio-cultural, technological);

- **PESTEL** (political, economic, socio-cultural, technological, environmental (or ecological), legal);

- **PESTLIED** (political, economic, socio-cultural, technological, legal, international, environmental (or ecological), demographic);

- **STEEPLE** (socio-cultural, technological, environmental (or ecological), economic, political, legal, ethical).

Description of the technique

PESTLE analysis provides a framework for investigating and analysing the external environment for an organisation. The framework identifies six key areas that should be considered when attempting to identify the sources of change. These six areas are:

Political: Examples of political factors could be a potential change of government, with the corresponding changes to policies and priorities, or the introduction of a new government initiative. These may be limited to the home country within which the organisation operates, but this tends to be rare these days since many changes have an effect in several countries. The development of bodies such as the European Union and the growth of global trade and multinational organisations have changed the scope of political activity. This has increased the possibility of political issues arising that may impact upon the organisation and how it operates.

3

Economic: Economic factors may also be limited to the home country, but as global trade continues to grow, economic difficulties in one nation tend to have a broad, often worldwide, impact. Examples of economic factors could be the level of growth within an economy, or market confidence in the economies within which the organisation operates. The 2008 sub-prime mortgage crisis in the USA, with its subsequent worldwide impact, is a good example of an economic situation that affected many organisations.

Socio-cultural: Socio-cultural factors are those arising from customers or potential customers. These changes can often be subtle, and they can be difficult to predict or identify until there is a major impact. Examples could be demographic issues such as an increase in the number of working mothers, or consumer behaviour patterns such as the rise of disposable fashion.

Technological: This area covers factors arising from the development of technology. There are two types of technological change: there can be developments in IT, and there can be developments in technology specific to an industry or market, for example enhancements to manufacturing technology.

IT developments can instigate extensive business impacts, often across industries or business domains and on a range of organisations. It is often the case that there is a failure to recognise the potential use of the technology – at least until a competitor emerges with a new or enhanced offering. For example, increased functionality of mobile technology or extended bandwidth for internet transactions can present opportunities to many organisations. However, the identification of such technological advances is critical if an organisation is to recognise the potential they offer.

Legal: It is vital to consider factors arising from changes to the law, since the last decade has seen a significant rise in the breadth and depth of the legal regulations within which organisations have to operate. Legal compliance has become such an important issue during this period that many business analysis assignments have been carried out for the purpose of ensuring compliance with particular laws or regulations. Some legal issues may originate from the national government but others, for example EU laws or global accounting regulations, may operate across a broader spectrum. One key issue when considering the legal element of the PESTLE analysis is to recognise laws that have an impact upon the organisation even though they originate from countries other than that in which the organisation is based. This situation may occur where an organisation is operating within the originating country or working with other organisations based in that country. Recent examples of this have concerned changes to international financial compliance regulations, such as the Sarbanes–Oxley Act in the USA and the Basel II Accord.

Environmental
(or Ecological):
Examples of factors arising from concerns about the natural environment, in other words the 'green' issues, include increasing concerns about packaging and the increase of pollution.

Using PESTLE analysis

The PESTLE analysis technique is usually used in a meeting or workshop where several ideas and opinions can be sought. Representatives from a range of functions should be present so that they can provide specialist information. For example, legal representatives would be able to provide information about changes to relevant laws and regulations. It is a good idea for departmental representatives to research any aspects that may impact the organisation prior to carrying out a PESTLE analysis. This could involve obtaining reports from research providers such as Dun and Bradstreet or Gartner.

The PESTLE technique is straightforward to use. Typically, each element will be considered in turn and any potential issues for that area documented. Once all of the elements have been considered, the factors listed are evaluated in order to identify those most likely to affect the organisation. This results in a list of key external influences that could cause it to take action – either to gain from an opportunity that appears to be present or to ensure that any threats are removed.

When using the PESTLE technique it is important to recognise that we are looking for factors that fit two criteria: they are outside the sphere of influence (i.e. control) of the organisation, and they will have some level of impact upon it.

It is essential to appreciate the importance of these criteria when using the technique. A common error is to identify a potential course of action for the organisation rather than highlight an external factor that will have an impact upon it. These external factors are shown as opportunities and threats in a SWOT analysis (see Technique 6), so when using PESTLE the focus should be on identifying external factors and not on deciding what to do about them. That analysis comes later. For example, in a retail enterprise:

- Environmental factors concerning the use of plastic carrier bags threaten to damage the market perception of the company, and thus constitute a threat to the business. This would be included in a SWOT analysis.

- Charging for plastic carrier bags is a possible response to the threat. This is neither an opportunity nor a threat, and would not be included in a SWOT analysis.

It is important to recognise the difference here, since leaping from a threat to a quick solution is not effective strategic analysis, and could lead to simplistic, ineffective solutions.

Another important aspect to recognise when using PESTLE is that its objective is to identify factors that could affect the organisation. It is therefore of little benefit to spend time considering whether a government initiative should be filed under

'Political', or whether 'Legal' would be preferable. The technique is invaluable in identifying factors to be considered, and if possible to be dealt with by taking action. The categorisation of these factors has little, if any, value.

Although the technique is usually seen as one where the external environment is considered, PESTLE may also be used to analyse influences operating within an organisation. This situation arises where issues or ideas concerning a particular function or department are under examination. An analysis of the external factors that may impact upon that department can help in a number of ways, from clarifying reasons for change to identifying options. For example, if a PESTLE analysis is carried out with regard to the human resources (HR) department there may be factors within the wider organisation that fit our two criteria – they are outside the department's control and are likely to impact upon its work. Perhaps there have been poor company results and the finance department has recommended to senior management that recruitment and training should cease for a six-month period. This decision will affect the work, but will be outside the control, of the HR department so it is an external factor to the department but an internal factor to the business as a whole.

Technique 2: Porter's Five Forces framework
Description of the technique
Porter's Five Forces analysis is also used to consider the external business environment, but it has a different focus from that of the PESTLE analysis.

Figure 1.1 Porter's Five Forces framework

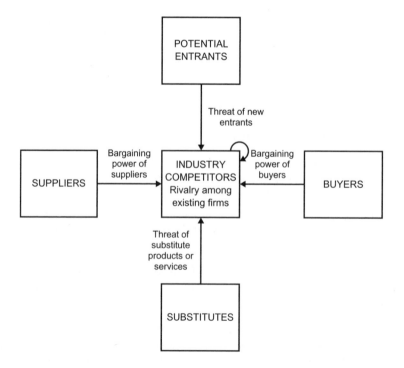

This technique examines the business domain or industry within which an organisation operates, and identifies the business pressures that may be brought to bear upon that organisation. The analysis derived from using the five forces framework is usually applied to a suite of products or services delivered by an enterprise.

Michael Porter divided the potential sources of pressures within an industry into five categories. These categories are set out in Figure 1.1, and the factors to consider in each case are described below.

Industry competitors: What is the level of competition for the products or services in this industry? Is the organisation in a good competitive position or is it a minor player? Are there several competitors that hold the power in the industry?

New entrants: Are there barriers to entry, such as the need for large amounts of money or expertise? Is it possible to start up an organisation offering these products or services without much financial support? What is the likelihood of new entrants coming into the industry?

Substitutes: What is the range of substitutes available? What is the position of the organisation when compared to the suppliers of these substitutes?

Buyers: How much choice do buyers have? Can they switch suppliers easily? Do they have the power in the relationship or are they locked in to the supplier?

Suppliers: How many suppliers are available? Is this a competitive situation where the organisation has a choice of suppliers? Do the suppliers have the power in the relationship because they operate in an area of limited supply?

The answers to these questions help to identify the factors within the industry or business domain that have the potential to impact upon the organisation, either positively or negatively.

Using Porter's Five Forces analysis

The first step in using this technique is to decide which industry or business domain the organisation operates within; this decision is extremely important when using the technique, as the results will vary considerably depending on the industry at the heart of the analysis. For example, if we are analysing a company selling expensive handbags, and we ask what industry this company operates in, it is possible to look at the question from two points of view:

- We could consider the company to be in the business of designing, marketing and selling handbags. In this case, the competitors are the other handbag companies, and the substitute products would include other products used to carry personal items – such as rucksacks and even plastic carrier bags. The industry is limited to products of a particular nature: bags.

- We could consider the company to be in the business of providing luxury giftware. In this case the competitors still include the other handbag companies, but they also include companies selling other luxury goods such as perfume and jewellery. The list of substitutes could extend to glassware or even donations to charity. Looked at like this, the industry is much larger, the potential market greater and the range of pressures that may impact upon the company more extensive.

Once the industry has been decided upon, the five categories are examined to identify the pressures that exist between the organisation and each of them.

Industry competitors: This is an examination of the other companies operating within the industry and the level of competition between them. Does our handbag company hold a powerful position or is it a minor player that is vulnerable to competitive moves?

New entrants: Could organisations operating in other, similar industries move into this area? For example, could an existing fashion company decide to develop a range of designer handbags? How great are the barriers to entry into this industry, and will they deter potential entrants?

Substitutes: As discussed above, what business pressures will arise from possible substitute products such as rucksacks?

Buyers: This could be an interesting area to explore for the handbag industry, as some high quality manufacturers restrict the sales outlets for their products and minimise the opportunities for buyers to shop around and compare prices. If this is a particularly desirable brand, the power of the buyer could be extremely limited.

Suppliers: Again, this could be an interesting aspect because some fashion brands are very exclusive and have a lot of power over their suppliers.

The answers to these questions help to identify the factors that have the potential to impact upon the organisation either positively or negatively. In this example we could identify that there are pressures, or threats, from competitors and new entrants, whereas the relationships with the buyers and the suppliers are in the company's favour – these present opportunities.

Five forces analysis requires knowledge about the industry and the different organisations or individuals that participate in its work. Areas such as substitute products can be difficult to analyse, and possible substitutes can be missed. At one time some industries had high barriers to entry because of the financial requirements, so new entrants were considered unlikely. However, the rise of businesses with access to funds, such as the major supermarkets, has meant that high financial requirements may not deter new entrants.

STRATEGY ANALYSIS – INTERNAL CAPABILITY

It is helpful to use a combination of techniques when analysing an organisation's internal capability, since just one technique would provide only limited information. Using a combination of the MOST and Resource Audit techniques that are described in this section, with possibly also the Boston Box, helps to provide a detailed picture of the areas where there is capability and those where there are weaknesses.

These three techniques help the analyst to identify areas that are strengths the organisation can harness, and those that are weaknesses that could undermine it. These strengths and weaknesses can later be combined with the opportunities and threats already described to build a SWOT (see Technique 6) for the organisation.

Technique 3: MOST analysis
Variants/Aliases
A variant is VMOST (vision, mission, objectives, strategy, tactics).

Description of the technique
MOST analysis is used to analyse what an organisation has set out to achieve (the mission and objectives) and how it aims to achieve this (the strategy and tactics). A MOST provides a statement of intent for the organisation, and is usually created following some strategic analysis activity. It is also used during the strategic analysis, since it can demonstrate strength within the organisation or expose inherent weaknesses.

MOST stands for:

- **Mission:** the rationale and direction for the organisation.
- **Objectives:** the goals that the organisation aims to achieve.
- **Strategy:** the medium- to long-term plans and actions that will enable the organisation to achieve its objectives.
- **Tactics:** the detailed, short-term plans and actions that will deliver the strategy.

Using MOST analysis
The use of MOST helps the analyst gain an understanding of two aspects: what the organisation wishes to achieve (its mission and objectives), and how it is going to do this (its strategy and tactics).

When examining the MOST for an organisation, the technique is used to identify strengths and weaknesses. This is done by considering the following areas:

Definition: Is there a defined MOST for the organisation? Is it complete and consistent, or are there elements missing or out of alignment with each other?

Clarity: Does the MOST set out a clear direction and plan that will enable the organisation's development and provide a focus for the work carried out?

Communication: Are the staff of the organisation aware of the MOST, and is it available as a context for the work they do?

Organisational commitment: Do the staff work to deliver the MOST? Do they agree with the content of the MOST and are they supportive of its intent?

If the answer to any of these question is 'no', then there is a potential for weakness in the organisation. For example, the senior management may have defined the MOST, but the staff might not agree with the direction and objectives, and as a result might not be motivated to deliver them.

If the answer to any of these questions is 'yes', there are potential strengths in the organisation. For example, the clear definition and planning as encapsulated in the MOST can help motivate the staff to work towards an agreed set of objectives.

MOST analysis can be a tricky technique to use when assessing internal capability. It is important to remember that merely defining and displaying a coherent MOST does not necessarily result in buy-in and motivation on the part of staff. The real strength is gained when the MOST provides a clear focus and direction for the organisation. Where there is no clarity or agreement, the MOST may mask some fundamental weaknesses.

Technique 4: Resource Audit
Variants/Aliases
The term 'resource analysis' is also used. Resources can be:

- tangible resources – financial and physical;
- intangible resources – technology, reputation and culture;
- human resources – skills, knowledge, communication and motivation.

Description of the technique
The Resource Audit is used to analyse key areas of internal capability in order to identify the resources that will enable business change and those that will undermine or prevent such efforts.

Figure 1.2 shows the areas analysed as part of the Resource Audit.

The five areas of resource to examine are:

Financial: The financial resources available – which may simply be the organisation's financial assets, but could also include the possibility of loans and credit. We need to consider whether the organisation is financially stable, and whether it has access to funds for investment and development.

Physical: The land, buildings and equipment available for use by the organisation, whether owned or leased.

Human: The people employed by the organisation, whether on a permanent or a temporary basis.

Reputation: The marketplace perception of the organisation, and the amount of goodwill, or alternatively, antipathy, generated by this reputation.

Know-how: The information held within the organisation, and the way it is used to support the organisation's work.

Figure 1.2 Resource Audit

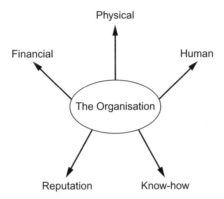

Using the Resource Audit

The Resource Audit is used to identify areas of strength and of weakness within an organisation. For each area listed, we need to determine whether the organisation has access to resources that will enable it to develop and grow, asking, for example:

- Does the organisation have access to financial resources that will enable the development of new products or services or is it in financial difficulty, lacking the ability to invest in new products or services?

- Does the organisation have access to land and buildings that will provide a basis for the development of new products or services, or is there a poor, underfunded infrastructure?

- Are the people working within the organisation motivated to deliver excellent products and services, or are they demotivated or complacent?

- Does the organisation have a reputation that will support the development of the market for its products and services, or is the brand devalued in a way that will hinder these efforts?

- Is the information held within the organisation used to inform decisions and operations? Is this information used to build a knowledge base that will support the organisation? Or is information used poorly, and accessed with difficulty?

Here is an example Resource Audit for a small consultancy company:

Physical: land: no land owned; buildings: no buildings owned – offices leased in Oxford and Bath; equipment: each employee has a company laptop and a personal mobile; supporting equipment: two printers and two projectors are available for use when necessary.

Financial: good financial control and stability. Ratios: profit on sales – 30%; liquidity – £1.5 current assets to £1 current liabilities; gearing ratio – 90%.

Human: staff of 25, including 18 consultants; two joint managing directors; all staff very motivated and committed to the company; all consultants highly qualified and skilled.

Reputation: good reputation in local area, and has won local awards; not known outside customer base and areas of operation.

Know-how: company makes extensive use of ad hoc information systems, but these are not well integrated.

The Resource Audit has well-defined areas to investigate, and can result in a clear assessment of an organisation's resources. However, each area may require significant time and effort if the Resource Audit is to be carried out thoroughly.

This technique may be used to examine internal resources at many different levels, ranging from an entire organisation to a localised team. The technique can be equally valuable when considering issues and problems right across an organisation, or looking at those that exist within a particular department or function. Either way, a Resource Audit will highlight where there are strengths that will enable the introduction of business improvement and where there are weaknesses that could undermine the new working practices.

Technique 5: Boston Box
Variants/Aliases
This is also called the **Boston Consulting Group matrix** or the **BCG matrix**.

Description of the technique
The Boston Box was developed by the Boston Consulting Group (hence, BCG matrix) to aid portfolio management. The box is a 2×2 matrix with four quadrants (see Figure 1.3). The axes represent low to high market growth and low to high market share. The quadrants represent the following areas:

Star: These are high-growth business units or products with a high percentage of market share. Over time the market growth will slow down for these products, and, if they maintain their relative market share, they will become 'cash cows'.

Cash cow: These are low-growth business units or products that have a relatively high market share. These are mature, successful products that can be sustained without large investment. They generate the income required to develop the new or problematic products that will become 'stars' in the portfolio.

Wild cat or problem child: These are businesses or products with low market share, but operating in high-growth markets. They have potential but may require substantial investment in order to develop their market share, typically at the expense of more powerful competitors. Management has to decide which 'problem children' to invest in, and which ones to allow to fail.

Dog: These are the business units or products that have low relative share and are in unattractive, low-growth markets. Dogs may generate enough cash to break even, but they do not have good prospects for growth, and so are rarely, if ever, worth investing in.

Figure 1.3 The Boston Box

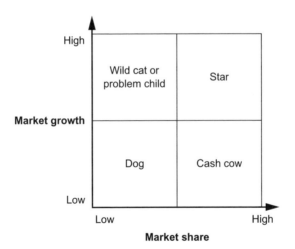

Using the Boston Box

The Boston Box is used to assess an organisation's products and services according to their market shares and their market growth prospects. The portfolio of products and services is examined, and each of them is placed within the most appropriate quadrant. This helps identify strengths and weaknesses within the portfolio. For example:

- When a product has been identified as a 'dog' it may be time to remove it from the portfolio. Even a limited amount of investment in a 'dog' may be a waste of finance that could generate greater benefits if spent elsewhere. Alternatively, it may be worth considering whether there is any action that could improve the situation – perhaps enhancing the product, or selling it in a different market in order to generate a higher volume of sales or greater profitability. Both of these courses of action would require investment, so the prospects for improvement would need to be assessed carefully.

- Where a product has been identified as a 'problem child', action to rectify the situation will need to be considered; with careful development it may be possible to move the product into a 'star' position. For example, it may be possible to change the approach to marketing the product in order to enhance the market's perception of it and thus increase sales.

One of the issues with the Boston Box is the level of granularity of the product assessment. There may be some products that do not fit neatly into a particular quadrant, but are on the cusp between two. When using this technique it is important that a commonsense approach is adopted and that other factors are taken into account. For example, if a product is assessed as having medium market share and low growth this might not be because of an inherent problem with the product. It could instead be a question of timing and market conditions. The action that would improve the situation might simply be to manage the product carefully until the market conditions change.

STRATEGY DEFINITION

Technique 6: SWOT analysis
Variants/Aliases
A variant is **TOWS analysis** (threats, opportunities, weaknesses and strengths).

Description of the technique
SWOT analysis is used to consolidate the results from the external and internal business environment analysis. SWOT (see Figure 1.4) stands for:

Figure 1.4 SWOT analysis

Strengths – will aid the development of the organisation	**Weaknesses** – will undermine the development of the organisation
Opportunities – available to be grasped by the organisation	**Threats** – presenting potential problems for the organisation

Strengths   the internal positive capabilities of the organisation, for example financial resources, motivated staff or good market reputation;

Weaknesses   the internal negative aspects of the organisation that will diminish the chances of success, for example out-of-date equipment and systems, unskilled staff or poor management information;

Opportunities   the external factors that present opportunities for success, for example social changes that increase demand for the organisation's services, or the development of technology to provide new service delivery channels;

Threats   the external factors that have the potential to harm the organisation, for example a technological development that could enable new competitors to enter the market, or economic difficulties leading to a reduction in market demand.

Using SWOT analysis

SWOT is used to summarise and consolidate the key issues identified when analysing an organisation and its business environment. It follows the use of techniques such as PESTLE (external) and Resource Audit (internal).

Once the SWOT has been developed it is then used as a means of evaluating the organisation's business situation and identifying potential strategies for the future. A standard approach is:

- Identify the new business improvements made possible by the opportunities defined in the SWOT.
- Identify the business issues that may arise from the threats defined in the SWOT.
- Consider the actions required to grasp the opportunities and address the threats.
- Identify the areas of strength that will enable the organisation to carry out these actions.
- Identify the areas of weakness that could undermine any action taken.
- Develop and evaluate strategic options for delivering success based on the previous steps.

SWOT analysis is often employed in workshops, where techniques such as brainstorming are used to identify the elements in each of the four areas. However, this approach is not rigorous and can be too informal to produce a comprehensive SWOT. There is the risk of missing significant factors, such as a looming threat or a major area of organisational weakness. A better approach is to use formal techniques to derive the SWOT, which helps to ensure that all relevant areas are considered and the key issues identified. Using techniques such as PESTLE, Porter's Five Forces and Resource Audit will provide a more analytical basis for this work, and will produce an enhanced SWOT with clear sources and derivation. Once the SWOT has been produced it is important to distinguish the key issues, since there may be a large set of entries, some of which are unlikely to yield more than minor changes. It is the key SWOT issues that should be examined in detail. These should form the basis for the strategy definition.

Technique 7: Ansoff's matrix
Variants/Aliases
This is also known as **Ansoff's Box.**

Description of the technique
Ansoff's matrix provides a set of strategic alternatives that may be considered by organisations when defining their business strategy. The box maps new and

---

Figure 1.5 Ansoff's matrix

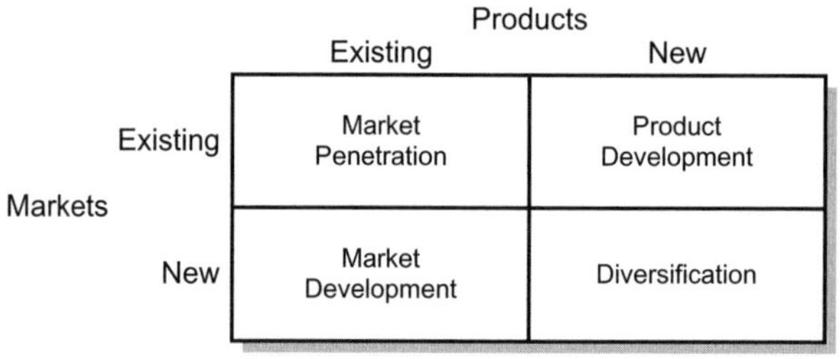

existing markets against new and existing products, creating a 2 × 2 matrix (see Figure 1.5). Four quadrants are created:

Market penetration:	This situation is where existing markets are targeted for greater penetration by existing products. In this approach, organisations decide to continue with their existing products and markets but to adopt tactics such as additional promotion, increased sales efforts or revised pricing approaches in order to generate increased market share.
Market development:	In this situation the organisation adopts a strategy of exploring other markets for its products. This may mean targeting new markets in other countries, or applying the products to different markets within the existing geographical areas of operation.
Product development:	This strategy involves developing new products or services, and targeting existing markets. Another approach to it would be to add further, related features to existing products and services.

Diversification: The most radical strategic alternative is to develop new products or services and target new markets. This is a risky strategy to adopt, since it does not use existing expertise or leverage the current customer base.

Using Ansoff's matrix

Once a SWOT analysis (Technique 6) has been completed it is vital that actions are identified to address the issues raised in the SWOT and determine an effective way forward. These actions may involve revisiting the organisation's strategy, and Ansoff's matrix provides a set of options that support this work. For example, if a weakness has been identified in the performance of the organisation's product range, two possible options from Ansoff's matrix may be considered: to adopt a market penetration strategy by initiating extensive promotional and sales activity, or to adopt a product development strategy by initiating the enhancement of the product portfolio.

Ansoff's matrix provides a means of identifying and evaluating the strategic options open to the organisation in the light of the information presented in the SWOT. Together these techniques are extremely powerful in ensuring that any strategic analysis is carried out in a formal, informed manner. The assessment of the advantages and disadvantages of the four options presented in Ansoff's matrix provides a systematic approach to strategy definition. The analyst can be confident that the business strategy that emerges from this work will be based upon firm foundations.

The strategy derived from the options provides information that will help the senior management to develop a new MOST (see Technique 3) for the organisation. While the 'mission' may still pertain, the business 'objectives' may need to be revised, the 'strategy' description will need to be changed and the 'tactics' that will enable the organisation to meet the objectives and deliver the strategy will need to be redefined.

STRATEGY IMPLEMENTATION

The implementation of business change is widely regarded as an extremely difficult activity, and success is often limited. Techniques such as the McKinsey 7-S (Technique 8) and the four-view model (Technique 9) provide a firm basis for identifying all of the aspects to be considered when implementing business change. These techniques may be used separately or in conjunction with each other. They are used to support two aspects of strategy implementation: identifying all of the areas that need to change and the range of actions to be taken within these areas, and cross-checking all of the changes to ensure consistency, completeness and alignment.

Technique 8: McKinsey 7-S

Description of the technique

The McKinsey 7-S model (see Figure 1.6) defines the areas of an organisation that need to be in alignment if it is to operate effectively. The model is used to

Figure 1.6 The McKinsey 7-S model

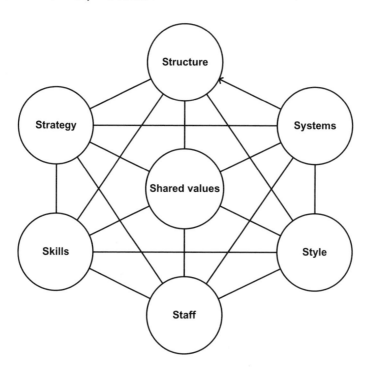

identify areas that need to change when implementing a business strategy, and areas that will be affected by proposed business changes.

The seven elements of the model are:

Shared values: the values that underpin the organisation and express the beliefs held by the people who drive it. These beliefs are inherent within the mission of the organisation (see Technique 3), and may also be analysed using the CATWOE technique (Technique 27), which is described in Chapter 3, 'Consider perspectives'. They are sometimes known as superordinate goals.

Skills: the skills required to carry out the work of the organisation. Key skills of particular staff may be defined, and these can be linked to the staffing categories.

Staff: the staffing requirements for the organisation, including the number and categories of staff.

Style: the culture and management style of the organisation. Contrasting examples of styles include 'mentoring manager/empowered staff' and 'commanding manager/instructed staff'.

Strategy: the defined strategy for the organisation. This is likely to have been developed following a SWOT analysis (Technique 6), and may be based upon Porter's generic strategies of market development or product development (Porter 2004).

Systems: the tactical and operational processes, procedures and IT systems that define how the work of the organisation is carried out. This definition should be in line with the organisation's strategy.

Structure: the internal structures that define the lines of communication and control within the organisation. Examples include centralised or decentralised control, and hierarchical or matrix management structures.

The 7-S model elements are sometimes categorised as 'hard' and 'soft'. The 'hard' areas are those that are more tangible and may be defined specifically; the 'soft' areas are less tangible and are more difficult to define precisely. The 'hard' group consists of strategy, structure and systems; the 'soft' areas are shared values, style, staff and skills. Although the 'hard' areas are more concrete, the 'soft' ones are of equal importance, and can cause problems if they are not recognised and considered when defining the changes to be made.

Using the 7-S Model

The 7-S model is used in order to consider an organisation holistically. It helps to ensure that all of the interdependent aspects that are required when working in a coordinated fashion are developed so as to achieve this. This can be extremely important when conducting an impact analysis following the definition of a business strategy. The model helps identify the areas affected by the new strategy, and highlights where action is needed and where difficulties can occur. Although the 'soft' areas are less tangible, the impact of a misalignment in them can be significant, and can create difficulties or even prevent the implementation of the business strategy. Here is example of such a situation:

- An organisation believes in delivering high-quality personal service.
- The organisation has a long history of employing highly skilled senior staff, many of whom have developed working relationships with their customers.
- In response to economic conditions, the organisation decides to adopt a strategy of market penetration, requiring a focus on selling high volumes at low prices.

The 7-S framework would help identify that the new strategy has not been aligned with the staff or shared values of this organisation, and is therefore unlikely to be implemented successfully.

Once a strategy has been defined for it, the 7-S model can be used to audit an organisation. The model provides a means of identifying which areas need to change in order that the tactics and operations will be in alignment with the strategy. The connections between the seven areas of the model emphasise the importance of alignment between these areas. This alignment between the 7-S areas needs to be assessed when identifying the required changes.

The McKinsey 7-S model helps ensure the successful implementation of business change. It provides a framework that supports the design of the seven key areas and the links between them. When using the model, it is useful to begin with one element and consider all related elements in the light of it. An effective approach is to begin by considering the Shared values defined for the organisation. The other elements are all linked to this, and they should all operate in sympathy with these values in the new organisation. The new strategy should align with these values, as should the structure of the organisation. For example, if this is an organisation that believes in empowering its staff, then this should be reflected in the management structure; we would not expect to see a tall structure consisting of several layers of management.

Technique 9: The four-view model
Variants/Aliases
The **three-view model** (people, process and organisation) is also used.

Description of the technique
The four-view model for business change sets out the four key areas to be considered when identifying the changes that need to be made to an organisation

---

Figure 1.7 The four-view model

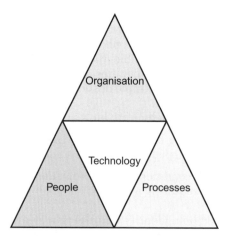

(see Figure 1.7). This model also applies when the changes are to be made to a business system within an organisation. The four areas are:

Organisation: the management structure, roles, responsibilities and resources;

Processes: the business processes used to deliver the organisation's products and services to customers, and to support its work;

People: the staff members responsible for implementing the business processes and carrying out the work of the organisation;

Technology: the hardware and software systems used to support the work of the organisation.

Using the four-view model

The technique is used as an aide-memoire when defining the elements that need to be considered during a business change process. For example, if the business processes are to be improved then their impacts upon the other three areas may change: the IT systems may need enhancement to support the new processes; the users – the people – may need to be trained and informed of their new roles; the management structure may need to be amended to reflect the revised roles and responsibilities. When defining changes to any part of an organisation or business system it is vital that the other three elements of the model are considered and the corresponding changes identified.

The four-view model is drawn to illustrate that a whole organisation or business system consists of four elements that need to work in concert. Changing one of these elements inevitably has an impact upon the other three, and all four aspects need to work together if the business changes are to be successful. A process that has been redesigned to be highly efficient will be diminished by untrained staff or poor-quality IT support; a highly motivated and skilled team of staff will fail to deliver optimum performance if the business processes they are operating are cumbersome and bureaucratic.

PERFORMANCE MEASUREMENT

Techniques 10 and 11: Critical success factors and key performance indicators

Description of the techniques

Critical success factors (CSFs) and key performance indicators (KPIs) are used to determine measures of organisational performance. CSFs are identified first, since they are the areas of performance that the organisation considers vital to its success. They are typically broad-brush statements such as 'customer service' or 'low costs'. Two types of CSF should be considered:

- Industry-wide CSFs – the areas of effective performance that are necessary for any organisation operating within a particular business domain or market sector. For example, all airlines have 'safety of operations' as a CSF – no airline that disregards safety is likely to operate for very long. These CSFs do not differentiate between organisations, but they allow them to continue operating.

- Organisation-specific CSFs – the areas of performance that enable an organisation to outperform its competition. These are the areas that it focuses upon as key differentiators. For example, Ryanair might claim that low cost of operation is one of the company's CSFs.

KPIs are related to the CSFs, and define the specific areas to be monitored in order to determine whether the required level of performance has been achieved. If an organisation has defined 'excellent customer service' as a CSF, the KPIs could include the volume of complaints received over a defined time period, and the percentage of customers rating the organisation 'very good' or 'excellent' in a customer perception survey.

Since KPIs are related to CSFs, they need to be defined for both the industry-wide and the organisation-specific areas.

Using the CSF/KPI techniques

Once an organisation has defined its MOST (Technique 3), the performance measures that will provide a detailed means of monitoring progress need to be determined. The CSFs are identified first, and the KPIs are defined in support of the CSFs.

The MOST for the organisation should help identify how it is positioned within the market; this should be underpinned by a set of organisational beliefs and priorities. These beliefs are those that the senior management feels are essential to its successful operation. The CATWOE technique (Technique 27), described in the 'Consider Perspectives' chapter, is helpful when considering the core beliefs of the senior management team. This information helps in the identification of the CSFs, which then leads on to defining the KPIs and the corresponding targets. This three-part approach is described in the following example.

If an organisation is positioned as a high-quality provider of services, the CSFs might include 'excellent customer service' and 'high-quality services'. There will be several KPIs to monitor the areas of operation that relate to achieving these CSFs. For example, the KPIs would need to monitor aspects such as the percentage of customer complaints and the percentage of repeat purchases. For each of these KPIs, a target and a timeframe would need to be set. Examples of these are:

- Fewer than 2 per cent of customers complain about the service received, when asked during the quarterly customer satisfaction survey.

- More than 60 per cent of customers purchase further services within 12 months of the initial purchase.

Technique 12: Balanced Business Scorecard
Variants/Aliases:

Organisations often have their own variants of the Balanced Business Scorecard (BBS), reflecting aspects of the organisation that are particularly important and that need to be monitored. An example is the area of risk: a financial services provider might be particularly keen to monitor this aspect of its business.

Figure 1.8 Balanced Business Scorecard

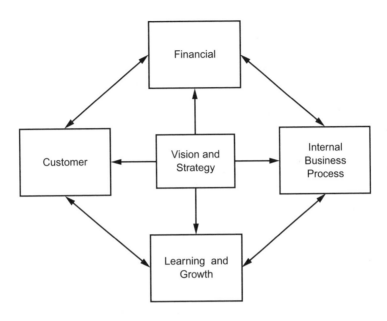

Description of the technique
The BBS was developed by Robert S. Kaplan and David P. Norton as a means of defining a framework of performance measures that would support the achievement of the vision for an organisation, and the execution of its business strategy (Kaplan and Norton 1996). Historically many organisations, and external stakeholders such as shareholders, have focused on their financial performance. However, financial measures have typically related to past performance, and the decline of financially stable organisations can be attributed to a lack of attention to areas of performance that will generate success in the future. The BBS identifies four aspects of performance that should be considered (see Figure 1.8):

Financial:	This aspect considers the financial performance of the organisation, looking for example at the profit generated by sales, the returns generated by the assets invested in the organisation, and its liquidity.
Customer:	Looking at the organisation from the customer perspective shows how customers view it. For example, the level of customer satisfaction and the reputation the organisation has in the marketplace are considered.
Internal business process:	This perspective shows the internal processes and procedures that are used to operate the organisation. For example, are the processes focused on reducing costs, to the detriment of customer service? Is the technology

	used well to support the organisation in delivering its products and services?
Learning and growth (also known as innovation):	The learning and growth perspective is concerned with the future development of the organisation. Examples of performance areas are the development of new products and services, the level of creative activity in the organisation, and the extent to which this is encouraged.

Using the Balanced Business Scorecard

The approach to identifying CSFs and KPIs defined earlier (Techniques 10 and 11) is usually used in conjunction with the BBS. The Mission and Objectives of the organisation (Technique 3) are used as the context in which to define the BBS areas. For example, if the Mission is to deliver good value, high quality services to customers, then the four BBS areas could measure performance as follows:

- **financial** – level of supplier costs;

- **customer** – prices charged in comparison with competitor prices;

- **internal** – quality checking processes;

- **innovation** – introduction of new products.

The BBS helps ensure that organisations will not focus solely on financial results, but will consider both their current performance and the factors that will enable continued success. The BBS is used to ensure that a complete view of the organisation's performance is measured and monitored. It is vital that all four areas are considered, not just one or two; omitting any of the areas is to risk undermining the performance of the organisation, and to increase the chance of business problems arising in the future.

REFERENCES

Kaplan, R.S. and Norton, D.P. (1996) *The Balanced Business Scorecard.* Harvard Business School Press, Boston.

Porter, M.E. (2004) *Competitive Strategy.* The Free Press, New York.

FURTHER READING

Grant, R.M. (2004) *Contemporary Strategy Analysis.* Blackwell, Oxford.

Johnson, G. and Scholes, K. (2008) *Exploring Corporate Strategy.* Prentice Hall, London.

Paul, D. and Yeates, D. (eds) (2007) *Business Analysis.* BCS, Swindon.

2 INVESTIGATE SITUATION

INTRODUCTION

This stage of the business analyst's work is concerned with uncovering problems and issues. It involves using a range of investigative techniques, and choosing those that are most appropriate to the situation being examined. It also involves documenting what has been found.

Three aspects of this stage are considered here:

- qualitative investigation;
- quantitative investigation;
- documenting the results.

Qualitative investigation (Techniques 13–15)

The techniques here are used to discover the widest possible range of facts and opinions about the issues. Facts are clearly important, but so are opinions. They help the BA to understand the people involved in the matter, and to begin to assess how receptive they are to change, to identify their hopes and fears about the situation, and to discover who may be 'allies' or 'opponents' in implementing change. This information is invaluable in the analysis and management of stakeholders, examined in more detail in the 'Consider perspectives' chapter. The qualitative techniques we review here are:

- interviewing;
- workshops;
- observation.

Quantitative investigation (Techniques 16–19)

In addition to qualitative information, it is also useful to get quantitative data to provide further insights into the business problems and issues. For example, how many invoices are produced per day? Per month? Per annum? Is there a peak at a particular time of the month? How much time is spent dealing with complaints, as opposed to taking new orders? What information is recorded on forms and reports at the moment, and who uses this? The qualitative techniques we present are:

- questionnaires;
- sampling;
- special-purpose records;
- document analysis.

Documenting the results (Techniques 20–22)

The simplest way of documenting the findings of the investigation is by writing a report of some sort. However, this is laborious and time consuming, and sometimes the real essence of a problem or issue can get lost in a great mass of text. As a supplement, or a substitute, for text we present here some more visual techniques:

- rich pictures;
- mind maps;
- context diagrams.

QUALITATIVE INVESTIGATION

Technique 13: Interviewing

Description of the technique

Interviewing is one of the main fact-finding, investigation or elicitation techniques used by BAs, and consists, usually, of one-to-one discussions with stakeholders in the business analysis assignment. Occasionally the BA may interview more than one person, and sometimes, too, more than one BA may be involved in a discussion, but one-to-one is the more usual situation.

A successful interview has three main stages, as shown in Figure 2.1.

Figure 2.1 The main stages of interviewing

Planning and preparation means answering two questions: Whom do I want to interview, and what do I want to ask them? Interviewees could be selected for a number of reasons, including these:

- They are senior managers who have commissioned the business analysis work and/or could have a significant influence on it.
- They are 'end users', the people whose jobs will be affected by the BA work and who can provide the analyst with detailed information.
- It is good politics to involve them, to keep them 'on-side' with the project.

Whatever the reason for the interview, the BA should create an agenda that is detailed enough so the interviewees can prepare themselves, and should send this to them in plenty of time. BAs may also perhaps create a more detailed list of questions for themselves.

Another aspect of planning is deciding when and where to conduct the interview. Of course, with senior managers, the BA might not have much choice, and might be told rather than asked when and where the interview can be arranged, but, otherwise, the following should be considered:

- Seeing people on their 'home turf' helps to put them at their ease, and, in addition, they will have documents and so forth readily to hand to show the BA. On the other hand, they might work in a distracting environment, and they may want more confidentiality than the workplace can provide.

- Distractions can be avoided and confidentiality provided by using the BA's office, or a neutral meeting room, but at the risk of making the interviewee more nervous.

- Interviews held first thing on Monday or the last thing on Friday are seldom very productive; the BA should try to find a time that fits around the interviewee's work commitments.

Follow-up after the interview includes sending interviewees a copy of the notes, and asking them to confirm the BA's understanding and interpretation. Apart from being good manners, this also helps in securing buy-in from the interviewee. These notes, incidentally, should be written up as soon as possible after the interview, while the discussion is still relatively fresh in the BA's mind.

Figure 2.2 The structure of an interview

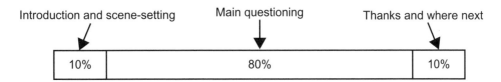

The interview itself is also divided into three parts, as shown in Figure 2.2.

During the introduction, the BA should thank the interviewee for participating, restate the purpose of the discussion and try to put the interviewee at ease. This is also a good time to start building the rapport with the person that will be invaluable later in the project, when you are trying to 'sell' and implement your solution. It is also a good idea at this point to mention that you will be taking notes, as this gives you 'permission' to pause from time to time in order to do so.

At the end of the interview the BA needs to do a few things. You should:

- Summarise the main points of the discussion.
- Make sure you have examples of any documents or forms mentioned in the interview (filled-in ones if possible, since these provide more information than blanks).
- Again, thank the interviewee for their time and their contribution to the analysis work.
- Provide some information about what happens next – interviewees often complain that they don't know where or how their information will be used.
- 'Keep the door open' with the interviewee in case you need to get further information.

Returning now to the body of the interview, this is where the main part of the questioning takes place. Needless to say, the BA should be careful to follow the agenda, but should also be prepared to go 'off piste' if necessary to follow up any particularly interesting points made by the interviewee.

There are various types of question that the BA may consider using, and each has its pros and cons. The main types are:

Open: These are questions such as 'Please tell me about …' and 'What are your views on …', and they serve to open up discussion and encourage the interviewee to speak. On the other hand, sometimes questions can be too open, leaving the interviewee a bit confused about what is wanted. An example might be 'Please describe the work of the invoicing section for me.'

Closed: These invite simple 'yes' or 'no' answers, and are generally to be avoided since they tend to close down conversation. However, they can be useful sometimes to get control over an over-garrulous interviewee, and where a definitive answer is required. An example is 'Does the invoicing section just deal with invoices?'

Limited choice: Here the interviewee is given a restricted set of options to choose from, as in 'Would you say the system is now better, worse or about the same as it was last year?' The downside of limited choice questions is the same as for closed ones – that they tend to shut down discussion – but they are sometimes useful if it is necessary to compare answers given by different interviewees. An example could be 'Are invoices produced before, after or on despatch of the goods?'

Leading: This type of question is often favoured by TV interviewers, and starts with something like 'Would you agree that …'. With a nervous or inexperienced interviewee, who might reply 'yes' just to be agreeable, these are dangerous; but they can sometimes yield interesting results when used carefully with more senior people to provoke a reaction. An example is 'Do you agree that the design of this invoice is a bit difficult for customers to understand?'

Probing: These are follow-ups to other questions, for example: 'So each invoice may cover more than one actual customer order?'

Link: These are the most difficult to use, as the BA is making connections between different parts of the interview. An example might be 'So you produce 1,000 delivery notes per week, and earlier I think you said there were 750 invoices per week; does this mean that some orders are sent out in more than one delivery?'

None of these types of question is 'right' in all circumstances, and the BA must be willing and able to use all of them at some time or other. In general, though, avoiding too many closed, limited-choice or leading questions is good, since these tend to close down the conversation, whereas open questions tend to keep it going.

While all this questioning is going on, the BA should be making notes of the conversation and should pause as necessary to facilitate this.

Using interviewing

To a new BA, conducting an interview presents a very great challenge, and even experienced BAs can have some difficulties on occasion. The reasons for this include:

- The BA is trying to do several things at once – listen to and understand the interviewee's answer, make notes, think about the agenda and frame the next question.

- Interviewees usually have much more subject-matter knowledge than do BAs. This can make the latter seem inexperienced, and lead them to ask apparently silly or obvious questions.

- Often the interviewees are busy, and resent giving up their time in this way.

- If the interview takes place in the interviewee's workplace, there may well be interruptions and distractions from colleagues or the telephone.

The truth is, though, that most BAs get better at all this with experience, and find their own ways round the issues. For example, one can turn the lack of subject-matter knowledge into an advantage by asking questions such as 'This may be a silly question, but …', and one can also build rapport with interviewees and get them 'on side' by deferring to their greater knowledge.

Note-taking is also difficult for new BAs, as it often seems to slow down the interview process. Actually this is not entirely a bad thing, since it can help to 'pace' the interview – and one can use the note-making pauses to think about the next question. Some people do not take conventional notes, but use mind-maps (see Technique 21) with the 'branches' – which they can prepare before the discussion – representing the main points of the agenda. They then populate these with details as the interview proceeds.

However difficult interviewing is, a successful BA **must** master the technique, since it is one of those most frequently used, and it also creates a wonderful opportunity to build good relationships with the key stakeholders, which are key to the success of every business analysis project.

Technique 14: Workshops

Variants and aliases
Variants include facilitated workshops, joint requirements planning workshops and IBM's Joint Application Development Workshops™.

Description of the technique
A workshop is essentially a gathering of a group of stakeholders in a project for the purpose of:

- agreeing the direction and scope of the project;
- identifying and agreeing business and/or system requirements;
- examining possible solutions to the requirements;
- reviewing and approving the products of analysis, for example the requirements catalogue and the requirements specification.

Workshops are particularly important when cooperative approaches to development are being employed, for example in Agile approaches such as Scrum or the DSDM Consortium's Atern. IBM has also for some years employed what it calls 'Joint Application Development' (JAD) workshops, and has trademarked this term.

The basic process for staging a workshop is shown in Figure 2.3, and in the pages that follow we will examine each stage in more detail.

Figure 2.3 Workshop process

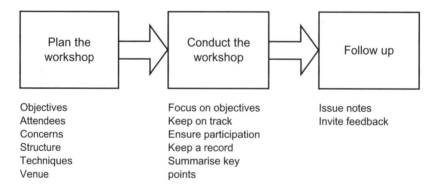

Plan the workshop	Conduct the workshop	Follow up
Objectives	Focus on objectives	Issue notes
Attendees	Keep on track	Invite feedback
Concerns	Ensure participation	
Structure	Keep a record	
Techniques	Summarise key	
Venue	points	

Plan the workshop
As with interviews, good planning is vital to the success of a workshop. The elements to think about at the planning stage are:

Objectives: The key question to ask is: 'Why are we staging this workshop?' Some of the possible reasons were outlined earlier, but it is important to be absolutely clear why this group of people has been brought together and what is the expected result. It may be that the outcome will be a set of detailed process models, or perhaps decisions will be made on the future of the project, or a signed-off specification of requirements produced. One common mistake is to make the objectives of a workshop too ambitious for the time available; this issue is discussed in the commentary below, under 'Using workshops'. Whatever the objectives are, they should be clearly stated on the agenda, which should be sent to the participants in enough time for them to prepare properly for the meeting.

Attendees: Clarity about the objectives should make it clear who the attendees should be. If the purpose of the workshop is to discover things, then priority must be given to people who have detailed knowledge on which to draw. If the workshop is expected to make decisions, then authority as well as knowledge is required. Sometimes knowledge and authority are not both found in one person, so the list of invitees may have to be widened to include more people. BAs organising a workshop must also decide whether they should facilitate the workshop themselves or ask a colleague to do so; the implications of this important decision are discussed below under 'Using workshops'.

Concerns: Once we know who the attendees will be, we need to try and find out what their concerns are likely to be, and thus from what 'angle' they will approach the workshop. This will enable the facilitator to think about what techniques to employ and how to manage the workshop.

Structure: The objectives will also point towards an appropriate structure for the workshop – getting all of the issues out on the table and assessing their significance before trying to find solutions, for example.

Techniques: The facilitator needs to consider the objectives and the attendees, and decide which techniques may be most appropriate to use. Some of these are considered below.

Venue: A suitable venue must be booked for the workshop. 'Suitable' covers various aspects, including size (not too cramped or too large, which would ruin the dynamic of the workshop), comfort (of chairs, temperature and so forth), convenience for the attendees, and services required (for example, catering and audiovisual equipment). A major decision is needed on whether the workshop should be held on site or off site, and some thoughts about this are given under 'Using workshops' later in this section.

31

Conduct the workshop
During the workshop the key elements for success include:

Focus on objectives:	It is the facilitator's responsibility to make sure that the agenda is followed and that the discussions are not allowed to drift off into irrelevancies. However, some latitude must be allowed, since it is not always clear initially where a particular point might lead, and the facilitator should not choke off any potentially promising lines of exploration.
Keep on track:	This is about making sure that the timetable is followed as far as possible. It can be very annoying to participants if a workshop appears to be bogged down on some point, or if they feel they are being 'railroaded' before they have been able to express their views.
Ensure participation:	In many ways this is the most important role of the facilitator – making sure that all of the people attending have a chance to participate. This may involve keeping the more vocal attendees under control and 'bringing out' the quieter, more reticent types.
Keep a record:	There is nothing more frustrating than attending any form of meeting and then finding afterwards that there is no record of what went on and, particularly, of what was agreed. This is true of workshops too, and someone must be deputed to keep a record of proceedings. If some of the diagrammatic techniques outlined later are used the records will create themselves, but otherwise someone needs to take the role of 'scribe', also discussed later.
Summarise key points:	At various stages during the workshop, and particularly at the end, the facilitator should summarise where discussions have got to and highlight any actions agreed. Doing this occasionally during the workshop helps participants to understand where they have got to and what they need to think about next.

Follow up
There are two vital responsibilities following the workshop:

Issue notes:	The notes should be issued as soon as possible after the workshop, before the 'trail has gone cold' and the attendees have had time to forget, particularly if they have any subsequent actions to take. Participants should be asked to correct any factual errors they spot, but they must be discouraged quite firmly from reopening issues that have been decided.
Invite feedback:	Feedback on the workshop should be sought, especially on the participants' experiences. This enables facilitators to hone their skills for future events.

Workshop roles

These are the main roles that need to be filled in a workshop:

Participant: What makes someone an effective participant in a workshop? It is difficult to generalise, of course, but some characteristics stand out, including:

- a willingness to contribute fully and to argue one's points;

- a good knowledge of the topics and issues to be explored and discussed;

- the authority to make decisions as necessary.

The last point is an important one. It is a waste of everyone's time if, at the end of a workshop, some of the people present will not (or cannot) bind themselves and their departments to the decisions made – 'I'll need to run it past my boss first.' In the process of organising the workshop it must be stressed to senior management that they need either to come themselves or to empower whoever they do send. There are some difficulties with this, however, and these are explored under 'Using workshops' later in this section.

Scribe: Someone needs to be responsible for making notes as the workshop progresses. For reasons we are about to explore, this should not, ideally, be the facilitator. Nor, where technical issues are to be discussed, can general administrators operate effectively as scribes, since they will most likely not understand a lot of the terminology used. The scribe therefore needs to be someone who has both an understanding of the topic under discussion and the close attention and note-taking skills required to keep an accurate record of proceedings.

Facilitator: The facilitator's role is clearly crucial to the success of the workshop. He or she must possess some necessary characteristics including:

- Good communication, and particularly listening, skills, so as to follow the discussion and make sure it is relevant to the workshop's objectives.

- Emotional intelligence', which, in this context, means being able to sense the mood of individuals and the meeting as a whole and to adjust one's own approach accordingly.

- Sufficient 'ego strength' to be able to manage the participants gently but firmly, to keep the more vocal ones under control and to draw out the less confident attendees.

It is a matter of some dispute whether the facilitator needs to have an in-depth knowledge of the subject of the workshop. One school of thought says that the aim of the facilitator is to be objective, and that this is difficult for a person who has knowledge – and therefore opinions – of the matters under discussion. On the other hand, and particularly where technical subjects are concerned, a facilitator without any knowledge is surely unable to gauge the significance and relevance of participants' contributions. What is not in dispute, though, is that the facilitator is there to help the participants to reach a conclusion – but not any particular conclusion. We have more to say about the BA as facilitator later in this section.

Ice-breaking techniques

Depending on the purpose of the workshop, and also on whether the participants already know one other, the facilitator may want to use some 'ice-breaking' techniques to help people to start working together. These have to be judged rather carefully, however, as some techniques can put participants off, especially in a rather conservative, formal organisational climate. To some extent the degree to which participants will 'play along' with a technique may depend on the authority and 'presence' of the facilitator.

Assuming that the climate is propitious, however, the following may be tried:

Personal introductions:	This is the most commonly used ice breaker, and simply involves asking all of the participants to introduce themselves and tell the rest of the group something about them. This can be broadened beyond the workplace by asking them to include an 'interesting fact', but some people feel a bit awkward about that. As a variation, participants can be asked to interview their immediate neighbours and then introduce them to the rest of the group. This gets some conversation going.
Fact or fiction:	Each person writes down four things about himself or herself, one of which is not true. Participants then read these out, and the rest of the group tries to identify those that are untrue.
Marooned:	The group is divided into teams which have to assume that they have been marooned on a desert island. Each team is asked to choose five items that they would have brought with them. They write their choices on a flipchart, and then debate their ideas with the other groups. This one is good because it does get some discussion going, which is, after all, the object of the workshop.
Bodyguards and assassins:	This one is more active, and it can also be used as an 'energiser' if there is a dip in concentration or enthusiasm. Everyone stands up and secretly chooses one other member of the group as a potential 'assassin' and another as a 'bodyguard'. They then have to move around the room, all trying at the same time to get away from their own 'assassins' and closer to their own 'bodyguards'. The exercise can cause great hilarity and encourage a warmer and more dynamic atmosphere.

Discovery techniques
Here are some techniques that can be used to uncover information and stimulate creative thinking.

Brainstorming: This is the technique that everyone remembers when thinking about workshops. It involves simply announcing a topic or posing a question, and inviting participants to shout out ideas. (Incidentally, in some organisations keen on political correctness, the term 'brainstorming' is thought to be rather insensitive to people with epilepsy, and 'thought showering' or 'ideas storming' are preferred.) Brainstorming works well when participants are comfortable with one other and not afraid of being criticised, but these ideal conditions do not always exist in a workshop. Where people do not know each other, or there are big differences in status between those present in the room, or the culture is not conducive to making mistakes, only the bolder participants are likely to contribute; this can skew the results of the workshop. In these situations, something like a Post-it exercise (see below) can be more productive. Another problem with brainstorming is that the scribe or the facilitator may not be able to keep up with the flow of ideas, and so their slowness actually acts as a brake on the creativity of the participants. It is vital, by the way, that all ideas are written down, partly so that they are not forgotten, but also so that those who suggested them do not feel slighted or excluded.

Round robin: Here the facilitator goes round the table from person to person and invites each to make a suggestion. This does have the virtue that everyone is explicitly invited to contribute, but sometimes more reticent people feel they have been 'put on the spot'. Again, Post-Its may be a better bet.

Post-it exercise: The idea here is that each participant is given a block of adhesive notes and is asked to write a suggestion on each one. The advantage of this over brainstorming is that each participant has time to think, and they do not have to expose their ideas immediately to public scrutiny. The facilitator can collect the Post-Its in various ways, including the 'Columns and Clusters' and 'Talking Wall' styles described next. An advantage of this approach over brainstorming is that it produces some quantitative, as well as qualitative, data; in other words, if several people write notes on the same topic, we get a sense that this topic is quite important. Also, the process is not slowed down by the need for the scribe or facilitator to write things down.

Columns and clusters: Once the participants have finished completing their Post-Its, the facilitator asks them to come up and stick them to the wall, starting a new column (or cluster) each time they believe they have introduced a new topic. Each person sticks up their notes in turn, and they can explain what they have written as they go along. Once the columns or clusters have been created, they can be reordered until the participants think they have them organised in a sensible manner.

Talking wall: This is like the Post-it approach (indeed, the little notes may be used with it), but it starts with several sheets of brown paper stuck to a wall. The facilitator asks the participants to write their ideas (or stick their notes) directly on to them.

Greenfield site: Here participants are asked to clear their minds of the baggage of history, and to imagine they are starting their organisation, department, process or whatever from scratch – on a greenfield site, in fact. If they weren't saddled with all their legacy approaches and systems, what would they do today?

Transporter: This one focuses on an organisation, or a group of people, or perhaps another nation, and asks: 'How would they do this in …?' Again, the idea is to get people to think in a different way about the issues, not constrained by the way things are done 'here, now and by us'.

Assumption reversal: Finally the participants could be asked to reverse their normal assumptions about a problem. For example, if the workshop starts from the premise that the organisation is the market leader in something, try assuming that it is one of the 'wannabees' instead.

Documentation techniques

The facilitator also needs to find some techniques for documenting the results of the workshop. Some of these are significant techniques in their own right, and hence are presented separately in this book. The possibilities include:

Notes on flipcharts: This is what seems to happen most frequently, and it has the advantage that all the participants can see immediately what is being recorded. Its success does rather depend on the scribe, or the facilitator, having reasonable handwriting, and it can slow proceedings down, particularly where the facilitator is also the one doing the writing.

Post-it notes: As we have mentioned already, one benefit of using these is that they are self-documenting, although at the end of the workshop someone will have to transcribe the results into the meeting notes.

Context and use case diagrams: These are very good for establishing the scope of a proposed IT system, and are covered in detail later in the book (Techniques 22 and 62).

Rich pictures: The idea of these is that they help participants to break away from the limitations of text. There is a description of rich pictures later in this chapter (Technique 20).

Mind maps: These represent the flow of thought, and provide a structure for organising the ideas of a group. They are described in detail later in this chapter (Technique 21).

Using workshops

Workshops have come to be the dominant technique for requirements elicitation and decision-making in projects, where once interviews seemed to reign supreme. The reasons are not hard to find: a workshop is less time consuming than a series of one-on-one discussions, especially in this time-pressured age; they give the opportunity to cross fertilise ideas and build consensus; and workshops somehow seem more democratic and transparent than decision-making by individuals behind closed doors. It should also be pointed out, though, that they are not always successful or universally accepted, and many people regard them as being just like any other meeting, and thus generally a waste of their time. Workshops, like any other technique, have their drawbacks, and some of the issues with them are examined next.

Right and wrong participants: The success of a workshop is very dependent on having the right people present. What 'right' means will obviously depend on the purpose of the workshop. If detailed information is required, then people who do the job, and can thus provide this, are needed; if decisions are needed, the workshop must include people who can make them. Sometimes it would be nice to have participants with both knowledge and authority, but this might mean including people who have different ranks within the organisation, which can make the dynamic tricky to manage. The facilitator can help here at the beginning by getting everyone to accept their equality within the workshop, and later by managing the workshop so that the most senior people do not unduly dominate proceedings.

The number of participants: A workshop can just be too big to manage effectively. Probably about a dozen is the maximum number of participants if each person is to contribute properly, and even this is a rather large group for a facilitator to manage. If large groups are unavoidable – perhaps because certain people insist on being present – then working in smaller subgroups and reporting back to the main meeting may be a good idea, though it will be difficult for the facilitator to manage and encourage all of the groups.

Over-ambitious agenda: Precisely because it is difficult to get a group of relevant people together in one place, there is a temptation to try and cover too much ground in a workshop. This can result in the agenda items not being covered properly, and the facilitator 'driving on' even though consensus has not been obtained on important matters, perhaps resorting to tactics such as voting, which achieve a decision but probably alienate some of the participants who were outvoted.

Duration: Winston Churchill is reported to have said: 'The mind can only absorb what the backside can endure', or something similar.

The point is that if a workshop goes on too long the concentration of the participants will waver, and they will become tired, bored and even fractious. The facilitator must sense when the energy is dipping, and call a break; and the workshop must finish on time. If, at the scheduled end point, agreement is very close, then an extension may be acceptable provided it is negotiated and agreed with the participants. Otherwise, unpalatable though it is, the only real answer is to reconvene – maybe with fewer people, just to finish off the remaining issues.

The venue:
The venue can have a significant effect on the dynamics of a workshop. For example, having too many people crammed into a small room with no daylight is hardly conducive to creative thought; but having a small group in a ballroom can be equally off-putting. The venue needs to be the right size, with comfortable seating, good lighting (preferably natural) and sufficient space to move around. It needs to be properly equipped with flipcharts, whiteboards, pens and so forth. Ideally refreshments should be available 'on tap', so that the facilitator can take breaks at a convenient time in the discussions, rather than at prearranged times. Similarly, workshop participants should not have to waste a lot of time getting served at lunch (or dinner, if it's a whole-day event).

One issue to be addressed is whether the venue should be on site or off site. On site is obviously cheaper and perhaps easier, though meeting rooms seem to be in short supply in many organisations. However, there is always the temptation for people to sneak back to their desks during breaks, just to check their emails, and this can make timekeeping very difficult. Also, people may 'pop in' to grab someone's attention, a further distraction from the main business of the workshop. An off-site venue obviously overcomes these problems, but expense has to be considered, and some places – hotels notoriously – are not as good at hosting business events (providing refreshments on time, and so forth) as they should be. And even off site, the availability of mobile phones and portable communication devices means that participants are not completely free of distractions.

Choice of techniques:
The facilitator must make sure that the techniques employed – especially those for discovery – are appropriate to the task in hand and the nature of the participants. Hard-nosed accountants, for instance, might be rather resistant to some of the 'softer' ice-breakers. The facilitator may, of course, wish to pull the participants out of their comfort zones, but this must be done deliberately and with a 'plan B' in mind if the attempt backfires. One thing that is a good idea in any case is to use a variety of techniques, so that participants do not get bored with yet another Post-it exercise or brainstorm.

Having a scribe:	Facilitating a workshop is a nontrivial undertaking. The facilitator has to manage the time, 'read' the people, phrase questions, watch the agenda, understand contributions, keep some people in line and draw others out, maintain their own 'presence' and composure and push the workshop forward all the time. This is hard enough on its own, but, if the same person is also keeping the record, it becomes very difficult indeed. For this reason, if at all possible the facilitator should recruit someone to act as scribe who can also, as it were, act as a 'deputy facilitator', drawing the attention of the facilitator to any points that have been missed in the heat of the moment.
The business analyst as facilitator:	BAs often end up facilitating workshops because they have convened them and have mastered the issues involved, but this is not necessarily a good idea. Apart from all other considerations, the BA has a personal interest in the outcome of the workshop and/or project and thus is not really objective (an important criterion for a facilitator). The facilitator may also have to act in the workshop to control participants, and this can make subsequent working relationships tricky. If at all possible, then, it is better to have an independent facilitator. If the budget will not run to hiring someone from outside, then maybe a BA from another project might be willing to act as facilitator; the favour can be returned at a later date.
Losing control:	Finally, nothing so destroys the benefit of a workshop, or puts people off attending further ones, than letting the whole thing get out of control – running over time, not covering important parts of the agenda, getting bogged down in trivia or irrelevances, or being dominated by the loudest voices rather than the most thoughtful brains. It is down to the facilitator to ensure that this does not happen, and that the workshop results in satisfactory conclusions for the participants.

Technique 15: Observation
Variants/Aliases
Observation comes in various forms, and several are discussed in this section. Variations on the observation theme include **structured observation, STROBE** (STRuctured Observation of the Business Environment), **shadowing, protocol analysis** and **ethnographic study**.

Description of the technique
Observation consists of BAs going and looking at work – business processes for example – for themselves. There are some very good reasons for it, including these:

- Business users often have trouble describing clearly or concisely what they actually do on a day-to-day basis, and it can be much more productive for the BA to watch what goes on rather then trying to elicit such information through interviews or workshops.

- Equally, tacit knowledge – which we might define as 'what we know but don't know we know' – by its very nature seldom comes to light in interviews or workshops, unless the BA is very skilful indeed or has a lot of domain knowledge to draw on. Watching people do their work can lead BAs to notice things that the business users may not have mentioned before, and they can follow this up by asking why these things are done and what value they add to the business processes.

- The fact that people do not necessarily do in practice what they have told the BA they do – or what, perhaps, the laid-down procedures say they should do – must also be faced. People are naturally inventive, and they find shortcuts to make their jobs easier. Sometimes these are a good thing and result in increased efficiency, but on other occasions problems arise because a defined procedure is not followed. In either case, these departures from the established procedures are unlikely to come to light unless the BA has a look to see what is happening in practice as well as in theory.

So observation is a valuable supplement to the primary elicitation techniques such as interviewing and workshops; and observation can spark off additional lines of enquiry and investigation for the BA.

The simplest form of observation consists of BAs just sitting with a user, or a group of users, and noting down what goes on and anything unusual that strikes them. Of course, common courtesy – not to mention maintaining good relations with the workers and perhaps with their union – dictates that this be agreed in advance with the people concerned and their managers.

As a more planned alternative to such an approach, we might employ structured observation, sometimes referred to as *STROBE*. Here the BA goes out with a checklist to look for specific pieces of information – for example, how many phone calls are answered each day, how many orders are taken, how far workers have to walk to access files, and so forth. This form of observation obviously depends on some preliminary investigations, probably via interviews or workshops, to identify what activities to look for.

Shadowing can take two forms. In one, the BA follows workers around and notes everything they do, thus obtaining a good overview of the pattern of work. In the other form, BAs take the role of an 'apprentice' and ask the worker to train them in the job, thus gaining personal insights into the details and challenges of the job.

Protocol analysis consists of workers performing their duties while providing the BA with a commentary on what they are doing.

The term *'ethnographic study'* originates from the world of anthropology, and means researchers spending a protracted time living with a group of people, such as an Inuit hunting band for example, immersing themselves in the culture and lifestyle. An anthropologist undertaking such a study is trying to discover things about the way the society works, what its norms are, where the power is in the group, what is acceptable and unacceptable behaviour, and so on. Although this might seem to be a world away from business analysis, in fact the approach can be very useful, since it helps BAs to understand the type of organisation they are studying, and into which they may later introduce new procedures, processes and systems. For example, a few days immersed in a high-energy sales team may reveal the hopelessness of trying to introduce procedures for capturing customer information through the use of detailed forms or input screens.

Using observation

So far we have been rather enthusiastic about the benefits of the various types of observation that a BA might consider using. However, there are several very practical issues to be borne in mind when planning the use of observation and, later, understanding and interpreting the results.

The first is what scientists refer to as the 'Heisenberg principle'. Loosely expressed, this means that the results of the observation are affected by the presence of the observer. If people know they are being watched, they may try to influence the results of the observation by, say, finding more work than they would normally have at that period or performing the work differently. Even if there is no deliberate intent to deceive the observer, the fact is that being watched is unnerving and people may find themselves behaving atypically because of this. Although the Heisenberg principle is real enough, however, it is also true that people soon get used to being observed, and either tire of trying to fool the observer deliberately or just revert to normal patterns of working. What this means in practice is that, to be useful, an observation must take place over an extended period; and the BA must be prepared to write off some of the earlier observations as part of the 'settling down' period.

Leaving aside the Heisenberg effects, though, having someone watching one's work does have the potential to interrupt 'business as usual' – especially if the observer is also asking questions all the time to find out what is going on. This is the main reason why it is important to set up the observation in advance by discussing it with the people affected and with their managers, explaining what it is for and what it is designed to discover. If this preparation is done properly, it should help to overcome a lot of the problems described so far.

Even if the observer intends to stay in the background and not to interrupt the work, this can be difficult to achieve. Often – and especially with clerical and 'knowledge' work – it is difficult for an observer to determine what is going on without asking. And how does an observer interpret the sight of people just sitting and apparently doing nothing at all? They may, in fact, be doing nothing – or, equally, they may be thinking through a particularly difficult business problem. The only solution to this is, of course, to ask what is going on or – as with protocol analysis – to ask the person to provide a running commentary; but sometimes people feel awkward or embarrassed about doing this.

When using a structured approach like STROBE the BA may concentrate too intently on the checklist and fail to spot something significant that is not listed on it. The BA therefore needs to be aware of this possibility, and be alert to something occurring that is relevant to the study even if it is not on the list.

When shadowing someone, another pitfall to think about is that the day, or the week, may not be a typical one. For example, there may be some cyclical peak or trough of work, and if the period of study happens to coincide with this, the results will not give a representative picture of work more generally. To avoid this, the BA needs to conduct some preliminary discussions with the workers and their managers and to select a study period that is reasonably typical. If an atypical period cannot be avoided – perhaps due to project time pressures – then other records may have to be consulted so that an adjustment can be made to the results.

It will have been apparent when reading the description above of ethnographic studies that this is likely to be a time-consuming exercise. Unfortunately such time is not often available in the hard-pressed world of work. This is a shame if significant business change is being proposed, the introduction of which will be immeasurably smoothed if the cultural context is properly understood.

It has to be acknowledged, too, that observation does not, of itself, yield reliable quantitative data; at best, it produces a view of the situation as seen by a – hopefully – impartial observer. If more 'hard' data is required, to be taken forward to a business case (perhaps to prove the value of tangible benefits), then a more quantitative approach, such as activity sampling, may be required.

Finally BAs need to be aware that informal observation can be combined with interviewing if the discussions take place at the subject's workplace. While giving full attention to interviewees and what they have to say, the BA should keep an eye open for what is going on around them, and look for any aspects of the working environment that may be relevant to the final business solution. It may have to cater for lots of interruptions, for example.

QUANTITATIVE INVESTIGATION

Technique 16: Questionnaires
Variants/Aliases
These can also be called **surveys**.

Description of the technique
Questionnaires are among the range of techniques that a BA can use to elicit requirements or gather other information, or to validate with a wider group of people the information already gained from smaller groups by using, for example, interviews or workshops (Techniques 13 and 14).

Questionnaires are probably best thought of as a second-line investigation technique, designed to supplement, test or amplify information gained first through other means. For example, the BA might already have convened a workshop with a few representatives of a particular job role, and may now wish to find out if what these people have said is typical of the wider population. Similarly a BA may want to see whether the views of a few interviewees are shared more widely.

However, there are some situations where the use of questionnaires becomes a primary fact-finding technique. This usually happens where the 'user population' is widely dispersed, and it is not practical to conduct lots of one-on-one interviews or a workshop; this occurs particularly with widely dispersed, for example multinational, organisations. If this really is the case, then the BA needs to be particularly aware of the limitations and difficulties of questionnaires, as discussed in the section below on 'Using questionnaires'.

The keys to success in the use of questionnaires include:

- Being clear about what purpose they are to serve. Obviously gathering data is one such use, but BAs may also use questionnaires to gain the involvement or engage the enthusiasm of a dispersed group.

- Being realistic in their scope. An unrealistic approach often leads to a questionnaire so long that few people bother to complete and return it.

- Designing the questionnaire, and particularly the questions, in a way that makes its purpose clear and its completion easy.

- Realising that low response rates are typical with many questionnaires; and thinking about how to factor in the possibly different views held by non-responders.

BAs planning to use a questionnaire should consider carefully how they are going to analyse the data once it is collected. For example, if we are asking the question 'Do you believe the situation is better, worse or about the same as it was this time last year?', do we want to know the mean response – the simple arithmetic average of all the responses, or the mode – the answer given by the highest number of respondents?

In terms of design, a questionnaire actually has four parts, as shown in Figure 2.4, and we shall consider each element in turn.

Figure 2.4 The elements of a questionnaire

Title	
Heading section	• Explanation • Incentive • Return
Classification section	• Categories • Ranges
Data section	• Questions • Possible answers • Comments

Title

Bearing in mind the low response rates typical of questionnaires, it is worth giving the document some sort of catchy title that engages the interest of the survey population. A title like 'Survey into business processes in the despatch department' probably will not achieve this, whereas 'Making the despatch work more interesting' just might.

Heading section

This section seeks to do three things:

- It should explain to the recipients what the questionnaire is about, and its importance.

- It should give some incentive for people to complete and return the questionnaire. In public opinion surveys respondents are frequently offered a place in a prize draw if they return the questionnaire, but this sort of incentive may not be appropriate, or available, in a BA study. Instead the BA needs to find some 'hook' for respondents, some way in which they can gain something from completing and returning the survey. This could take the form of a lessening of their workload, the removal of some tedium from their tasks, or something else that the workers may appreciate. (Incentives such as increased company profitability, although probably dear to the hearts of senior management, are of less direct interest to workers than the effect on their jobs.)

- Finally it should be clearly spelled out how and to whom the questionnaire should be returned. If the questionnaire is on paper, an addressed and, if relevant, stamped envelope should be included for the purpose.

Classification section

This section is needed when the BA wants to find out more about who is completing the questionnaire, and whether there are differences between the various groups of respondents. For example, are the views of men different from those of women? Do older people have different views from younger ones? Are there divergences between the ideas of senior managers and front-line workers?

Classification can be achieved in two ways:

- by asking people which of a number of groups they fall into (such as males and females, for instance);
- by offering ranges (such as ages 16–25, 26–35, and so forth).

Data section

This is the part of the document where the actual questions are asked. Three types of question might be posed (it is worth comparing this list with the broader set given in the earlier discussion on interviewing – see Technique 13).

Open: Open questions invite free-format answers. They allow respondents to state their real views, but the answers can be difficult to analyse.

Closed: These questions ask for simple 'yes/no' answers, and can be used to secure definitive information. It is a good idea to offer 'don't know' as another possible answer, since respondents may resent being forced into a 'yes/no' choice with which they do not agree.

Limited choice: Here a set of choices is offered, such as a range of monetary values.

Where closed and limited-choice questions are used, respondents should also be provided with the chance to make comments that explain their choices.

Using questionnaires

One real problem with questionnaires is the low response rate typically experienced. In commercial situations the researchers can offer some sort of incentive for the return of the questionnaires; an entry in a prize draw for example. BAs might have to find some other incentive, such as the potential benefits to the respondents' jobs.

Another issue to consider with poor response rates is how to interpret the results that are obtained. Is it safe, for example, to assume that the people who responded are typical of the larger population? Probably not; it is just as likely that those who returned their questionnaires had a particular axe to grind. What this means is that a small sample has to be 'taken with a large pinch of salt'.

To increase the likelihood that people do respond to questionnaires, respondents are sometimes guaranteed anonymity. However, this can be compromised by questions asked in the classification section of the questionnaire. For example, if we ask for grade, age range and gender, we may have narrowed the respondent population to the point where specific individuals can be identified.

Another problem with the classification section is that some respondents react adversely to some types of question: those relating to salary range, for instance, seem to be particularly unpopular. Before using a specific classification, therefore, the BA needs to be certain that it really is necessary to classify respondents in this way. It may also be advisable to add to the classification section an explanation of why the questions are being asked.

The phrasing of each question should also receive careful consideration, and it is a good idea to test questions out on a small sample of respondents before using the questionnaire more widely. For example, if we asked 'Have you recently stopped smoking?', the answer 'no' would be the same for people who have never smoked, those who gave up a long time ago, and those who continue to smoke. What's more, what does 'recently' mean in this situation? Some poorly phrased questions may, in fact, be impossible to answer sensibly, and this can antagonise respondents – and cause them not to complete the questionnaire.

Even if most of a questionnaire contains closed or limited-choice questions, respondents should be given some open questions, or at least be allowed some comments, so that they can qualify their responses; otherwise, they may feel that their views are being inaccurately represented, which, again, can worsen the response rate.

Nowadays, of course, we are not limited to sending out paper questionnaires, and online surveys can be very effective – especially as we can get at a large population relatively easily. However, online surveys must be carefully designed for ease of use and navigation. Respondents are easily put off by surveys that are hard to use or difficult to understand, or that do not allow for changes of mind. The best principles of good web design should be followed in the creation of online surveys.

Technique 17: Sampling
Variants/Aliases
Related techniques are **activity sampling, work measurement** and **record sampling**.

Description of the technique
Sampling is one of the techniques that can be used to obtain quantitative data during a business analysis assignment – particularly data about how people spend their time. This is valuable because it enables the BA to understand where the real problems and issue lie, and it also provides input to the business case for change.

One of the problems with the information gleaned from interviews and workshops (Techniques 13 and 14) is that it is, to some extent, subjective – it represents the views and opinions of individuals. These individuals may see something as a great problem that, when it is subjected to measurement, is found to be irritating but not really significant in terms of the time spent. Observation will help to put these views into perspective, but there is nothing like measurement to get to the real heart of a problem.

We may also employ special-purpose records to get quantitative data, but, as we show in the description of Technique 18, they do rather depend on the memory and the goodwill of the people completing them; the memory in that they need to remember to complete them, and the goodwill in that they have to complete them accurately. These difficulties are overcome with sampling, though it does have some problems of its own, which we discuss later in this section.

Before embarking on a sampling exercise the BA needs to prepare the ground. To do this:

- Talk to the managers of the department or area concerned, and also the people working there, to explain the purpose of the exercise. Where the workforce is unionised, the agreement of the trade union representatives will also be needed.

- Find out what activities are likely to be seen during the sampling period, and check whether the period is a reasonably typical one (not hitting an atypical year-end period, for instance).

- Decide the sampling interval. To get a reasonable picture of the work, something like once every 15 minutes is usually good enough.

Based on this information a sheet like that in Figure 2.5 can be created, to record the results of the exercise. In this case the samples are for a section within a bank call centre that fields certain types of customer enquiry.

Figure 2.5 Activity sampling sheet (completed)

Date/time	Person						
4th January	Angie	Jack	Tom	Claire	Petra	Darren	Tracy
09:44	1	1	2	1	4	5	6
10:00	1	5	2	4	7	4	1
10:33	4	4	2	1	1	6	7
10:55	1	1	4	1	1	1	1
11:21	1	4	2	4	4	1	5
12:17	6	6	2	1	6	1	4
12:19	6	6	4	1	6	1	1
13:08	4	4	6	6	1	6	6
13:22	4	1	6	6	1	6	6
13:28	5	1	6	6	1	6	6
13:37	3	1	6	6	1	6	6
14:26	3	1	2	1	5	7	1
15:14	3	4	2	4	4	1	4
15:57	4	4	4	1	6	1	7
16:20	3	1	2	2	1	1	5
16:39	3	1	2	2	1	4	4
17:08	3	1	2	4	1	5	6

<u>Activity codes</u>

1 = Amending account details   2 = Setting up new account   3 = Setting up new standing order

4 = Making interaccount transfer   5 = Discussions with supervisor   6 = Not working

7 = On other work

It will be noticed that in Figure 2.5 there are roughly four observations per hour, but they are not exactly at 15-minute intervals. This is to avoid the possible problem where the intervals coincide with some regular process and thus give a skewed result.

On the first day of the survey the BA turns up at the intervals stated, and notes down what each person is doing during each timed observation. With clerical work it is sometimes hard at first to see what someone is doing (it is usually easier with manual work).

Once the day's observations have been made, the results are summarised on an analysis sheet like that in Figure 2.6.

Figure 2.6 Sampling analysis summary sheet

Date	4th January			5th January			6th January		
Activity	**Number**	**%**	Moving avge %	**Number**	**%**	Moving avge %	**Number**	**%**	Moving avge %
1	40	34	34	32	29	21	28	27	30
2	12	10	10	15	13	12	12	12	12
3	6	5	5	8	7	6	7	7	6
4	24	20	20	20	18	19	22	22	20
5	7	6	6	9	8	7	8	8	7
6	26	22	22	25	22	22	20	20	21
7	4	3	3	3	3	3	5	5	4
Total observations	119			112			102		

The next question to be addressed is: how long should the sampling exercise last? Statistical formulas can be used to determine the size of the sample (Wood 2003; Rumsey 2003), but a pragmatic approach is to calculate a 'moving average' at the end of each day (in other words, an average of all the observations so far); when this moving average settles down, the sample size is probably big enough. We can see in our example that the averages settle down quite well after three days, so that probably gives us a reasonable picture of the pattern of work.

The analysis sheet thus gives us a view of how the staff in our call centre spend their day. If the figure for 'not working' seems rather alarming at 21 per cent, we need to remember that, with a eight-hour day, an hour for lunch and two 15-minute coffee breaks, we would expect to lose just under 20 per cent anyway, so this result seems about right. We can see that amending customers' account details is the most significant activity, followed by making transfers. If we want to improve the efficiency of the section, therefore, it is on these processes that we need to concentrate our attention.

Using sampling
As we have seen, the use of sampling techniques gives us reasonably reliable quantitative data with which to plan the business analysis work (in other words, to select which are the most significant activities to study), and also provides input to the business case by giving a picture of the situation 'as is'.

We can combine sampling data with information gleaned from other sources to measure transaction times. For example, during the three-day exercise shown in Figure 2.6, a total of 6.72 hours was spent setting up new accounts (7 people × 8 hours per day × 12%). If we find out that 40 new accounts were opened in that period, we get a time of about 10 minutes per transaction (6.72 hours × 60 minutes divided by 40). We can compare this time with that for any improved process that we may propose, and thus offer the decision-makers a properly costed and justifiable tangible saving as part of the business case.

Two issues that do worry people with sampling are that being watched in this way can be unnerving for the workers, and that the workers may behave atypically (particularly by working faster or slower than usual) precisely because they are being measured. These are real possibilities, but practical experience suggests that people get used to the sampler's presence, which they soon begin to ignore; and again people rapidly tire of trying to distort the survey, and settle back into their usual pattern of work. If the BA does suspect some problem like this in the early stages of the project, one answer is to extend the study by a couple of days and discard the first two days as a settling-down period.

Technique 18: Special-purpose records
Variants/Aliases
Timesheets are often used for this.

Description of the technique
Often in business analysis work it is useful to gather quantitative as well as qualitative data. For example, if we are examining the work of a complaints-handling section, it would be useful to know how many complaints are made, what they are about, how long it takes to respond to them, and so forth. One method of getting such data is to conduct an activity-sampling exercise (Technique 17). However, activity sampling is time-consuming for the analyst and can be unnerving to the people being studied. The use of special-purpose records, whereby business users keep a tally of what they have been doing, is an alternative way of collecting such information.

Let us continue to use a complaints-handling section as our example. We could devise a special-purpose record for it, which in its simplest form might look like that shown in Figure 2.7.

Figure 2.7 Special-purpose record for complaints handling

Issue	Mon	Tue	Wed	Thu	Fri
Non-delivery	卌II	IIII			
Late delivery	III	II			
Wrong product	II	III			
Defective product	II	I			
Poor service	III	II			
Other	III	卌			
Daily totals:	20	17			

In Figure 2.7 we have listed six categories of complaint that might be handled. To identify these we would previously have conducted an interview with the section manager, or perhaps held a workshop with some members of the section. The latter is a particularly good idea, since it gives the BA an opportunity to explain why the exercise is being conducted, and the importance (for the participants' jobs, ideally) of the results.

The subjects are then asked to use a 'five-bar gate' system to record every time they get a call, and, at the end of each day, to total how many complaints of each type they have dealt with.

A more elaborate timesheet is shown in Figure 2.8, where the subjects are asked to assess, at the end of each day, how much time they have spent on various sorts of activities; such timesheets are often used already in organisations such as consultancy firms and law offices, where clients are charged on the basis of the amount of time spent on their business.

Using special-purpose records

The most obvious downside of special-purpose records is that they may not be completed accurately. One reason for this is that people forget to do it until the end of the day – probably because they are very busy doing their actual work – and then just make something up to keep the pesky BA happy! Another possibility is that people deliberately inflate the results, and this is very likely when they are worried about retaining their jobs or are angling for an increase in staffing levels or improved compensation. There is no sure-fire way of avoiding this, but the BA can often improve accuracy by building a good relationship with the subjects beforehand and explaining why accurate information is important for all parties.

A well-designed form can aid completion, by being easier to fill in and making the whole exercise look more professional. In addition, it's a good idea not to ask

Figure 2.8 Detailed weekly timesheet

Issue	Mon	Tue	Wed	Thu	Fri
Non-delivery	1.00	1.25			
Late delivery	0.50	0.50			
Wrong product	0.50	0.50			
Defective product	0.50	0.25			
Poor service	0.75	0.50			
Other	0.75	1.50			
Daily totals:	4.00	4.50			

for too many different things on one form, since this adds to the burden of completing it. If a wide variety of information is required, consider giving different sheets to different subgroups of subjects, so each person can concentrate on a narrower set of information.

Technique 19: Document analysis

Description of the technique
Document analysis is the systematic examination of data sources, usually forms, but also screen layouts and reports if there is an existing system, to analyse the data requirements of a proposed computerised information system.

The starting point for document analysis is to discover worthwhile data sources to examine. In the early days of IT, such sources would always be physical things, usually forms, ledgers and so forth. Today, where one is more likely to be moving from an existing IT system to a newer one, the range of sources can also include screens and reports from the current system.

The information shown on each document is examined systematically and recorded on a form like that shown in Figure 2.9.

The heading rows of the document specification are used to record information that enables the document to be identified. These include the name of the document, its file reference, a short description, its stationery reference (if relevant) and its size. We also record how it is currently prepared – in this case by hand. The remaining information to be recorded includes:

Filing sequence: This provides insights into how the users will want to access this information once it is computerised; although, of course, unlike manual filing, an indexed computer system allows the information to be accessed in a variety of ways.

Figure 2.9 Example of a document specification form

Document specification				
Project ID and name: *P027HR System Study*				
Document name: *Training record sheet*	**Project file reference:** *Doc 10*		**Description:** *Record of training courses* *attended by employees*	**Sheet:** *1 of 1*
Stationery ref: *Form TR01*	**Size:** *A4 (landscape)*	**Number of parts:** *1*	**Method of preparation:** *Handwritten*	
Filing sequence: *Alphabetical by surname*	**Storage medium:** *Loose-leaf cards*		**Prepared by/maintained by:** *HR clerk or HR manager*	
When created: *When employee joins*	**Retention period:** *3 years after leaving service*		**Storage location:** *HR Department*	
Volumes per: *Month*	**Minimum:** *0*	**Maximum:** *10(new employees)*	**Average:** *3*	**Growth rate/** **fluctuations:** *Not applicable-* *volume fairly* *static*
Users/recipients: *Personnel Department* *Line Manager* *Line Manager* *Subject*	**Purpose:** *Review training* *Review training* *Appraisal* *To check*		**Frequency of use:** *As required* *As required* *Annually* *As required*	
Data item:	**Format/description:**		**Value range:**	**Sources of** **data:**
Name	*Alphanumeric(25). First and surname*		*Any*	*Application form*
Payroll number	*Numeric(6)*		*00000–1999999*	*Application form*
Date of course	*Numeric(6) (DD/MM/YY)*		*Dates*	*HR clerk*
Name of course	*Alphanumeric(50)*		*Any*	*Brochures*
Training provider	*Alphanumeric(50)*		*Any*	*Brochures*
Result if tested	*Alphanumeric(4)*		*Pass/Fail*	*Training provider*
Comments				*Not used*

Storage medium:	This shows how the information is stored at the moment – and identifies the source from which the new computerised files will need to be created.
Prepared by / maintained by:	Here we show who records the information initially and who maintains it. Again this gives us information about who will need to have access rights once the system is computerised.
When created:	This helps to identify the business event that causes the information to be recorded initially.

Retention period:	Now we begin to understand how long information will need to be held and to be available in our computerised system.
Storage location:	This indicates where the forms (if that's what they are) are stored at the moment, and thus the location from which they will have to be obtained for data creation.
Volumes:	Here we can record the number of new documents per month, per year or whatever, and what the overall growth in numbers is. This, clearly, is of some importance in working out how much space must be reserved in the system for the data.
Users / recipients:	Apart from the people who record the information initially, we are also interested in who needs to access it and for what reason. Again this will influence the access privileges we define for the computer system.
Data item information:	Finally, for each data item on the form, we record its name, its format and description, whether there are defined ranges within which the values must fit, and where the data comes from. This is extremely useful in modelling the data for the proposed system (for details of which, see Techniques 63 and 64, entity relationship modelling and class modelling), and, again, in sizing the proposed system.

Using document analysis

Some commonsense has to be used in the selection of data sources to be documented in this way. We do not necessarily need to examine every form, screen or report currently used. Instead we need to select those that will give us the best overall picture of the proposed system's data requirements.

Some BAs may feel that such detailed work on data is not really part of their job, leaving this to the systems analysts or even the developers. However, it must be remembered that the BA probably has the closest contact with the system's proposed users and is therefore in the best position to search out the relevant data sources.

DOCUMENTING THE RESULTS

Technique 20: Rich pictures

Description of the technique

Rich pictures were popularised in the soft systems methodology, put forward by Professor Peter Checkland and his associates in the 1980s (Checkland 1993). The idea is to capture in pictorial form the essential elements of a business issue or problem, to facilitate a more holistic understanding and analysis of it. There are no rules as to what may or could be captured in a rich picture, nor about what symbols should be used, so it is a very free-format technique indeed. Typically, though, the sorts of things we want to represent in a rich picture include:

- the principal actors in the business process or system;

- the views, ideas and concerns of those actors;

- anything we know about the structure of the organisation (including its actual structure – hierarchical versus flat for instance – but also issues like its geographical location, fragmentation across sites and so forth);

- impressions of the business processes – bureaucratic at one extreme, or very informal at the other, for example – and the IT systems that support them;

- an impression of the culture and climate of the organisation: for example, is it a supportive environment or a blame culture?

The best way of understanding the technique is to look at a rich picture, so one is presented in Figure 2.10.

Figure 2:10 Example rich picture (of a sales organisation)

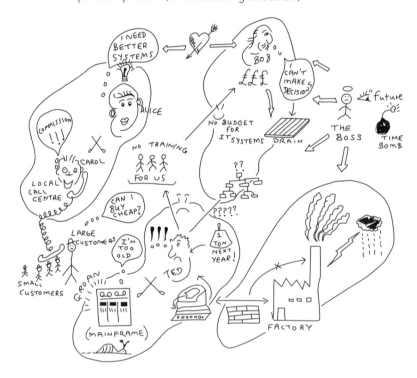

Although Figure 2.10 may appear somewhat whimsical at first, it does in fact contain a vast amount of information that would probably take many pages of text to capture. For example:

- Bob is extremely concerned that money is going down the drain in the firm;

- Alice is frustrated by the inadequacy of the IT systems;

- the IT systems are both old and slow (notice the snail);
- the boss sees the future as a ticking time-bomb, if the organisation does not improve its performance;
- there seems to be an overall lack of training within the firm;
- there is a black cloud hanging over the firm's factory – mainly because the sales people reckon they get lower prices and better service by going to outside suppliers;
- there is tension between Carol and Alice (the crossed swords), but Alice seems to see eye-to-eye with Bob (the heart);
- there is a bit of a query about where Ted (the head of IT) fits into the organisational structure.

In effect, then, this rich picture is a 'brain dump' of everything the BAs have discovered in their initial studies, and it also provides a 'shopping list' of issues that need to be investigated further. For example, is it true that the factory does a worse job than do outside suppliers, or does this just represent the prejudices of the salespeople?

Using rich pictures

Rich pictures, like the mind maps we discuss next, seem to arouse strong reactions when people are first introduced to them. Some people love the freedom of expression they permit, and relish the way they avoid the tedium of long textual descriptions of problems and issues. Others, however, find this very freedom somewhat unnerving and prefer more structured diagramming techniques, such as those found in the IT world.

It is also true that not everyone is equally gifted with drawing skills. Drawing is essential to the use of rich pictures, but if one cannot, for example, draw people as in Figure 2.10, stick figures will do just as well.

An element of this may be related to organisational culture, too: a highly visual technique like this might be just the thing in a creative organisation like an advertising agency – but perhaps less acceptable in a staid law firm?

The authors have used rich pictures very successfully for many years, for example to bring together and summarise the results of several interviews conducted by different analysts. We are not so sure, however, that rich pictures necessarily provide a particularly good method of communication back to the business stakeholders, since what is clear to the author of a rich picture may be very obscure to someone else viewing it. Again, this might depend on the culture of the organisation being studied.

We would urge BAs at least to give rich pictures a try, to see if they will work for them, in their environment.

Technique 21: Mind maps
Variants/Aliases
Similar techniques include **semantic networks, webs** and **concept maps**.

Description of the technique

The basic concept of a mind map as a visual representation of a set of ideas, words, things or tasks and the relationships between them is actually quite ancient but their popularity at the present time is probably due to Tony Buzan, an author and broadcaster on psychology, who, in his TV programmes and books, has introduced them to a wide public (Buzan 2006; Buzan and Buzan 2006). Mr Buzan's organisation has registered the term 'Mind Map' as a trademark in the UK and the USA.

A mind map can be used in several situations, including team building and other cooperative endeavours, for note taking during interviews or other meetings, and, of course, in workshops. It is probably in the interview or workshop situation (Techniques 13 and 14) that most BAs will make use of the technique.

Figure 2.11 presents an example of a mind map, in this case one showing the development, content and presentation of a business case. This mind map has been developed on a computer, but, more often, they are created by hand, probably on a flipchart or whiteboard during a meeting or workshop.

The mind map starts with a central idea, in this instance that of a business case. This represents the 'trunk' of the model. It then shows the subsidiary themes, the main 'branches' of the idea – in this example the main components of a business case. These branches can then be developed into more and more detail.

Figure 2.11 Example of a mind map

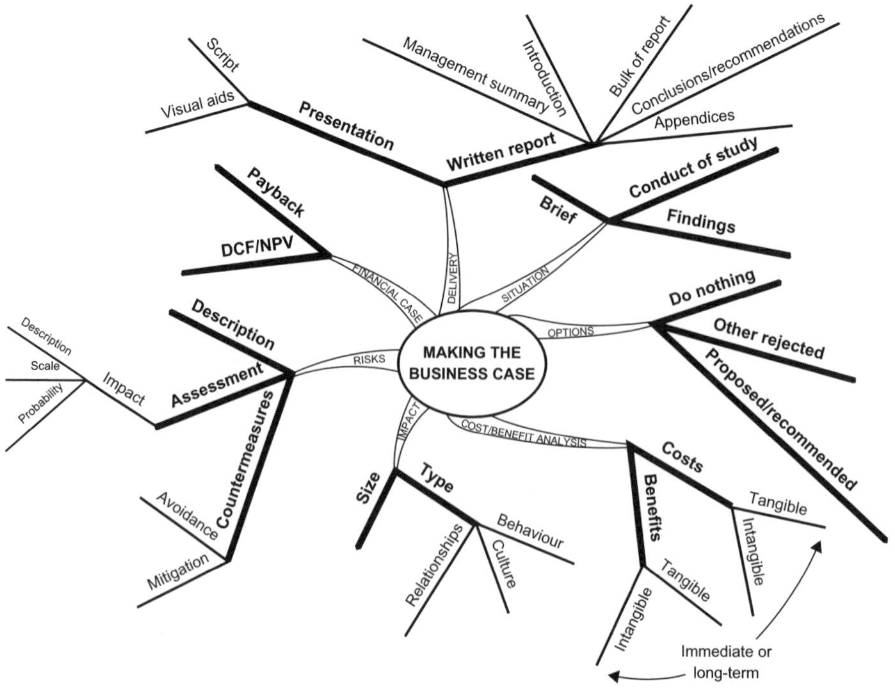

Notice, too, how cross-connections can be made between the different 'twigs', as with that between tangible and intangible costs and benefits at the bottom right of the diagram.

This example uses only words, but mind maps can be even more powerful if images are used as well or instead.

When using it to support interviewing, the BA can create the outline mind map – the trunk and main branches only – from the agenda and then populate the rest of the diagram with information supplied by the interviewee. Because only a few words need to be written down, this can simplify note taking and allow for greater eye contact with the subject.

When it is used during a workshop, the facilitator can create the mind map as participants suggest ideas. Alternatively, or additionally, participants can be put into smaller groups and asked to explore particular aspects of the issue under discussion and present their findings back in the form of mind maps.

Using mind maps

Tony Buzan claims that mind maps work because they reflect the way the human mind organises information – a central theme leading to subsidiary concepts and thus down into lower and lower levels of detail. It is fair to say that his claims are not necessarily supported by other experts in thinking and, when this book was being written, somewhat of a controversy was raging on Wikipedia about the effectiveness of mind maps.

Not everyone gets on with mind maps. One of the present authors, for example, does not find them particularly intuitive or useful, although this may be due to a lack of persistence in working with and mastering them. Those who do like them, however (a group which includes the other two authors), seem to like them very much and find them a very powerful alternative to conventional note taking. Certainly they provide focus, clarity and brevity where more conventional notes, though containing the information, sometimes obscure key issues with irrelevant detail. It may be that whether one 'gets' mind maps has something to do with individual thinking styles – whether one thinks in words or in pictures, for instance – although Mr Buzan's view seems to be that they are suitable for everyone. Our advice would be to try the technique – and maybe persist with it for a while if it is not instantly accessible.

Technique 22: Context diagram

Description of the technique

The idea of a context diagram has appeared in various 'structured' approaches to development over the years. Both Tom DeMarco and Edward Yourdon, for instance, pioneers of structured methods, refer to context diagrams in their books (DeMarco 1978; Yourdon 1989), and these diagrams also appeared in the Structured Systems Analysis and Design Method (SSADM) in the guise of a 'level 0' data flow diagram (SSADM Foundation 2000). What we shall describe here, however, is the latest manifestation of a context diagram within the Unified Modeling Language (UML) (Arlow and Neustadt 2005).

The essential idea of a context diagram is that it shows a proposed (or existing) IT system in relation to the wider world – to the people and other systems with which it must interface. The system itself is regarded as a 'black box' with things (yet to be defined) going on within it. Later we can go inside the 'black box' and define these things in more detail.

The basic technique is quite simple, and an example of a context diagram is shown in Figure 2.12. The proposed system is drawn as a box in the centre of the diagram. Around it are positioned the 'actors' with which it is expected to interact by receiving input or providing output. Actors in this case include:

- user roles – a person or job title within or outside the organisation (the latter category including customers, for example);
- other systems;
- time.

Figure 2.12 Context diagram

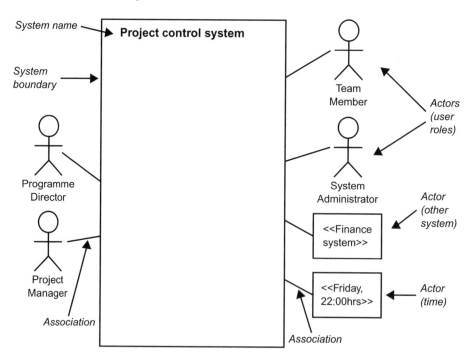

The 'user role' type of actor is usually represented by a 'stick person' with the name of the role underneath. These symbols can also be used for other actors, too, but that might look a little odd. Instead a box can be used, as in Figure 2.12, showing the name of the system. A box can also be used for time, with, if it is known at this stage, the time or date that actually triggers processes within the system.

The 'association' – the interaction – between the actors and the system is indicated by a line between the actor and the system boundary. Notice that the line is not arrowed, since it does not show the flow of data. It just shows the existence of a relationship between the system and the actor.

Using context diagrams

Context diagrams can be developed by BAs based on the research they have done through interviews, workshops and so forth. Having drawn a diagram a BA then needs to review it with the various actors to check that it does represent their understanding of how they will use the proposed system. If the system is replacing an existing one, study of that earlier system's documentation will also reveal the various interfaces that will be needed, particularly with other systems and with time.

However, context diagrams are also a powerful tool for use during a workshop with the various stakeholders (Technique 14). The BA (or other facilitator) can draw a box representing the proposed system on the whiteboard or flipchart, and then ask participants to shout out the names of the actors they think need to interact with it. Alternatively participants can be invited to come up and add actors themselves. This way, the group can generate very quickly a diagram that shows the scope of the proposed system and the way it fits in with the wider world. If time permits, the group can then go on to explore the types of function within the system with which each actor will interact – and thus begin to develop a more detailed use case diagram (Technique 62).

REFERENCES

Arlow, J. and Neustadt, I. (2005) *UML 2 and the Unified* Process, 2nd edition. Addison Wesley, Upper Saddle River, NJ.

Buzan, T. (2006) *Use Your Head*. BBC Active, London.

Buzan, T. and Buzan, B. (2006) *The Mind Map Book*. BBC Active, London.

Checkland, P. (1993) *Systems Thinking, Systems Practice*. Wiley, Chichester.

DeMarco, T. (1978) *Structured Analysis and System Specification*. Yourdon Press, Englewood Cliffs.

Rumsey, D. (2003) *Statistics for Dummies*. Wiley, Hoboken.

SSADM Foundation (2000) The *Business Context* volume of *Business Systems Development with SSADM*. TSO, London.

Wood, M. (2003) *Making Sense of Statistics: A Non-mathematical Approach*. Palgrave Macmillan, Basingstoke.

Yourdon, E. (1989) *Modern Structured Analysis*. Prentice Hall International, Englewood Cliffs.

FURTHER READING

Paul, D. and Yeates, D. (eds) (2007) *Business Analysis*. BCS, Swindon.

Skidmore, S. and Eva, M. (2004) *Introducing Systems Development*. Palgrave Macmillan, Basingstoke.

Townsend, J., Donovan, P. and Hailstone, P. (2009) *The Facilitator's Pocketbook*. Management Pocketbooks, London.

Yeates, D. and Wakefield, T. (2004) *Systems Analysis and Design*, 2nd edition. FT Prentice Hall, Harlow.

3 CONSIDER PERSPECTIVES

INTRODUCTION

One of the key aspects of business analysis is working with stakeholders. Stakeholders can support or resist change, they can clarify or confuse requirements, and they have knowledge that the analyst needs to acquire. As a result, the importance of working closely and effectively with stakeholders cannot be overstated.

Once an investigation of the business situation has been carried out the BA needs to take time to think through the issues that have been raised. At this point thinking through the information gained and the perspectives of those providing that information can be invaluable in uncovering inconsistencies, hidden agendas and personal priorities. Failing to think about these points, or delaying this thinking until a problem arises, can derail or undermine later work. Potential impacts could be the rejection of a business case, requirements conflicts, or, even worse, the failure of new processes and systems.

The process for working effectively with stakeholders has three major steps:

- stakeholder identification;
- stakeholder analysis;
- stakeholder management.

Stakeholder identification (Techniques 23–25)
Stakeholder identification involves considering all of the major groups that could have an interest in the business situation or project. This is done in order to identify the stakeholders within these groups who may have working links or interests with the area under investigation.

There are three techniques that are used to identify the stakeholders for a particular business analysis assignment:

- stakeholder nomination during interviews or workshops;
- background research through document analysis;
- the stakeholder wheel.

Identifying the stakeholders is extremely important if conflicts are to be avoided later in the project. Many initiatives have been derailed when an alternative point of view has emerged, sometimes at a late stage. Identifying the interested parties early on will help analysts to understand the range of views, and, where necessary, handle the differences.

Stakeholder analysis (Techniques 26–29)

Stakeholder analysis is concerned with examining all of the stakeholders or groups of stakeholders and categorising them according to factors such as their level of influence and their areas of concern. It is important to carry out this analysis, since this will provide a means of deciding the stakeholder management strategies to be adopted.

There are four major techniques that are used to analyse stakeholders:

- the power/interest or power/impact grid;
- CATWOE, VOCATE or PARADE;
- business activity modelling;
- RACI or RASCI.

Analysing stakeholders is the key to working well with them. This is essential if business analysis work is to be successful in delivering business improvements. Early analysis of stakeholders can prevent the occurrence of many problems, in particular:

- late (too late!) emergence of conflicts;
- misunderstandings about business needs;
- implementation of poor solutions;
- communication problems;
- resistance or even antipathy.

Stakeholder management (Techniques 30–32)

Stakeholder management provides the basis for ongoing work with the stakeholders during a project. It involves identifying and implementing management strategies that enable analysts to deal with a range of stakeholders. These management strategies are based upon the categorisation that has been carried out during stakeholder analysis. They have to be supplemented by additional techniques that help during the stakeholder management process. These techniques assist with influencing stakeholders, negotiating with them and managing conflict between them.

Three techniques that help with managing stakeholders are covered in this section:

- stakeholder management planning;
- the Thomas–Kilmann conflict mode instrument;
- principled negotiation.

STAKEHOLDER IDENTIFICATION

Technique 23: Stakeholder nomination

Description of the technique
It is relatively easy to identify an initial set of stakeholders, and this is done mainly through stakeholder nomination. The project sponsor is a key stakeholder, and is usually one of the first individuals to interview in order to engage in discussion about the project. During this interview the sponsor should be able to specify the key managers and business staff who need to be involved in the business analysis work.

Using stakeholder nomination
This approach usually works in a hierarchical fashion: the sponsor identifies key managers, all of the managers identify key members of their teams, and so on. A hierarchical approach is helpful because the managers are able to identify the individuals they feel would best fulfil the role required by the analyst, and they can also give permission for their staff to spend time working on the project.

Relying upon individuals who have been identified by the sponsor or another senior manager can be extremely risky, however. Sometimes the sponsor or managers will identify people who are sympathetic to their views and ideas, resulting in a limited analysis with the risk that important details are omitted. Furthermore, a more systematic approach, such as the Stakeholder wheel described below, helps to ensure that all stakeholder views are considered – even those stakeholders who, at first sight, do not appear to be relevant.

Technique 24: Background research
Variants/Aliases
This is also called **report analysis** or **background reading**.

Description of the technique
There are many reasons for initiating a business analysis project. These include a change in business strategy, a request from a senior manager, changes to a related business area, and legal or regulatory changes. One may even follow on from a feasibility study. This usually means that documentation exists to explain why the business analysis is required. There may also be a Terms of Reference statement for the study, or formal project documentation such as a Project Initiation Document. Examining such documentation will often provide information that will help the analyst uncover a wide range of stakeholders, including those working outside the area under investigation. For example, a feasibility study might have included discussions with managers and staff from areas of the organisation that, at first sight, appear to be unrelated to the project, or the source of the original idea might be an external stakeholder such as a major customer or supplier. Any individuals or groups identified when examining background documentation should be entered on the list of initial stakeholders.

Using background research
It is important to locate the documents that could be helpful in identifying stakeholders, and sometimes these are not obvious. If there are pre-project or project documents then they should be made available to the analyst.

However, sometimes work has been done by a different team or under the authorisation of a different sponsor, and it can be difficult to find the related documents. The key approach here is to find out if there have been any other studies looking at similar areas, and obtain copies of the documentation that was produced.

Other documents that are often found within organisations and can be useful when identifying stakeholders are Organisation Charts or Project Structures. The Organisation Charts will show where stakeholders sit in the organisation, and can be the source of valuable information. For example, there may be work areas that have not been mentioned previously but are potentially linked to the business situation under investigation, or may be affected by any recommendations. Any such stakeholders need to be identified and categorised during stakeholder analysis.

One tool that can be extremely useful for stakeholder identification is the Organisation Diagram (Technique 35). It is described in full in Chapter 4, 'Analyse needs', since its primary use is in the analysis of business process improvements. This diagram includes an analysis of the external suppliers of resources to the organisation, and the customer groups that receive products, services and information. The breakdown shown for these groups can provide a great deal of insight into these stakeholders and their perspectives. In addition, the diagram shows the organisations that are competitors, some of whom may be stakeholders for a particular business analysis assignment.

Technique 25: The stakeholder wheel

Description of the technique
As mentioned earlier, a systematic approach to identifying stakeholders can yield great benefits, particularly when used in conjunction with the personal identification and background research described above. The primary technique we favour to help with systematic stakeholder identification is the stakeholder wheel.

The wheel identifies the range of stakeholder groups, and adds structure to the process of identifying them. Without this structure, the stakeholder identification activity usually involves identifying individuals or groups through discussions with other individuals or groups. While this can generate knowledge about many stakeholders, there is a danger that the focus will be on the internal ones, and that some stakeholders may be missed and, as a result, their viewpoints might not be considered.

The stakeholder wheel is shown in Figure 3.1. It defines the groups within which we need to look for stakeholders, and includes both internal and external ones.

The groups in the wheel are:

Owners: Depending on the sector in which the organisation operates, these could include, for example, shareholders, trustees or government ministers.

Managers: These are the senior and middle managers with responsibility for running the organisation, monitoring progress and delivering the results required by the owners.

Employees: These are the operational staff, with responsibility for delivering the products and services of the organisation.

Regulators: This group covers external bodies that set and enforce regulations to which the organisation must adhere.

Suppliers: External organisations or individuals that provide products and services to the organisation are listed as suppliers.

Partners: These are other organisations that work with the organisation being analysed, to deliver complementary or supplementary products and services.

Customers: The recipients of the organisation's products and services are listed as its customers.

Competitors: This group consists of other organisations that deliver their version of the products and services to the same set of customers.

Figure 3.1 The stakeholder wheel

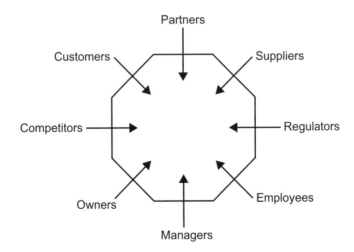

Using the stakeholder wheel

The wheel is used by looking systematically at each group and checking for the stakeholders that may exist there. Within each group it may be possible to use the earlier techniques of personal identification and background research

(Techniques 23 and 24) to find the stakeholders. It is likely that several of the stakeholders in the groups identified in the wheel will not have been found initially. In essence, the wheel is a form of checklist that helps the analysts ensure that stakeholder groups are not missed. It also prompts the analysts to consider the different constituencies with an interest in the project, and the nature of that interest – an aspect that is vital when analysing stakeholder views. This topic is discussed in the later sections of this chapter, under 'Stakeholder analysis' and 'Stakeholder management'.

The internal stakeholders – the managers and the employees – may be identified by the sponsor or other managers, or by examining documentation such as the Terms of Reference or a Feasibility Study, or even an Organisation Chart. While, initially, the BA will focus on the internal stakeholders, it is important that analysts look beyond the internal organisation and consider external stakeholders.

The external stakeholders are often less obvious to identify, and this is where the stakeholder wheel can help enormously by setting out the key groups to examine. It is vital that each of these groups is considered in the light of the organisation's activities and the area under particular examination. For example, the suppliers might seem obvious – the other organisations that supply products and services to ours. However, we need to consider the specific areas of supply: raw materials, products, advisory or consultancy services, finance, potential employees, IT services. If, for example, an organisation is involved with arranging conferences, the suppliers could be varied and numerous – including suppliers of food products, keynote speakers and venues. When planning changes to the organisation one would have to consider whether these suppliers would be impacted by those changes, and how interested they would be in them. A high impact is likely to ensure a high level of interest. It is possible that some impacts might mean the loss of particular suppliers, and if there is the potential for this to happen, it is vital that it be taken into account as early as possible. The loss of an excellent conference venue would cause a great deal of additional work for the organisation in our example.

STAKEHOLDER ANALYSIS

Technique 26: Power/interest grid
Variants/Aliases
Aliases for this technique are the **influence/interest grid** and the **P/I grid**. A variant is the **Power/impact grid**.

Description of the technique
The power/interest grid is a two-dimensional matrix, and stakeholders are plotted on the matrix. The simplest form of the grid uses a 2×2 matrix as shown in Figure 3.2.

The grid categorises stakeholders into the following four groups:

High power /   The key stakeholders who need to be managed actively.
high interest: These are the people who need to be kept informed of each step in the project, and whose views need to be taken into account. They will be instrumental in achieving the project outcomes.

High power /   The senior stakeholders who usually only need to be kept
low interest: satisfied that the work is travelling in the right direction. If the analyst wishes them to become more active, they may need prompting to exert their influence.

Low power /   Typically the stakeholders who will have to operate the new
high interest: business system. This may lead to changes to their roles, responsibilities and skill requirements. Consequently these stakeholders are highly interested in the changes that they will encounter – or even have imposed upon them. However, as they are likely to be working at an operational level, they will have little power as individuals to influence any decisions.

Low power /   The stakeholders who are on the fringes of the study.
low interest: They might be external suppliers of commodity products or infrequent customers, and as a result they do not exercise a great deal of influence, if any, over the organisation. However, these stakeholders, while being interested in the ways in which the organisation works with them, are unlikely to be concerned about, or even aware of, its internal operations.

Figure 3.2 Power/interest grid

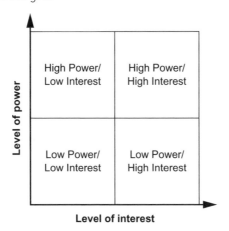

A more complex version of the grid uses a 3×3 matrix and is shown in Figure 3.3. It divides the stakeholders and the management strategies into more categories.

Figure 3.3 Extended power/interest grid

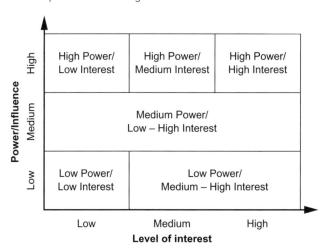

This version of the grid categorises stakeholders into six groups. These are similar to the ones from the simpler version of the matrix, but some key areas are different:

High power / high interest: These are the key stakeholders who require constant, active communication and management.

High power / medium interest: These are the stakeholders we need to keep satisfied, so that they will not intervene – unless a situation arises where that is precisely what we require. Careful management of stakeholders with this level of power is needed, so that any of their interventions serve to support the work rather than add further complication.

High power / low interest: These stakeholders may be far removed from the area of study, or may be too senior for it to have reached their notice. However, within organisations there are often incidents that bring seemingly minor issues to the attention of more senior stakeholders: for example, where a customer involves a regulator or a solicitor, or where a senior manager is let down by poor information. For these reasons it is important that analysts be aware of the stakeholders in this category, and ensure that they are not provoked into action where it is not desired.

Medium power /low to high interest: These stakeholders often include middle managers from across the organisation, or some of the more important customers and suppliers. External regulators may also fall within this category. The interest levels of the stakeholders in this group are likely to fluctuate depending upon several factors, such as the direction the work is taking, the decisions that are being made, the visibility of the study or even external factors, such as the economic situation. It is important to be aware of these stakeholders and keep a watchful eye on their interest and opinions. As before, it may be that we want to manage their level of interest such that they provide support when required.

Low power / low interest: These are the stakeholders who do not have a direct interest or involvement in the business situation, so little effort needs to be spent on managing them.

Low power / medium to high interest: These stakeholders are the business staff who will operate any new processes and systems. They need to be kept informed, and, if possible, kept on side. As the people who are often affected most directly by a business change project, their interest is likely to grow as the work advances. While they generally have little power individually, their power can increase dramatically if the analysts require assistance from them to obtain detailed information, and the implementation of changes can be severely compromised without their help. It has been said that in the absence of information chaos develops; this should be borne in mind with regard to these stakeholders, since their worries and concerns may extend far beyond the reality. This can only be countered by providing sufficient information to keep as many of the fears as possible at bay.

Using the power/interest grid

Each category of stakeholders will need to be managed in a different way to take account of their level of power and interest. In the power/interest grid the stakeholders are grouped into either four (if the 2×2 matrix is used) or six (if the 3×3 matrix is used) categories. Since the latter is an expansion of the former, we will look at the six possible categories:

Manage actively: These are the high power / high interest stakeholders. They need to be closely involved at all stages of the project and in any key decisions. If a recommendation is to be made, these stakeholders need to be aware of the recommendation, and should have approved its inclusion in the list. They should support any proposals made. The stakeholder management strategy to be used here involves the analysts working continuously and closely with these key players. Nothing should come as a surprise to them in a public forum; all recommendations should have been discussed with them, and actions agreed, in advance.

Keep satisfied: These are the high power / medium interest stakeholders. They need be kept informed where necessary so that they do not begin to develop an unhelpful interest in aspects of the project – and possibly delay, or even reverse, progress. Where there are any issues that will be of interest to them, the analysts need to ensure that they will support the approach taken. This may require analysts to hold meetings with these stakeholders, or at the very least talk to them, in order to explain the desired course of action and take note of any issues or objections.

Watch: These are the high power / low interest stakeholders. These stakeholders are usually at such a senior level that the business analysis work is of little interest to them. However, care needs to be taken to ensure that they do not have their interest aroused. This could occur if an issue becomes high profile within the organisation, typically where another stakeholder has decided to raise it, perhaps by harnessing more powerful groups such as the organisation's owners or even the media.

Keep onside: These are the medium power stakeholders, with a range of levels of interest from low to high.

Keep informed: These are the stakeholders in the low power and medium to high interest category. These stakeholders are typically the business staff who will apply the new processes and use the new IT features. Although their requirements are discussed early on in the project, it is usually the case that they have change done to them and have little, if any, power to influence decisions. Theirs is probably the least comfortable position among all the stakeholders, so management of the relationship is very important if changes are to be understood thoroughly and implemented effectively. If people know change is coming without any idea of the nature and extent of that change, then the rumour mill can begin and all sorts of scenarios be imagined. It is far better to ensure that there is regular communication with these stakeholders so that they are kept as informed as possible.

Ignore: These are the stakeholders with low power and low interest. The changes are likely to have little impact upon them, and hence they do not require a great deal of consideration at the moment.

Stakeholder analysis needs to be carried out regularly throughout the project, since stakeholders are liable to move around the grid. Some will become more interested as the work progresses and they begin to perceive that the changes will affect them. Others may become more powerful, possibly through internal promotion or transfer. Another possibility is that some individuals acquire influence through gaining the confidence of a key stakeholder.

Although individuals working at an operational or even middle-management level can have little influence, they can achieve power by banding together. Some stakeholders may gain influence by leveraging other organisations, for example trade unions or staff associations, or even by approaching the media. In other situations they gain influence because there is strength in numbers. It is important not to dismiss individual stakeholders as unimportant – you never know when they have a good friend, or even a partner, in a more influential position. With the advent of internet communication and the availability of networking systems, it is all too possible for individuals to form a pressure group and gain a lot more power very quickly.

A variant of this technique is the power/impact grid, which is used when planning the implementation of change. This version of the grid helps to identify how to manage the stakeholders by recognising the level of impact the change will have upon them and the level of control (power) they have over the situation. The understanding and insight this provides will help in ensuring that stakeholders are managed effectively and the emotional impact of change is considered.

Technique 27: CATWOE
Variants/Aliases
Variants include **VOCATE** (viewpoint, owner, customer, actor, transformation, and environment), **PARADE** (perspective – or point of view, activity, recipient, actor, decision-maker and environment) and **Root definition** (in the Soft Systems methodology).

Description of the technique
One of the key reasons for managing relationships with stakeholders is to ensure that we understand their ideas, priorities and wishes before we put forward recommendations, or, even worse, implement business changes. Understanding what the key players want is vital if the work is to go in the right direction. The following quotation explains why this is so important.

'Would you tell me, please, which way I ought to go from here?'

'That depends a good deal on where you want to get to,' said the Cat.

'I don't much care where –' said Alice.

'Then it doesn't matter which way you go,' said the Cat.

'– so long as I get SOMEWHERE,' Alice added as an explanation.

'Oh, you're sure to do that,' said the Cat.

(*Alice in Wonderland*, Lewis Carroll)

One of the most important features of stakeholder analysis involves uncovering the direction each stakeholder believes the organisation should take. As the quotation above so eloquently explains, if you don't know where you are aiming to go, you are sure to get somewhere but that is all that can be guaranteed. The question is, can we afford such a lack of direction in today's business world? The answer is surely 'no'.

Most of the stakeholders for a project will have ideas about the direction it should take, the requirements to be addressed, the options for improvement and the solutions that should be adopted. However, these ideas originate from their personal concerns, beliefs, values and priorities, and they often form the basis for strongly held opinions from which deviation is difficult if not impossible. A failure to understand these views can result in serious problems later in the project as the differences of opinion develop into conflicts. This may be seen in the different priorities placed upon business requirements, or even the emergence of contradictory requirements.

The CATWOE technique was created by Professor Peter Checkland and his team at Lancaster University (Checkland 1981) and is an excellent approach to understanding what the stakeholders value and the impact this will have on the direction of the project. The acronym represents the following elements:

Customer(s) the beneficiary or recipient of the outputs of the business system;

Actor(s) the roles that perform the transformation (the main business processes);

Transformation the core process that delivers the services to the customer;

Weltanschauung the underlying set of values, beliefs and priorities that
or world view explain the existence of the transformation;

Owner the individual or group with the authority to change significantly, or even close down, the business system;

Environment the rules and constraints that have to be taken as a given (that is, those that cannot be changed) within the environment surrounding the business system.

Using CATWOE
The key to the CATWOE technique is the 'W', which Checkland called the *Weltanschauung* or world view. Understanding a stakeholder's world view is a fundamental step in understanding the perceived needs, priorities and values, and uncovering these helps to reveal hidden agendas. Where this is not done, and the world view not uncovered, the opportunity for resentment, misunderstandings and even conflict exists.

Once the world view has been defined, the analysis should move to the transformation. This defines the core activity that is carried out in line with the world view. A common example to look at is the world view of sales people. This centres on selling and earning commission. When the sales team thinks about what the business system under consideration should be, their focus is on making sales in order to ensure that as much commission as possible is paid. If this is the world view, it follows logically that the transformation is to take a customer, make a sale and produce a customer who has made a purchase. In an extreme case, some salespeople believe that making the sale is the sole purpose of the business system, and delivery of the purchased goods is not on their 'radar'.

Thus the transformation is 'make sale', without specifying what is being sold or how the products or services reach the customer.

The next natural progression is to identify the customer targeted by the transformation. This can be a critical part of using the technique, since it can uncover exactly where the focus of the stakeholder lies. In a situation such as our sales scenario the customer could be the salesperson, and the beneficiary from the transformation could be seen to be the salesperson with the commission.

The next aspect to consider is the actor profile. The actors are the roles that perform the transformation, and analysts often complete this with little insight, simply offering 'management and staff' as actors. This valuable aspect of the technique is therefore completely dismissed, and may as well be left uncompleted. The more insightful analyst, however, understands that the definition of the roles begins to highlight the skills required – something that is very useful during later analysis.

The owner of the business system under consideration is the next entry. The owner is the person or group of people who can instigate change, define policy or impose closure of the system. In some systems this entry can be vital, for example where conflicts have arisen because a lack of direction from the owner has allowed different world views to emerge and take hold.

Finally the environment is defined. The environment surrounds the business system defined in the transformation, and imposes rules and constraints. One way of analysing it is to use the PESTLE technique (Technique 1), which provides a framework for exploring different aspects of it. Something to remember is that a business system targets external customers, and these customers must be willing to take part in the system for it to be able to operate. This willingness to take part can be seen as a constraint in the environment.

As an example, a CATWOE could be developed to analyse the perspective of the operations director of a high-street clothes store. As discussed earlier, we would begin by considering the director's world view on the business. In this instance, the director feels the business will succeed if the focus is on designing and selling inexpensive fashionable clothing, because this is what is desired by the target market – young consumers who are interested in fashion. This director does not include the manufacture of the clothes in the world view. The transformation will be the core process required to fulfil this view, in this case to sell inexpensive, fashionable clothes. The customer is the young, fashion-conscious consumer, and the actors will be clothes designers, fashion buyers, sales staff and store managers. The owner could be the director, but for a high-street store is more likely to be the board of the company. The environment will include factors such as the economic situation, market desire for inexpensive fashion and consumer concerns over fair trade issues. This worked example has developed the CATWOE by beginning with the core elements, the W and the T, and then progressively defining the others. The example is documented using the CATWOE structure as follows:

C young consumers who require fashionable clothes at affordable prices;

A clothes designers, fashion buyers, sales staff, store managers;

T   selling inexpensive, fashionable clothes;

W   the opinion that there is a desire from young consumers for inexpensive, fashionable clothes, and the company will be successful if we satisfy that demand;

O   the board of the company;

E   the economic situation, market desire for inexpensive fashion, and consumer concern over fair trade issues.

CATWOE can be used at various stages and for many purposes during a project:

- as a means of understanding a stakeholder's view of a business system, in order to develop a conceptual model that may be used to analyse the gap between current and desired systems;

- as a means of analysing the source of potential or actual conflict between stakeholders;

- as a means of considering different priorities assigned by stakeholders to options, business needs or requirements.

It is sometimes useful to consider all of the CATWOE elements, and this is particularly the case when the analyst is trying to use stakeholder perspectives to derive conceptual models of business activities. However, the technique can be equally helpful when used less formally to consider stakeholders' world views. It is often a means of uncovering the root causes of disagreements.

The Soft Systems methodology, created by Peter Checkland and his colleagues (Checkland 1981), refers to a 'root definition'. This consists of the six CATWOE elements, assembled into a paragraph that encapsulates the stakeholder's perspective. In the case of our high-street clothing retailer, the operations director's perspective could be turned into a root definition like this:

> [XYZ] is a company controlled by its board (O) where clothes designers, fashion buyers, sales staff and store managers (A) work to sell inexpensive, fashionable clothes (T) to young consumers who require such fashionable clothes at affordable prices (C). This reflects the desire of those consumers for inexpensive, fashionable clothes, and the company will be successful if we satisfy that demand (W). The company operates against the background of the economic situation, the market desire for inexpensive fashion, and consumer concern over fair trade issues (E).

In this example we have included the *Weltanschauung* explicitly in the root definition. However, it is common practice to omit it, since it can be inferred from the remaining five elements.

Our experience is that using CATWOE in its bullet-point form is best for the actual analysis of the stakeholders' perspectives, but that turning the results into root definitions is useful when we want to present the perspectives back to the stakeholders to check that they do, in fact, reflect their view of the situation.

Technique 28: Business activity modelling
Variants/Aliases
This is also known as **BAM**. Related terms include the **conceptual model** and the **logical activity model**.

Description of the technique
A Business Activity Model (BAM) builds on the 'transformation' element of the CATWOE technique (Technique 27), and presents a view of the high-level business activities that we would expect to see in an organisation that espouses the world view captured in the stakeholder perspective. The model shows these high-level activities and the logical dependencies between them. This conceptual, or idealised, view can then be compared with the actual situation (perhaps captured in a rich picture – Technique 20) to identify areas where, potentially, the performance of the organisation could be improved.

In a business analysis project, the BAM is created after the initial investigation of the situation has taken place and the stakeholder perspectives have been analysed. The BAM is used in gap analysis and the identification of options for business improvement. The high-level activities represented in the BAM can, if this is useful, be examined in more detail through business process models or swimlane diagrams (Technique 37).

The BAM is built at the level of **what** the organisation does, not **how** it does it (which is more the province of business process models). Essentially, there are five types of business activity that are represented:

Do: These are the primary tasks of the organisation – the things that it has been set up to do. Usually there are very few 'doing' activities on a BAM. For example, a training and consultancy firm might just have 'deliver training' and 'provide consultancy' as its 'doing' activities; a supermarket would have 'sell groceries'; and so on.

Enable: These activities obtain and, where relevant, replenish the resources needed to perform the primary task. Resources include people, materials, customers and so forth. So, for our training company, 'enabling' activities might be 'create training course' and 'advertise courses'. For the supermarket, we would have 'advertise products', 'buy groceries', 'transport groceries to stores' and 'establish stores'.

Plan: In building a BAM, it is assumed that the basic strategic planning has already taken place. The 'planning' activities on a BAM are the more detailed ones associated with putting the strategy into effect. Examples for the training organisation would be 'decide courses to offer' and 'decide skills required for trainers'; for the supermarket, 'planning' activities would include 'decide store locations' and 'plan product range'. 'Planning' activities should include setting targets against which progress can be monitored.

Monitor: These activities monitor the achievement of the performance measures that have been set during the planning activities. The modelling convention is to show that the 'monitoring' activities are dependent on the 'doing' activities (the primary tasks). This is on the basis that the 'doing' activities are dependent upon the 'enabling' activities and that these dependencies carry forward to the 'monitoring' activities. Also, performance monitoring can only take place once the business system has undertaken some primary task activity.

Control: Finally, there is little use in monitoring progress unless controlling action is also taken if something is not going according to plan. There are two ways of showing 'control' activities on a BAM. Either a 'control' activity is associated with each 'monitoring' activity, or all 'monitoring' activities feed into one 'control' activity. Over the years we have come to favour the second approach, since, in a real-world situation, managers usually take action on the basis of issues that concern several areas of performance.

In diagrams, instead of showing links back into the rest of the BAM (which would result in an incomprehensible 'plate of spaghetti' appearance), the convention is that a 'lightening strike' symbol comes out of the bottom of 'control' activities. This indicates that controlling action feeds back into the model wherever it is necessary.

Using business activity modelling

There is no universally agreed convention for the symbols used on a BAM. Essentially only three symbols are needed, one for the activities, another (an arrowed line) indicating the logical dependencies between them, and the 'lightening strike' described above. Soft Systems specialists typically use 'cloud' symbols to indicate the essentially conceptual nature of the model. The authors tend to use ellipses, since these are somewhat easier to find in popular drawing packages and take up less room on the screen or page. It is a good idea to avoid rectangles or squares, which make the diagram look too much like a conventional process model.

It is best to start at the centre of the model, with the 'doing' activities – remember that there will only be one or two of these primary tasks on each model.

Having identified the 'doing' activities, next give some thought to the resources that will be needed to carry them out. What these resources are will vary from one organisation to another, but typically they will include some of these:

- staff;
- suppliers;
- products and services;
- production processes;
- delivery processes;
- premises;
- infrastructure;

- marketing channels;
- distribution channels;
- finance.

There may be several connected 'enablers' associated with each resource. For example, with staff, enabling activities might be:

- recruit staff;
- train staff.

We can now work backwards to the 'planning' activities for each stream of enablers. For example, with staff there will usually be:

- plan numbers and types of staff required (which includes the competencies they will need);
- plan recruitment methods;
- plan training.

Thinking about what measures should have been set in the 'planning' activities, we can now identify what 'monitoring' activities are required. For our staff example, these might include:

- appraise staff performance;
- monitor staff satisfaction.

Finally, one or more 'control' activities can be put in place, to take action if the organisation's performance – as measured by the 'monitoring' activities – falls short of the targets set in the 'planning' activities.

Figure 3.4 shows a BAM built according to these principles, in this case modelling the CATWOE for the operations director of the high-street clothing retailer.

When building a BAM it can be useful to apply a numbering system to the activities for identification and cross-referencing purposes, and to indicate the type of each activity as we have done here, where E1 is an 'enabler', M1 a 'monitoring' activity and so forth. It is good practice to give each activity an active name in the form of a verb followed by a noun.

It needs to be appreciated that what is being built in a BAM is a conceptual model of the activities we (the BAs) would **expect** to see in place, given the business perspective and particularly the world view from which it has been created. It is emphatically **not** a model of what is happening now in the organisation. The whole point of creating the BAM is to find out if there are gaps between what should be happening and what is happening now, which can be explored and bridged. This, in turn, means that the BAs must seek to divorce themselves from what is happening now and use their creativity and business knowledge to think about what, conceptually, should be going on.

Figure 3.4 Business Activity Model for a high-street clothing retailer

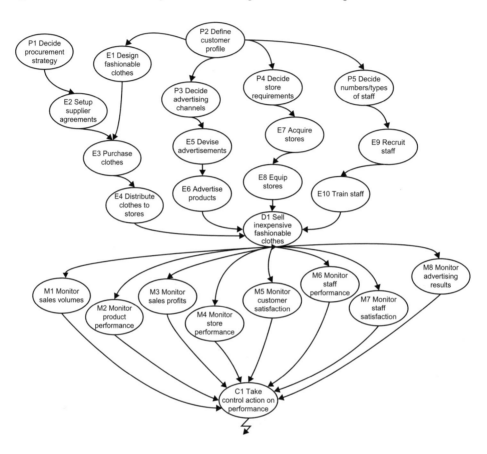

If there are several different world views evident from the organisation's key stakeholders, it will probably be necessary to build several BAMs to explore each business perspective. The best thing to do next is to hold a workshop with these stakeholders and facilitate a discussion in order to develop the BAM that represents a consensus view of the business. This might involve combining two or more BAMs, or resolving conflicts between the different views. If no agreement can be obtained this way, it may be necessary to refer the issue to the project sponsor, or even more senior management, for a decision on the way forward. Ultimately a consensus BAM must be agreed upon to provide a basis for further work such as gap analysis (Technique 40), which is explored when we cover the 'Analyse needs' stage of business analysis in Chapter 4.

Technique 29: RASCI charts
Variants/Aliases
Variants are **RACI (responsible, accountable, consulted, informed)** or **ARCI (accountable, responsible, consulted, informed)**.

Description of the technique

RASCI charts are used during business analysis assignments or business change implementations, to record and assess the stakeholders' roles and responsibilities with regard to a business problem, a business process or a task. The RASCI acronym represents the following categories:

Responsible: the person required to own a particular problem, process or task;

Accountable: the person ultimately accountable to the business for the area under consideration, and responsible for approving the completed work (the Responsible stakeholders report to the Accountable stakeholder);

Supportive: people who can provide resources or other forms of support during the project and the change implementation;

Consulted: people who can provide information or capability necessary to complete the work;

Informed: people who must be notified of the results, but who do not have to be consulted about the work.

Using RASCI or RACI charts

A RASCI chart is a matrix that is used to list all of the tasks to be carried out within a project or a business process. The stakeholder roles are plotted along the top of the matrix, and the set of tasks along the vertical axis. Each task is then analysed using the RASCI headings to determine the role of each stakeholder with regard to that task. Figure 3.5 shows a sample RASCI chart.

Figure 3.5 RASCI chart

	Project Sponsor	Project Manager	Business Analyst	Operations Manager	Sales Clerk
Record Customer Orders			I	A/S	R/C
Document Requirements	A		R		C
Plan Stage	S/C	A/R	I	I	
Approve Request for Change	A	S	R	C/I	C/I

Recording stakeholders and their responsibilities on RASCI charts helps to provide a clear view of the people we are dealing with in a particular project, what we can expect them to deliver or make available, and how we need to communicate with them. These charts are related to the power/interest grid in that they inform the analysts about the stakeholders, so the information can be used to supplement that on the power/interest grid. The RASCI chart helps the analysts understand the stakeholder responsibilities and identify who should be approached in a given situation. For example, if authorisation is required for a particular decision, this will need to be referred to the Accountable stakeholder; if the analysts need access to some members of staff they will need to look for Supportive stakeholders working in that area.

RASCI charts also help the analyst to ensure that all stakeholders are clear about their roles and their responsibilities. For example, if a stakeholder is said to be in the Consulted category, it may be useful to list all of the responsibilities that this brings.

When producing a RASCI chart it is useful to adopt the following steps.

- Identify the areas of work to be carried out. Allocate each area of work to a row on the chart. It is useful to choose an active verb when naming a task. For example, terms such as 'document', 'monitor' and 'check' are helpful, since they give a sense of the activity to be carried out.

- Identify the stakeholders who will be involved in the project or business process. Allocate each stakeholder to a column, and annotate each column along the top of the chart.

- Consider each task in turn to decide where the RASCI elements reside. For example, identify the stakeholder who is Accountable for the task, the stakeholder who is Supportive of the task, and so on.

- Review the completeness of the RASCI chart. Is someone Accountable for each task? Is a stakeholder Responsible for completing the work of each task? Is there a stakeholder who has too much responsibility? Are there stakeholders who can be Consulted about tasks? It is accepted good practice to have only one stakeholder Responsible for each task, since this indicates that there is an owner for the task. It is also beneficial to have few Accountable stakeholders on the chart, so as to avoid confusion over where the authority for a situation resides.

Using the stakeholder analysis techniques
We can use the power/interest grid, supplemented by the RASCI chart, to recognise the key stakeholders that we should consider when undertaking the CATWOE analysis (Technique 27). The CATWOE technique provides a means of understanding personal agendas, priorities and values. However, an analysis of all stakeholders or stakeholder groups would be time consuming and, more importantly, would result in a lot of diverging views that could cloud the real issues. As analysts are usually working within a limited timescale, information about categories is extremely useful to help prioritise this more detailed stakeholder analysis work. The identification of key stakeholders helps to make this work more manageable and highlights the important conflicts – those that need to be addressed if the business improvements are to be achieved.

One of the key aspects of stakeholder relationship management is to recognise that all stakeholders are individual people. As the saying goes, 'people buy from people', and this applies to messages and information as well as products or services. Stakeholders are not automatons who will always behave in a predictable manner and can be treated in a generic fashion. If we want to work effectively with them we need to begin by recognising that they are individuals, and aiming to view situations from their perspectives. The CATWOE technique helps us understand the stakeholders' perspectives – their view of the area that is under investigation. Some time spent thinking about what stakeholders value in a situation, and considering their priorities, can provide excellent insights into how they need to be approached, what information they require and which concerns should be taken into account.

CATWOE, supported by the other stakeholder analysis techniques, is used to develop a diagrammatic view – the BAM. The business activity modelling technique can be difficult to apply in practice, since it requires BAs to 'step back' from the existing situation and model what the perspective indicates ought to be happening in the organisation, rather than what is actually happening. There is also a tendency to model activities at too low a level – for example, by having three activities called 'sell over telephone', 'sell over internet' and 'sell face to face', where, probably, just 'sell goods' would be more correct. Sometimes there is a need to split activities in this way, but usually it is better to work at a higher level of aggregation. Another problem is that practitioners can confuse this approach with building process models. As we have explained, the BAM shows **what** is going on, whereas a process model explores **how**. It can sometimes be useful, however, to 'drill down' inside an activity on a BAM, using a process model in order to understand why the activity is not satisfactory at the moment.

This set of techniques supports various aspects of stakeholder analysis. They are particularly effective at the following points during business analysis projects:

- when investigating business situations and analysing issues and problems;
- when analysing value propositions for internal and external customers;
- when building conceptual activity or process models;
- when identifying and negotiating conflicts;
- when carrying out gap analysis;
- when producing business cases – and considering the options and how to encourage 'buy in'.

STAKEHOLDER MANAGEMENT

Technique 30: Stakeholder management planning
Variants/Aliases
Another term used in this context is **stakeholder map**.

Description of the technique

The stakeholder analysis work contributes to the ongoing management of stakeholders during a project. A stakeholder management plan provides a means of capturing all of the information, and setting out the actions to be taken with regard to each stakeholder. The plan consists of an assessment for each one, and the areas to be included in each assessment are as follows:

Name of stakeholder: the name and possibly the job title of the stakeholder;

Current level of power or influence: an assessment of whether the stakeholder's power is low, medium or high (from the power/interest grid);

Current level of interest: an assessment of whether the stakeholder's interest is low, medium or high (from the power/interest grid);

Issues and interests: a summary of the major issues of concern to the stakeholder, and the areas of particular interest, possibly also including a list of the priorities, values and beliefs identified during CATWOE analysis;

Current attitude: an assessment of the stakeholder's attitude towards the project, possibly standardised using a classification scheme, such as:

- Champion or Advocate: a stakeholder who will promote the project actively;

- Supporter or Follower: a stakeholder who supports the project but will not be particularly active in promoting it;

- Neutral or Indifferent: a stakeholder who is not particularly in favour of or against the project;

- Critic: a stakeholder who is not in favour of the project but will not work actively against it;

- Opponent: a stakeholder who will work actively to oppose the project and impede progress – likely to have a personal agenda resulting from perceived negative impact of the project;

- Blocker: a stakeholder who opposes the project, typically because of reasons unconnected with it.

Desired support: assessment of the contribution that the stakeholder could provide to the project;

Desired role: the role and responsibilities that the stakeholder could perform for the project – an assessment that might be linked to the RASCI chart;

Desired actions:	the actions the stakeholder could carry out in order to progress the project;
Messages to convey:	the key issues to be considered when communicating with the stakeholder, and the nature of the message we wish to put across;
Actions and communications:	the stakeholder management approach to be adopted with this stakeholder. This will be linked to the strategies defined in the power/interest grid. For example, if this is a key stakeholder, we may wish to define a communications plan setting out the frequency and means of communication. This might include regular meetings and formal written reports.

Using stakeholder management planning

The stakeholder management plan is used to summarise all of the important information about an individual stakeholder or a group. It forms the basis for developing documents such as a stakeholder communication plan, where the means of communicating with the different stakeholders are defined. The stakeholder management plan helps the project team decide the most appropriate means of communicating with the stakeholders, and the timing, duration and frequency. Key stakeholders will be part of a regular, ongoing communication process, typically combining meetings with written communications. Some powerful stakeholders will need to be treated with care to ensure that their priorities are understood and addressed, even if this means managing their expectations towards alternative solutions. Less powerful stakeholder groups will also need to be considered carefully, to ensure that communication with them is as informative as possible, and the amount of support retained for the project is maximised.

As mentioned earlier, one of the fundamental issues with stakeholder management is that stakeholders change, and this can affect many of the areas we have been analysing.

- They may become more powerful through forming groups or gaining influence through more senior stakeholders.
- As the project progresses and the extent of the impact becomes clearer, their interest levels may rise significantly.
- Their priorities and beliefs may change. This can be difficult to identify, since these are often affected by influences outside the project or even the organisation. For example, the sudden global economic crisis changed the world views of many individuals as financial security became a major issue.

For these reasons, the stakeholder management plan needs to be kept under review and the analysts need to be alert to any changes that should be handled. An example of an extract from a stakeholder management plan is shown in Table 3.1.

Table 3.1 Example of a stakeholder management plan

Name/role	Steven Lewis, Marketing Director
Power/influence level	High power
Interest level	High interest
Issues and interests	Developed recent revised marketing strategy. Keen to develop web-based marketing approach; sponsoring the change programme to develop this. Likes original and creative ideas.
Attitude	Champion
Desired support **Desired role**	High level of support required (and will be provided). Has been allocated Project Sponsor role and is likely to be proactive in performing this role.
Desired actions	Needs to ensure that the Board are informed and support the project. Needs to ensure that resources, in particular the operations staff, are made available to the project when required.
Messages to convey	Need to emphasise understanding of his requirements, in particular those related to delivering web-based marketing using innovative concepts.
Actions and communications	• Discuss objectives, timescale, etc., and create Project Initiation Document (with Project Manager). Gain agreement. • Explain Project Sponsor responsibilities. • Set timescale for regular meetings.

Technique 31: The Thomas–Kilmann conflict mode instrument
Variants/Aliases
This is also known as the **Thomas–Kilmann Instrument (TKI)** or the **Thomas–Kilmann conflict model**.

Description of the technique

The Thomas–Kilmann conflict mode instrument sets out five positions that may be adopted by people in a conflict or negotiation situation. These five positions represent alternative preferences individuals have when dealing with such situations. This model is shown in Figure 3.6.

Figure 3.6 Thomas–Kilmann conflict mode instrument

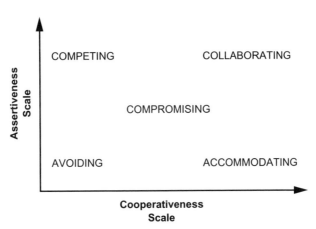

The five positions represent the following approaches:

Avoiding: Unassertive and uncooperative. This stance is based upon a refusal to acknowledge that a conflict exists, often in the hope that if ignored the situation will resolve itself. This can be appropriate in minor situations, but where another stakeholder feels there is a genuine issue, anyone taking this stance may be perceived to be awkward and to be failing to address the issue. People taking an avoiding position may also build up resentment because they have repressed their concerns; ultimately, this could lead to a more serious conflict, sometimes over a trivial issue.

Accommodating: Unassertive and cooperative. In this position stakeholders have acknowledged their concerns and the existence of the conflict, but have decided to give way to the ideas or requests from other parties. People taking an accommodating position may be content with this approach, but might feel sometimes that their voices are unheard, even when they make good suggestions. A history of accommodating can exacerbate this situation, such that they are habitually ignored by the other stakeholders.

Competing: Assertive and uncooperative. Stakeholders who adopt a competing position are keen to focus on their own ideas and concerns and may pay little attention to the other stakeholders' needs. Sometimes this is an effective way to deal with a situation, but it is likely to cause resentment in the long term.

Compromising: Moderately assertive and moderately cooperative. This is often the approach that people recommend – meeting all parties in the middle. However, some stakeholders, particularly those with a competing preference, do not like compromise since it means giving ground on some issues. One view of compromise is that everybody loses, although a more positive view is that everyone gains something. Compromise is often an effective approach to resolving conflicts or negotiations but it is important that everyone feels content with the result. If this is not the case, then resentments can fester in the longer term.

Collaborating: Assertive and cooperative. Sometimes known as the 'win, win' scenario, collaboration is the ideal outcome to a situation, since all participants feel that the result is beneficial for them. Creative suggestions that provide alternatives to those put forward by the stakeholders can provide the basis for collaborative solutions. However, it is not always possible to achieve this, and in such situations a compromise may the best outcome that can be achieved.

Using the Thomas–Kilmann instrument

Some stakeholders believe that there are only two positions to be taken when negotiating or in a conflict: the 'soft' approach, where you can't win and so give in to your opponent, and the 'hard' approach where you concede little, if anything. The Thomas–Kilmann approach sets out three other possible positions, and helps to encourage participants to consider other options that might provide a route to consensus. Positioning the avoiding, collaboration and compromise approaches so clearly adds alternatives to the two extreme positions and can form an excellent starting point for debate. Merely opening up the discussion can sometimes provide a softening of firm positions, which is usually helpful when seeking consensus or compromise alternatives.

In some situations the Thomas–Kilmann model can be a useful way of assessing the significance of the issue under discussion and deciding whether there is more to be gained by agreeing on a proposed solution or by spending time finding an outcome agreeable to all. If the issue is minor it might be resolved over time, and an avoidance position could be the best approach. If one stakeholder feels very strongly about a particular point of view and the others are less concerned, it may be easier to allow that stakeholder to carry the day. It could bring other advantages in the future if someone has been allowed a 'win' in one situation.

Technique 32: Principled negotiation

Description of the technique
The principled negotiation technique was developed by William Ury and Roger Fisher (Fisher and Ury 1982). There are four main points that define this approach:

People: Consider the people and separate them from the problem. Considering stakeholders as people rather than an amorphous group is always a good approach in a conflict or negotiation situation. In negotiating, terms such as 'the other party' are often used, and, while this can help us to distance ourselves from the individuals within this group, there are also risks because it can lead us to ignore personal feelings and beliefs. When we are negotiating it is important to remember that we are dealing with people who experience emotions, hold beliefs and are from differing backgrounds. If the negotiation does not meet their needs they may react unpredictably or emotionally, they may try to find other routes to influence the outcome – such as seeking support from senior managers – and they may harbour resentment, leading to problems in future negotiations.

Interests: Focus on the stakeholders' interests and priorities rather than their positions. People often set out their positions rather than the reasons behind these positions. Examining the interests involves asking questions and uncovering the reasons behind the positions.

Options: Consider a variety of options before making any decisions. People often set out what they want the solution to be, rather than the problem that needs to be addressed. While the suggested solution may be feasible, there might be alternatives that address a wider range of needs. Broadening the discussion to include the identification and consideration of other options can help to break a stalemate.

Criteria: Set criteria upon which the decision will be based. Agreed criteria will provide an objective approach to selecting the way forward. The process of defining the criteria will provide a means of incorporating the needs of the people involved in the negotiation.

Using principled negotiation
It is common in negotiations to find that participants take up positions, argue over those positions and then become entrenched in them. The discussion focuses on why they cannot move or change position, and the more they justify this, the greater becomes their sense of being right. They concentrate on achieving their aims at the expense of everyone else's. Inevitably the issue of 'saving face' enters the discussion, and the chances of reconciling the parties' interests become remote. Principled negotiation attempts to avoid this situation developing.

Failing to consider the people, and to appreciate the part that emotions and beliefs play in a negotiation, can be disastrous. Unfortunately this is not uncommon; the people and the problem become entangled as one, and the negotiation process includes emotional responses to practical issues. Where there is a conflict situation the first step is often to blame the people involved rather than finding the root of the problem and sorting it out. This blame focus can be very destructive, and can harm working relationships with colleagues and stakeholders.

There are three aspects to consider about the people:

Perception: How do the people view the situation? This involves trying to understand the stakeholders' emotions and beliefs about the situation – the CATWOE technique (Technique 27) can be extremely useful here. While this may not change the other views, it will lead to a greater understanding, and perhaps open up ideas that will address the issue.

Emotion: The way that people feel during negotiations can often be as relevant as what they say. It can be very valuable to acknowledge those feelings and recognise that they are important. Sometimes it is helpful to allow people the opportunity to pour out their grievances or anger so that the resentment doesn't fester inside them. A small gesture, such as listening carefully or even proffering an apology, can often help to defuse the situation.

Communication: Effective communication is very important in negotiations. This means using clear language that will encourage everyone to contribute. Active listening is vital, not only to help with understanding but also to foster good working relationships. This can be a great help in providing a positive basis for negotiations. Additional ways to communicate well during negotiations include:

- acknowledging what has been said, and, where necessary, asking for clarification;

- phrasing comments without apportioning blame – for example, 'I felt let down' rather than 'you let me down';

- speaking purposefully, and setting out the reasons for providing information.

The focus on the interests rather than the positions held is a vital shift in emphasis, which can help with the development of positive solutions that address everyone's needs. The interests can be uncovered by asking questions such as 'Why?' and 'What benefit would this give you?' They can also be uncovered by asking 'Why not?' For example, if a party sets out as a position 'I must have my telephone repaired by tomorrow,' the interests are uncovered by asking 'Why?' or 'What benefit would you derive?' This moves the conversation on to the interests of the party, which increases the understanding of the problem and possibly opens up alternative solutions. Sometimes the interests are common to the other stakeholders in the group, so an area of agreement is found.

We can begin to consider options to address the situation, once the interests of the parties have been explored. Brainstorming (see Technique 14) can be useful here, because it can help to increase creativity and encourage the suspension of judgement. This last point is critical if people are to be engaged in identifying options without fear of criticism or objections. Once the options are identified, they can be evaluated to see how well they address the interests that have been explored previously. Where options meet shared interests and provide mutual gains there can be a basis for compromise or even collaboration.

The final aspect of this approach is to set objective criteria against which we can measure each option. An objective evaluation of the options will help to ensure that the focus is on the problem and on everyone's interests.

The principled negotiation approach can help to achieve positive outcomes from negotiation or conflict situations. An additional aspect of it, also developed by Fisher and Ury (1982), is known as Best Alternative to a Negotiated Agreement, or BATNA. The BATNA approach helps stakeholders to consider other alternatives, by thinking about what else they could do if the negotiation does not meet their needs. For example, someone selling a house needs to decide at what price it would be better to take an alternative course of action such as building an extension, or even consider rental options. The alternative actions are the person's BATNA.

This approach helps everyone focus on producing a true standard against which any proposed agreement can be measured. It is extremely helpful to think about this in advance and have it in mind during the negotiation. Sometimes in negotiation situations people feel under pressure to accept the deal that is on the table, only to regret this afterwards. Deciding on a BATNA in advance helps protect them against being pressurised into accepting the unacceptable.

Aligned to the BATNA is the warning level. This is the limit at which it is time to stop negotiating and consider whether the BATNA would be preferable. For example, in our house sale situation the sellers set a price that represents their warning level, and any offer at or below that level leads them to consider whether their BATNA is preferable. This is an excellent sanity check that helps avoid rash decisions.

Fisher and Ury (1982) stated that 'If you have not thought about what you would do without a negotiated agreement, then you are negotiating with your eyes closed.'

Using the stakeholder management techniques

Stakeholder management is an essential element of business analysis and business change projects. There are many aspects to stakeholder management, and the techniques described here provide approaches that will help with some of them.

- The stakeholder management plan provides a formal framework for documenting information about stakeholders and deciding the best actions to take.

- The Thomas–Kilmann instrument provides insights into stakeholders' conflict and negotiation preferences and the possible outcomes that might be achieved.

- The Fisher and Ury negotiation approach provides a more detailed process for conducting effective negotiations with stakeholders.

Used together, these techniques will help BAs to work effectively with their stakeholders in order to deliver the required business outcomes.

REFERENCES

Checkland, P. (1981) *Systems Thinking, Systems Practice.* John Wiley and Sons, Chichester.

Fisher, R. and Ury, W. (1982) *Getting to Yes: Negotiating Agreement Without Giving In.* Hutchinson, London.

FURTHER READING

Checkland, P. and Scholes, J. (1999) *Soft Systems Methodology in Action.* John Wiley and Sons, Chichester.

Patching, D. (1990) *Practical Soft Systems Analysis.* Pitman Publishing, London.

Ury, W. (1991) *Getting Past No: Negotiating with Difficult People.* Random House, London.

4 ANALYSE NEEDS

INTRODUCTION

Early approaches to business analysis used a systematic process for improving existing business systems. This typically involved analysing and documenting the existing situation and then adding in additional requirements that would solve current problems. Although this view of business analysis often gave rise to incremental improvement, it did not take account of broader stakeholder visions for the business system. As a result, the focus on addressing problems meant that greater opportunities were sometimes missed.

Over time business analysis work has evolved to take account of approaches based upon systemic thinking. The framework shown in Figure 4.1 reflects this.

Figure 4.1 Systemic analysis approach

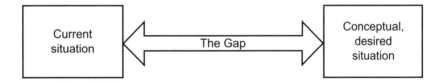

In this framework the conceptual view of a business system is contrasted with the view of the current situation. This chapter explores a range of techniques that support this approach, and covers the following areas:

- organisation modelling;
- business process analysis;
- business change identification.

Organisation modelling (Techniques 33–35)
Organisation modelling is concerned with analysing the organisation-level processes that deliver beneficial outcomes to customers. This section presents the following techniques to help with this analysis:

- value proposition analysis;
- value chain analysis;
- organisation diagrams.

Business process analysis (Techniques 36–39)

In Chapter 3, 'Consider perspectives', we saw how a Business Activity Model (Technique 28) could be used to develop a conceptual view of a desired situation. The Business Activity Model may be used to show a conceptual view of an entire business system, and its focus is upon **what** should be in place to fulfil a given world view. Business process analysis complements this view by providing a representation of **how** activities are carried out. The business process models are underpinned by an understanding of the business events the organisation has to deal with and the business rules that constrain the operations. The techniques covered in this section are:

- business event analysis;
- business process modelling;
- business rules analysis;
- decision tables and decision trees.

Business change identification (Technique 40)

Possible business changes are identified by contrasting the current and desired views of the business system. The technique used to do this is called 'gap analysis', since it focuses on examining the gaps between the desired and existing situations. Actions will need to be taken to close the gaps and thereby change the business system. These actions can be formed into options for business change, which are evaluated in order to decide the best way forward.

ORGANISATION MODELLING

This section is concerned with the techniques that provide the analyst with an organisational context for deriving a desired view of processes. The analyst needs to develop an understanding of the organisation, its external business environment (as discussed in Chapter 1, 'Business strategy and objectives'), and the views of customers. This information is essential when considering business process improvements.

Technique 33: Value proposition analysis

Description of the technique

Value propositions are the customer perspectives with regard to an organisation. They summarise why customers choose to work with certain organisations, and what the customers want from each of them. Where there is a competitive market the value propositions also help to identify why a customer would purchase from one supplier rather than another.

As examples of value propositions, we consider the reasons why different groups of customers choose to buy their weekly food shopping from one supermarket rather than another:

- One group requires a supermarket where the prices are competitive and the range of products extensive.

- To another group, reasonable prices are important, but high product quality is vital.

- A third group requires a supermarket that is local and does not require them to travel. Price is a factor, but location and ease of travel are more important.

Understanding value propositions can be extremely helpful when improving processes, since they highlight what the recipients of the processes consider important.

Using value proposition analysis

When analysing value propositions, the first thing to consider is the identification of the customers. Customers tend to fall into three categories:

Owners or senior managers:	These are the individuals or groups who have invested in the organisation and those who are responsible for running it; in some cases they are the same people. In a private-sector organisation the owners are the people who expect a return on their investment, usually in the form of dividends. They are interested in the financial performance of the business. In a public-sector organisation the owners are the ministers responsible for the areas covered by its activities – for example, state pensions. They are also interested in the financial performance, but from a budgetary perspective rather than that of the payment of dividends, and they are interested in other aspects of performance as well, such as the quality of service delivered. In a not-for-profit organisation the owners are the trustees or committee members who are responsible for running it. They are interested in wise spending of a tight budget, and in the ability of the organisation to generate funding for future spending on good causes.
Partners or resellers:	These are the representatives from intermediary companies who work collaboratively with the organisation to sell or deliver the products or services. They are interested in their financial rewards from working with the organisation, and in the level of service they can provide to their customers.
End customers:	These are the beneficiaries of the products and services. They have a direct interest in what they pay for the goods, and in the quality of products and services that the organisation delivers.

The three types of customer and the areas of performance required are shown in Figure 4.2.

Figure 4.2 Types of value proposition

		CUSTOMERS		
		Owner	Partner	End Customer
VALUE CATEGORIES	Timing	Timing of receipt of financial reports and returns	Timing of receipt of information or goods	Timing of receipt of product/ service
	Financial	Level of dividend	Discount rate	Price of product/ service
	Quality	Reputation of organisation	Quality of service to partner	Quality of product/ service

The three value categories shown in Figure 4.2 highlight the key areas where customers have a requirement that they would like the organisation to meet. A combination of these factors helps to define each value proposition. For example, an end customer will require an organisation to provide a product that is usable, received when promised and priced at an acceptable level. A comparison of these factors may cause customers to switch suppliers if they feel their value proposition is better met elsewhere. Similarly, owners who are investors will want to feel that this is a reputable organisation that delivers good financial returns and provides timely reports to its investors.

Value proposition analysis is used to highlight what an organisation, or part of one, is required to deliver by its customers. The range and nature of those customers, and of the value propositions they have, is also clarified by this analysis. It is vital that the analysts are aware of the value propositions when they are analysing and improving the business processes, since this will enable them to ensure that any improvements meet the needs of the customers. Sometimes organisations are focused on processes that support internal requirements, such as cost reduction. While these may be required by customers of the owner type, they are rarely concerns for the end customers – those who purchase the goods and services. Understanding the range of value propositions, and the potential for conflicts between them, helps to provide analysts with a rounded view of the areas of performance to be addressed by the processes.

Technique 34: Value chain analysis

Description of the technique
The value chain was developed originally by Michael Porter (1985) and shows the different organisational activities that are grouped together to deliver value to customers. The value chain is a useful technique for business analysts who are working on business process improvement assignments. Understanding the 'value' that the organisation delivers to its customers, and the activities that contribute towards delivering this, is very powerful. It provides a view of the organisation's processes that helps the analyst ensure there is a customer focus when changes to the organisation are being considered. The original value chain devised by Porter is shown in Figure 4.3.

Figure 4.3 Porter's value chain

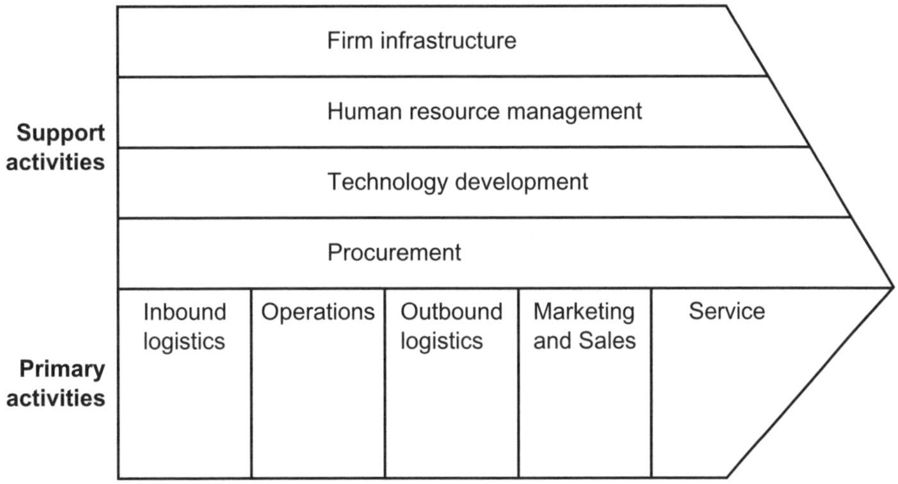

The primary activities in the value chain represent the key areas that need to work together to deliver an output of value to the customer. When building an organisational view of business processes, the five categories of primary activity in the value chain may be used to identify the key processes. For example, in a manufacturing company the activities may be considered as follows:

Inbound logistics: the activities that are concerned with obtaining raw materials and other items required to produce the goods;

Operations: those that are concerned with producing the goods;

Outbound logistics:	those that are concerned with distributing the goods to customers;
Marketing and sales:	those that are concerned with designing and promoting the products, and taking orders from customers;
Service	the post-sales activities that are connected with customer service and support.

While this is a useful approach for a manufacturing company, an amended view of the value chain primary activities is required if we are using it to analyse a service organisation:

Inbound logistics:	the activities that are required to develop or design the services to be delivered;
Operations:	those that are concerned with delivering the services;
Outbound logistics:	those that are concerned with distributing the services to customers – often merged with the operations activities;
Marketing and sales:	the activities that are concerned with designing and promoting the products, and taking orders from customers;
Service:	the post-sales activities that are connected with customer service and support.

When using the value chain for business analysis work, for example when analysing an organisation's processes in order to improve them, it is usually sufficient to consider the primary areas of activity. We can use these categories to identify the key areas of process required in a value chain to deliver the organisation's services, and these then provide the context for further process improvement work. However, the value chain also includes areas that comprise support activities. These represent the internal functions that offer support to the primary activities. They are:

Procurement:	the activities required to procure supplies of goods and services consumed by the organisation;
Technology development:	those required to develop and implement technology utilised by the organisation;
Human resource management:	those required to develop and maintain the workforce;
Firm infrastructure:	those required to develop and maintain the physical infrastructure required for the organisation.

If analysts are required to investigate the support activities, the approach we recommend is to model the value chain of the support activity area. For example, if the project is to study the HR work, the value chain will comprise the high-level HR processes, and the customers will be the internal management and staff of the organisation.

Using the Value Chain

When building an organisational view of processes using a value chain, we find the easiest approach is to begin with the operations area. This is very similar to finding the primary 'doing' activity on a Business Activity Model (Technique 28). In essence, you ask the question 'what is this value chain for?' As an example, if you ask this question about an examination body, the answer could be 'Examine candidates'. Having started with this, the next area to look at is the inbound logistics. The question to ask here in this example is 'What do we need to do in order to provide our qualifications?' Here we would think about activities such as 'Define qualification syllabus', 'Write examinations' and 'Set up examination schedule'. These are all examples of activities that should be carried out in order to examine the candidates. Moving on to outbound logistics, the next question to ask is 'What do we do after we have examined the candidates?' At this stage in the example there is an activity that is concerned with distributing our service to the customer – we need to deliver the result of the examinations. So the activity could be called 'Issue examination results'.

We have now identified the primary activities in the first three areas, so our value chain is as shown in Figure 4.4.

Figure 4.4 Partial value chain of primary activities – example

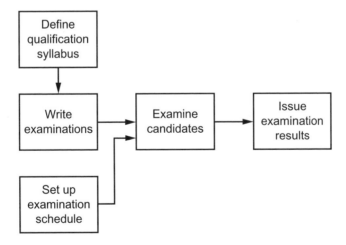

The next area to consider is the marketing and sales area. There are two separate aspects to this. First we need to think about the promotional and market research activities; secondly we need to consider the sales activity. In an examination body there may be a need to ensure that the potential candidates and their organisations are aware of the qualifications offered and the route to achieving them. The activity required here could be named 'Promote qualifications', and there could also be an activity called 'Research qualification requirements'. The sales area would be concerned with signing up candidates rather than the more traditional sales activity of taking an order or a booking. We could call this 'Register examination candidate'. The final area concerns service, so we could have activities such as 'Handle candidate appeals' and 'Resolve candidate queries'. The value chain would then look as shown in Figure 4.5.

Figure 4.5 Value chain for an examination body

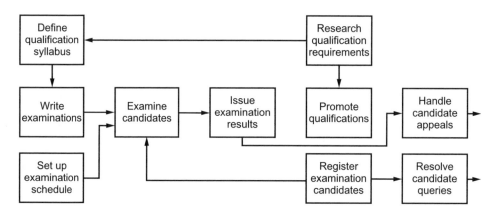

This model provides a high-level process map for the organisation and gives the analyst an excellent view of the areas that need to work together in order to provide value to the customer. This model also enables the analyst to consider, typically with the business managers, the areas that are of high priority or are known to be struggling. Further analysis of an area of process can be carried out using supplementary techniques such as business event analysis and business process modelling (Techniques 36 and 37). Both of these are described later in this chapter.

Technique 35: Organisation Diagram
Variants/Aliases
Organisation model is a related term.

Description of the technique
This technique was described by Paul Harmon (2007) in *Business Process Change*. The Organisation Diagram pulls together the external business environment and the internal value chain, and provides a view of the high-level processes and the forces that impinge upon the successful delivery of the value chain.

Four aspects of the external environment are modelled: the external business factors such as those found using PESTLE analysis (Technique 1); the competitors offering alternative products or services; the suppliers of resources; and the customers who are the beneficiaries from the value chain.

These external environmental views are shown in Figure 4.6 for our examination body example.

Figure 4.6 Organisation Diagram showing external environment

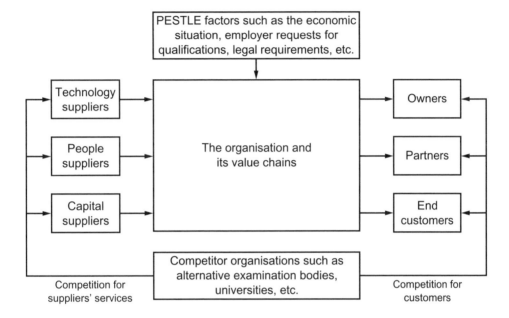

An Organisation Diagram helps to show what the organisation is facing in its external environment. In the example in Figure 4.6 the following aspects are modelled:

- PESTLE factors such as the economic situation that may affect the ability of employers or individuals to pay for the qualifications;
- the suppliers of resources such as technology – perhaps for online examinations or marking – and people – perhaps markers and examination writers;
- competition from other examination organisations that could attract customers, and could employ the examination body's suppliers such as the markers;
- the customers with their different value propositions, for example employers of potential candidates or even the candidates themselves, all needing to be targeted by the processes in the value chain.

The Organisation Diagram is completed by showing the value chain within the box representing the organisation. Figure 4.7 shows an example of a completed Organisation Diagram.

Figure 4.7 Completed Organisation Diagram

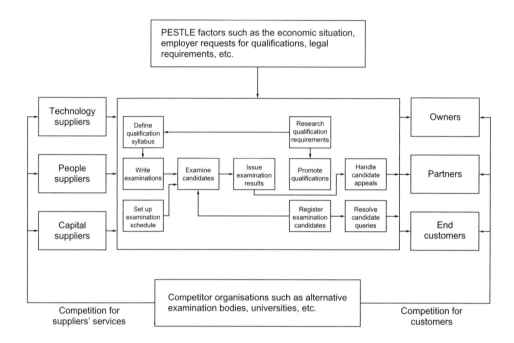

Using the Organisation Diagram

The Organisation Diagram offers a number of benefits to the analyst. The discussion and thought required to develop the diagram helps to clarify the priorities and issues that the business processes need to address. For example, it may highlight where the internal processes are not aligned with the external environment or the customers' value propositions.

The Organisation Diagram itself can be seen as the top level in a business process hierarchy, and therefore provides a context for future process improvement work. Each area of process can be examined separately by considering all of the business processes required to deliver the work of this area. The analysis of these processes requires an understanding of business events, covered later in this chapter, since these will help in the identification of the set of business processes. The value chain also helps with the development of the process hierarchy if each of the value chain processes is allocated a reference number. This number provides a basis for cross-referencing the lower-level, detailed process models and documents.

A further benefit of the Organisation Diagram is that it helps the analyst communicate with the business managers and staff by setting out clearly the areas of work, providing a basis for discussing a range of process-related areas, and supporting the prioritisation of process improvement efforts.

BUSINESS PROCESS ANALYSIS

Business process analysis provides a view of an organisation that is focused on the customer. This is often contrasted with the functional view, which tends to be focused upon internal objectives and is often referred to as 'silo thinking'. Over the last twenty years or so, the business process view of organisations has increased in popularity, particularly when considering business improvements, as it removes the silo effect experienced when the focus is on the internal departments or functions.

Technique 36: Business event analysis
Variants/Aliases
Variants of this technique include **system event analysis** and **business process triggers**.

Description of the technique
Business events are occurrences to which an organisation needs to respond. For example, if a membership society receives an application from someone wishing to become a member, it will need to be able to respond to this request. The receipt of the membership application is a business event, and the response will be one of the organisation's business processes. If the Identity and Passport Service receives a passport application, the agency will need to invoke a process to handle this application. In this case the receipt of the passport application is a business event, and the response is the corresponding process.

Business event analysis is concerned with examining a business system or an area of activity in order to identify the events the organisation needs to handle. There are three standard types of event, and we usually consider these types as a framework for thinking about events. They are:

External events: the occurrences that take place outside the organisation or business area. External events typically originate from the external stakeholders, so it is often useful to begin by identifying the relevant stakeholders. The stakeholder wheel (Technique 25) discussed in Chapter 3, 'Consider perspectives', is one technique that can be used to identify the initial set of external stakeholders. Once we have identified them we can think about the reasons they would want to contact them, what information they would want to provide or obtain, and what products and services they would want to receive. This approach enables the analyst to identify an initial set of external events, each of which will need to be handled by the organisation.

Internal events: the occurrences that take place inside the organisation or business area. Internal events originate typically from the management of the business area, but can also originate from the members of staff. Again it is helpful to begin by identifying the stakeholders – this time the relevant internal stakeholders. Once they have been identified, the events that they need the business area to handle can be considered. A key area concerns decisions.

The managers of the organisation will make decisions regarding its operation, and these will need to be enforced. This means that there need to be organisational responses, in the form of business processes, to handle the decisions. These may affect limited areas: an example is the reallocation of a piece of work from one staff member to another. This requires a process to update any records regarding the allocation of the work and to communicate the change to any interested parties. However, a decision can have a variety of different effects, so it may require more work to ensure that all affected areas are updated. In this case it will require a process that is longer and more detailed. Examples include a decision to introduce a new pricing structure or a new product range.

Time-based events: the regular occurrences that take place at predefined times. Time-based events often result from legal regulations or business policy. An example that affects all organisations is the financial reporting cycle, which specifies set timings for reports. A further example could be an internal policy that requires that management reports have to be produced and distributed to specified stakeholders at a set time each week, such as every Monday morning. Another form of time-based event occurs where actions are required in advance of another business event. For example, there may be a requirement to issue information two weeks prior to a senior management meeting.

Business event analysis provides a means of breaking down the work of an organisation or business area into discrete areas. This is invaluable in supporting an organised, structured analysis of the business processes and the tasks they comprise. The identification of the business events is the first step in this approach. Following on from that, the analyst needs to consider the outcomes desired from the events. For example, if an event is identified in which a customer complains to an organisation about the delivery of a service, the outcome should be the resolution of that complaint. So the second step is to consider the outcome required once a business event occurs. The third step is to model and analyse the business process that will be triggered by the event and will deliver the outcome. Business process modelling is the next technique described in this chapter.

Using business event analysis
Business events provide a framework for analysing business systems. They help to clarify for the analyst all of the different components of the work carried out within a particular area. They also help with uncovering tacit knowledge, since they provide a basis for identifying situations that the business user may not have mentioned or even considered important.

It is often helpful to begin by building a context diagram like that in Figure 4.8. This diagram can be used to show the relevant stakeholders, both internal and external to the organisation, that have been identified for this area of business activity. Once we have identified the stakeholders the next step is to consider the types of events each stakeholder will require the business system to handle. This helps in the identification of the individual events.

Using the context diagram in Figure 4.8, we might identify the events shown in Table 4.1.

Figure 4.8 Context diagram supporting event identification

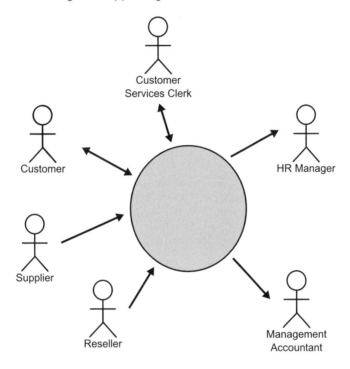

When documenting the events we name them so that they reflect what has occurred. For example, there is an external event called 'issue of invoice reminder'; this name expresses an incident that the business area needs to deal with. It is good practice to name events in this way, so that the name indicates something that has happened or that needs to happen. Time-based events typically fall into the latter category.

Once the business events have been identified they can form the basis for partitioning the business area under investigation. Each event handled by the business area can be analysed separately. For each of them, we consider factors such as these:

• Who is responsible for the business response (the process)?

• What is the desired outcome?

• What is the required timescale to achieve the desired outcome?

• Who is involved in carrying out the work?

• What are the alternative scenarios to be explored?

Consideration of these aspects for each event allows the analyst to focus on the partitioned area without the introduction of other aspects that could cause confusion or obscure the issues.

Table 4.1 Examples of business events

	Stakeholder type	Events
External events	customer	purchase of business service
		amendment of service purchase
		purchase cancellation
		complaint
		receipt of customer registration
		submission of request for quotation
	supplier	receipt of quotation
		delivery of goods
		submission of invoice
		submission of payment confirmation
		issue of invoice reminder
	reseller	request for discount rate
		request for service information
		provision of service feedback
Internal events	management accountant	revision of quotation format
	HR manager	staff member allocated to training course
Time-based events	management accountant	end of month reconciliation
	staff member	production of weekly allocation report

Business events can be analysed at a number of different levels. As shown above, they can be used to identify processes and partition a business area. The business area under investigation might be a high-level process such as that shown on an Organisation Diagram (Technique 35), or it could be a business activity from a Business Activity Model (Technique 28). In these cases the response to the business event will be documented as a business process model or swimlane diagram (Technique 37).

At a lower level of detail business events can be used during the analysis of the individual tasks or activities from within a business process. This can be a useful aspect to consider, since each individual task will also be initiated by a business event, and, just as an organisation has to initiate a business process in order to handle an event, an individual member of staff has to recognise that a task needs to be initiated when the relevant event occurs. Failing to recognise when a piece of work needs to be carried out can cause problems for organisations. An analysis of the events that trigger a task helps to clarify this and to ensure that the staff are aware of what needs to happen in response to an event.

If the business events trigger, or are required to trigger, IT system responses they are often referred to as 'system events'. Whether we are dealing with business or system events, there is one constant principle: when an event occurs it requires a response, and that response can be analysed to consider whether it is adequate and supports the business objectives. The response is what the organisation does when it encounters an event; this response may be automated, manual or a combination of both automation and manual action. Business process modelling (Technique 37) is often used to carry out the detailed analysis once the events have been identified. Other approaches that may be used to analyse the event are scenarios or use cases (Techniques 50 and 62).

Technique 37: Business process modelling
Variants/Aliases
Models like this are also known as **swimlane diagrams** or **process maps**.

Readers will also come across the terms 'workflow model' or 'workflow diagram'. A workflow system is one where the operation of a business process is managed, monitored and controlled by a computer system. For example, a document is scanned at the start of the process and then various actors are prompted to do something with it. Workflow models are, in our opinion, just another use of the basic process modelling technique rather than a separate or distinctive technique.

Description of the technique
Business process models show several of the key elements of a business process:

- the business event that initiates the process;

- the tasks that make up the process (these are the pieces of work that are carried out by an actor at a point in time, and are sometimes called 'activities' – we prefer 'tasks' in order to avoid confusion with the activities on a Business Activity Model);

- the actors that carry out the tasks or activities (these actors may, in automated or semi-automated processes – for example, workflow systems – include IT systems);

- the sequence or flow of the tasks;

- the decisions that lead to alternative process flows;

- the endpoint or outcome of the process;

- optionally, the timeline for the process.

There are numerous approaches to business process modelling, and each has its own notation set. The approach we favour uses the UML notation for the activity diagrams (sometimes known as cross-functional diagrams). Figure 4.9 shows this notation set.

Figure 4.9 Business process notation set

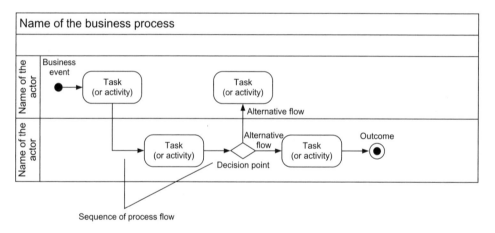

The business process models are built from the initial list of business events described earlier. The response to each event is modelled by building a business process model. In building this the analyst often uncovers additional business events, for which further business process models will need to be built.

Using business process models
Business process models are used for many purposes, including:

- to document an existing process for accreditation purposes;

- to use as a basis for training members of staff;

- to understand how the process works and where the problems lie;

- to provide a basis for business process improvement;

- to identify who is involved in the entire process;
- to show the sequence of process flow and the alternative flows.

When building a business process model it is important that the analyst understands the event that initiates the process, the required outcome and the possible alternative outcomes. The model is then built by considering each task within the process in turn. The event will trigger an actor to carry out the initial task. On the conclusion of that task, the responsibility for the next piece of work will pass to another actor and the flow should be represented on the model. If the work can be passed to more than one actor, the decision point, with the reasons for the different work flows, is shown. The analysis of the tasks and their outcomes continues until the endpoint of the process is reached for all alternative paths. Once the model has been produced it may be useful to add the timeline for the process, showing which tasks need to be carried out within a defined timeframe.

Business actors have to be involved in building the business process models. They have the detailed knowledge of the work they carry out, the sources of any information and the sequence of tasks in the process. They should also understand why alternative sequences will be required, and the rationale for decisions. Most business processes will be carried out across business functions and teams, so there may be several actors involved with each process. The analyst needs to ensure that the views and knowledge of all relevant actors are incorporated into the business process model, so the models are usually developed in a workshop environment (Technique 14). As a visual documentation technique, business process models are extremely useful when building a consensus view of processing.

Building the process hierarchy
The business process modelling technique is often used in a hierarchical fashion. The high-level view of the business processes – from the value chain (Technique 34) or the activities in the Business Activity Model (Technique 28, in Chapter 3) – form the top level of the hierarchy. If this is a large and complex area of processing, it is sometimes useful to build an intermediate model showing the key actors, processes and sequences of work. The next step downwards, below the intermediate model if one has been produced, is to build a business process model that represents the detail of the process – its actors, tasks, decisions and flows of work. At the bottom level of the hierarchy are the tasks – the individual boxes on the process model. These are also analysed and documented.

When building a hierarchy of process it is important that a numbering system is adopted. This system should allow traceability from the high-level area of process or activity down through the hierarchy to the tasks at the bottom level. A suggested system is illustrated by the example shown in Table 4.2.

Documenting tasks
There are several possible approaches to documenting tasks, some using text and some a combination of text and diagrams. A typical approach might be to use the activity modelling notation from the UML to show the series of steps carried out, and the decisions made, during the task. This is essentially a flowchart showing

Table 4.2 Example hierarchical numbering system

Level	Process number	Process/task name
Organisation	1	Sell products
Business process model	1.2	Record customer order
Business process model	1.4	Handle customer complaint
Task	1.2/1	Record customer contact information
Task	1.4/5	Issue customer refund

how the task is carried out and which business rules are applied during this work. It can also be useful to consider the following areas for each task:

- the event that initiates the task;
- the actor who is responsible for the work;
- the information required to carry out the task (it is important to note that this is sometimes part of the initiating event, but it may equally be additional information that is accessed while carrying out the work);
- the possible outputs from the task;
- the timing and quality performance measures that the actor has to adhere to when carrying out this work.

Rationalising process models

Business process models are often produced in such detail that they show all of the individual tasks, plus the details of each task. For example, there might be a swimlane with a series of steps, as shown for the event organiser in Figure 4.10.

This approach to modelling processes usually leads to large, complex models that are of little use for their primary purposes – communication and improvement. It is better practice to show one task for a series of steps, and then analyse the task in greater detail separately as described above. This way the model is readable and easily understandable, and each area of work that needs particular attention can be focused upon separately. The revised swimlane is shown in Figure 4.11.

A similar approach applies when documenting the decisions that an actor takes when choosing between different courses of action while carrying out a task. As long as the courses of action are all carried out by the same actor, the analysis of the decisions and the rules that govern them can be contained within the task analysis.

Figure 4.10 Business process model with detailed steps

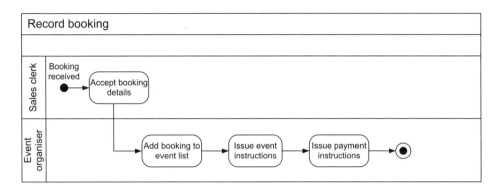

Figure 4.11 Business process model showing rationalised steps

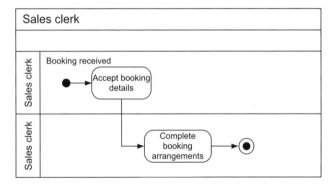

Process performance measures
As discussed earlier, business process modelling shows a cross-functional view of the organisation and enables the organisation to focus on the customer. This focus provides a basis for considering the measures to be applied to the actors' performance. The performance measures related to the process need to be defined such that they contribute to meeting the customer's required value proposition. For example, if a purchase has to be registered, organised and delivered within three days, each element of the process needs to be set a timescale so that, when taken collectively, the total time corresponds to this figure. If the delivery task will take two days, then this might mean that the overall timescale cannot be met. An effective approach to defining performance measures is as follows:

- Identify the customer's requirements, for example as encapsulated in the value proposition.
- Define the performance measures to be achieved by the entire process.

- Analyse each task to set the individual performance measures.

- Ensure that the task performance measures will collectively meet the overall business process performance measures.

Each business process sets out a parcel of work that should be the responsibility of a nominated individual. This individual is then responsible for achieving the defined performance measures. Each task, together with its own performance requirements, is the responsibility of the actor carrying it out, and this is shown clearly on the model.

Technique 38: Business rules analysis
Variants/Aliases
A related term is **constraints analysis**.

Description of the technique
Business rules underpin the way an organisation carries out its work. They are the basis for the decisions that are made, which in turn determine the information that is distributed and the sequence of tasks.

Business rules apply at a number of different levels, and can originate from external and internal sources. The major categories of business rule are:

- legal and regulatory constraints;

- organisational policy constraints;

- operational procedures.

Legal and regulatory business rules originate from external sources. As discussed in Chapter 1, the legal and regulatory issues facing organisations are numerous and increasing. These constraints impose decisions on all parts of an organisation; areas affected include accounting and payment procedures, health and safety requirements and employment rights. Where constraints of this kind exist the analyst needs to be aware of them, because they have to be complied with. There is little point in trying to find options for improvement if the current approach is determined by laws and regulations.

Organisational policy constraints are defined internally, and also impose rules upon the organisation. These policies may relate to areas such as:

- payments, cancellations and refunds;

- appeals and complaints;

- pricing and discounts.

There is likely to be little gain from challenging policy constraints. They are usually linked to the MOST for the organisation (Technique 3), and help in the delivery of its strategy. It may be helpful, however, to verify that a business rule really does originate from the organisation's policies. Sometimes rules are presented as policy when in fact they are only based upon long-standing practice.

In this case the analyst may be able to uncover unnecessary constraints and the opportunity for improvement.

Operational procedures are also defined internally, and are the business rules that are most likely to be open to challenge and amendment when pursuing organisational improvement. Typical operational procedures include rules for determining customer discounts or benefits, or for accepting orders or bookings. These procedures have often developed over time, and may be based upon personal preferences or individual views rather than business needs. Detailed analysis can also uncover discrepancies in the way that different members of staff apply operational procedures. Ultimately, operational procedures may need to be considered in the light of the business objectives and strategy in order to determine whether they should be revisited and improved.

Using business rules analysis

Business rules are important because they govern the work of the organisation. Hence, it is vital that they are considered during business process modelling work. They need to be documented so that the analysts can understand the impact of the rules and whether or not they are open to discussion or challenge.

Business rules are encountered at many points during business process improvement. They can constrain the value chain by imposing an overall sequence on the high-level processes; they can constrain the business processes, represented in the business process models or swimlane diagrams (Technique 37), by imposing a need for a particular task to be carried out by a particular actor or at a set point in the process, or even to be carried out at all; finally, they can constrain the procedures followed during a task, by imposing rules upon which decisions are based.

When modelling processes or analysing tasks we can uncover the business rules by asking about:

- the reason for deciding upon a particular course of action;
- why the work is carried out in a particular sequence;
- the transitions between tasks or the steps within a task (are there any circumstances under which these transitions would not take place, or there would be an alternative task invoked)?

For example, we could have a process that contained the following sequence of tasks:

- record ticket booking;
- issue tickets.

In this example, the stated sequence of tasks is not open to question but we could consider why there are two separate tasks, and ask whether they could be carried out at the same time. If we investigated what could prevent the issue of the tickets and cause a task other than 'issue tickets' to be invoked, we might find that:

- The tickets could be available as an email download, and hence be issued with the booking confirmation during 'record ticket booking'.

- The customer might not be eligible to attend – possibly on age grounds – and so the booking would have to be rejected.

Investigating such questions helps to uncover the business rules that apply to the processes. In the example above, the business rules might be age related, as suggested – perhaps this is an event with a lower age limit of 18 years. Another potential eligibility rule could be that when there is a group booking there has to be at least one person over 21 years old. Alternatively, there could be a prerequisite – for example, to attend a radio show a person might have to submit questions in advance in order to gain attendance information. Examining the transitions between tasks and steps will help to uncover the tacit knowledge about the business rules.

Business rules and modelling data

Business rules do not just impact upon the business process analysis – they are also key to understanding how the data in the organisation needs to be organised. When modelling data, the business rules govern aspects such as which items of data can be grouped together because they are in one-to-one correspondence, and the ways in which these data groups are associated with each other – for example, is there an association between two data groups, and, if so, what are the rules that govern it? If we consider the ticket example above, in many ticket booking systems the number of tickets associated with one customer is limited to a maximum number. In this situation, the business rules could state that a customer must hold a minimum of one ticket and a maximum of four tickets.

Data modelling, the business rules shown within data models, and techniques for modelling data are explored in further detail in Chapter 6, 'Define requirements'.

Technique 39: Decision tables and decision trees

Description of the technique

A decision table shows a set of conditions that may be combined in different ways in order to determine the required courses of action. Decision tables provide a clear and unambiguous means of documenting conditions and the resultant actions to be taken.

Consider the following rules for determining rail fares as an example:

All passengers travelling after 10 am are allowed to purchase off-peak tickets; tickets for travel before 10 am are charged at the full price. All passengers aged 60 and over are allowed a further 20% discount on the ticket price charged.

We have two conditions here:

- Is the time of travel after 10 am?
- Is the passenger aged 60 or over?

There are four possible prices charged:

- full price;
- full price less 20% discount;
- off-peak price;
- off-peak price less 20% discount.

While this information can be written in text, a decision table presents these conditions and actions in such a way that the information is clear and unambiguous. The decision table is divided into four sections: the condition stub, the condition entries, the action stub and the action entries. The conditions that determine the actions are listed in the condition stub. Combinations of the conditions are identified and expressed as condition entries. The actions that can be taken are listed in the action stub. The relevant actions for each condition set are identified in the action entries. Figure 4.12 shows the structure of the decision table.

Figure 4.12 Decision table structure

CONDITION STUB	CONDITION ENTRIES
ACTION STUB	ACTION ENTRIES

The most frequently used type of decision table is known as a limited-entry decision table. In this table the conditions are expressed as questions that have a 'yes' or 'no' answer. Each combination of answers to the conditions results in a specified action; there is an action for each possible combination.

We can show the rail fare example given above as a decision table.

First we list the conditions, as in Table 4.3.

Table 4.3 Condition stub in a decision table

Condition 1	travelling after 10 am?
Condition 2	aged 60 or over?

Next we work out the number of possible combinations of conditions. This can be calculated by using the formula (2^c) where c is the number of conditions – two, in this example. This formula ensures that all of the table entries have been expressed. In this example, the existence of two conditions generates 2^2 combinations of conditions – four combinations in total. The easiest way to identify all possible combinations is to use the following approach:

Condition 1: Answer Y for half of the number of combinations and N for the other half. In our example this would be as in Table 4.4.

Condition 2: Answer Y for half of those combinations where Y was answered to condition 1, and N for the other half; repeat this. In our example, this would result the entries in Table 4.5.

Table 4.4 Decision table condition entries – one condition

Condition 1	travelling after 10 am?	Y	Y	N	N

Table 4.5 Decision table condition entries – two conditions

Condition 1	travelling after 10 am?	Y	Y	N	N
Condition 2	aged 60 or over?	Y	N	Y	N

This approach always provides the correct number of condition combinations. Where there are three conditions we would expect to see 2^3, i.e. eight, combinations of conditions. This would result in the entries shown in Table 4.6.

Table 4.6 Decision table condition entries – three conditions

Condition 1	Y	Y	Y	Y	N	N	N	N
Condition 2	Y	Y	N	N	Y	Y	N	N
Condition 3	Y	N	Y	N	Y	N	Y	N

Once the condition entries have been made, the next step is to identify all possible actions and record them in the action stub. It is helpful if the entries are in the sequence in which they are to be applied. For our example the actions are listed in Table 4.7.

The action entries for the combination of conditions are now indicated in the decision table. The complete decision table for our example is shown as Table 4.8.

Table 4.7 Action stub in a decision table

Action 1	off-peak price less 20% discount
Action 2	off-peak price
Action 3	full price less 20% discount
Action 4	full price

Table 4.8 Decision table with two conditions

Condition 1	travelling after 10 am?	Y	Y	N	N
Condition 2	aged 60 or over?	Y	N	Y	N
Action 1	off-peak price less 20% discount	✓			
Action 2	off-peak price		✓		
Action 3	full price less 20% discount			✓	
Action 4	full price				✓

A more complex decision table using the case where there are three conditions is given as Table 4.9. As discussed above, where there are three conditions the number of combinations is calculated by using the formula 2^3, resulting in eight combinations.

Table 4.9 Decision table with three conditions

Condition 1	travelling after 10 am?	Y	Y	Y	Y	N	N	N	N
Condition 2	aged 60 or over?	Y	Y	N	N	Y	Y	N	N
Condition 3	holder of discount railcard?	Y	N	Y	N	Y	N	Y	N
Action 1	off-peak price less 20% discount	✓	✓						
Action 2	off-peak price less 10% discount			✓					
Action 3	off-peak price				✓				
Action 4	full price less 20% discount					✓	✓		
Action 5	full price less 10% discount							✓	
Action 6	full price								✓

Sometimes there is redundancy within the decision table. This occurs if two or more different combinations of conditions lead to the same actions. In Table 4.9 this can be seen in the first two condition columns – as long as the passenger is travelling after 10 am and is aged 60 years or over, action 2 applies. The discount railcard answer does not have any effect. This also occurs when a passenger aged 60 or over travels before 10 am. In these circumstances we can consolidate the entries to simplify the table. The decision table is amended to remove the redundancy by combining each set of two columns in which condition 3 has no effect. The resulting decision table is shown as Table 4.10.

Table 4.10 Decision table with rationalised conditions

Condition 1	travelling after 10 am?	Y	Y	Y	N	N	N
Condition 2	aged 60 or over?	Y	N	N	Y	N	N
Condition 3	holder of discount railcard?	–	Y	N	–	Y	N
Action 1	off-peak price less 20% discount	✓					
Action 2	off-peak price less 10% discount		✓				
Action 3	off-peak price			✓			
Action 4	full price less 20% discount				✓		
Action 5	full price less 10% discount					✓	
Action 6	full price						✓

Sometimes decision tables can become extremely complex. Given the exponential effect of additional conditions, if there were five or more of them we would end up with a large and unwieldy decision table. In this situation we recommend using a hierarchy of tables. The most important conditions are combined in a high-level table, where the actions refer to lower-level table(s) showing the additional conditions and actions.

Extended-entry decision tables
An extension to the decision table approach involves using condition entries that are expressed as values. If we consider the consolidated limited-entry decision table in Table 4.11, we can see that the decision table approach does not work very well in this situation. There is only one action for each condition, so the decision table looks over-complex as a means of representing the situation.

An alternative approach, using the extended-entry decision table, is shown in Table 4.12. This decision table shows the conditions and the corresponding actions more clearly.

Decision trees
Decision trees provide an alternative means of showing a set of conditions and how they are combined to determine the action to be taken. The diagram

Table 4.11 Decision table with exclusive conditions

Condition 1	ticket purchase < 2 days in advance?	Y	N	N	N
Condition 2	ticket purchase 2–10 days in advance?	–	Y	N	N
Condition 3	ticket purchase 11–20 days in advance?	–	–	Y	N
Condition 4	ticket purchase > 20 days in advance?	–	–	–	Y
Action 1	no discount	✓			
Action 2	discount 10%		✓		
Action 3	discount 25%			✓	
Action 4	discount 50%				✓

Table 4.12 Extended-entry decision table

Conditions	how far in advance ticket is purchased (days)	< 2	2–10	11–20	> 20
Actions	% discount	0	10	25	50

begins at a point called its root, and is developed by using branches that represent the responses to each condition and ultimately the actions to be taken. Figure 4.13 shows the rail fare example (with two conditions) in a decision tree format.

Figure 4.13 Example decision tree

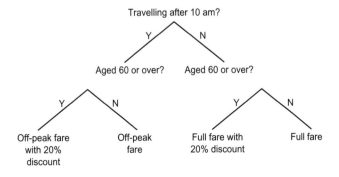

Using decision tables and trees

Decision tables and decision trees are useful when trying to define clearly a set of conditions, how they work in combination and what actions should be taken on encountering a given set of conditions. There is a close link between the business rules discussed earlier and the use of decision tables and trees. Essentially, decision tables and trees provide a means of documenting business rules that allows for complex combinations of different conditions to form composite rules.

An alternative approach is to show the conditions using a form of flow chart. However, this can result in a lengthy diagram that can be difficult to read. Such a diagram shows the business rules and the pathways that result from applying them. However, where there is the possibility of several combinations of conditions, it can result in a lengthy and complex diagram.

A decision table is concise and clear, and the technique allows for complex combinations of conditions. As a result, they are invaluable when defining detailed procedures where business rules have to be applied in combination. This may be needed when documenting the procedural details relating to tasks that are to be carried out by business staff, or when documenting the business rules to be applied by IT systems, for example when carrying out calculations or deciding on courses of action.

The formula to calculate the number of combinations of conditions is also useful in uncovering situations that the business user might not have considered. This can help to reveal new facts about business situations that might not have been disclosed to the analyst without prompting.

Experience has shown that the detail of decision-making, involving the application of specific, often complex, business rules, is frequently overlooked during the analysis of processes and systems. Techniques such as decision tables and decision trees help to clarify the business rules and the resultant actions and to uncover tacit knowledge about decision-making.

BUSINESS CHANGE IDENTIFICATION

Technique 40: Gap analysis

Description of the technique

Gap analysis is concerned with examining the two views of a business situation – that of the situation as it exists and that of the conceptual, desired situation – in order to identify the differences between them. These differences provide the basis for defining the actions to be taken in order to implement the desired view. The exact approach taken to gap analysis depends upon the techniques used to represent the two views, but a typical approach is as follows:

1. Investigate and model the existing situation. Typically this involves the use of diagrammatic techniques such as rich pictures and mind maps (Techniques 20 and 21), since these are effective in representing the range of issues that may be inherent within an existing situation, including cultural and

personal issues. A set of 'as is' business process models (Technique 37) can also be used to represent a view of the existing situation. However, whereas aspects such as business culture, stakeholder disagreements or priorities, and voiced opinions are represented in techniques such as rich pictures, they would not be shown in the business process models. Where business process models are used to document the existing situation, supplementary techniques would be required to show these additional issues.

2. Analyse perspectives and develop a representation of the desired situation. It is important to use techniques that provide a conceptual representation of a desired, future business situation. Business activity modelling (Technique 28) is often used for this purpose, since it provides an holistic view of a business system and is a conceptual modelling technique. The 'to be' business process models also provide a conceptual view, but purely from a process perspective rather than that of an entire future business system. While process models provide a detailed view of the desired business processes, they focus on how the work is carried out and do not cover all of the required areas, such as the planning and enabling activities. As a result, it is preferable if they are used to supplement, or are supplemented by, other techniques.

3. Compare and contrast the two views, to identify the differences and the actions that would be required in order to move from the existing situation to the desired business system.

The gap analysis technique contrasts the existing and desired views by considering the following questions:

- Do the desired activities exist in the current business system?

- Do the current activities work well or are there problems?

- How extensive are the problems with the current activities?

In order to carry out this analysis, each of the activities on the Business Activity Model should be classified into one of the following categories:

- existing and satisfactory;

- existing but not satisfactory;

- not existing.

Once the activities have been classified, they can be prioritised for further, more detailed, analysis. It is possible that some areas are of low priority – perhaps because there is little room for improvement or because they are not within the scope of the study – in which case they will not be the immediate focus of the work. Where an activity is to be analysed further, the following areas should be considered for that activity:

- What work should the activity address, as compared with the current work?

- How important is this area, and how imperative is it to business success?

- What business events should the activity handle?

- What are the gaps between the current and desired processes to handle these business events? Is there a current process defined to carry out this activity and handle this event?

- Are there any standards adopted when performing this activity, and are there any required standards?

- Are there any performance measures to be monitored, and are there any to be defined?

- How well do the IT systems support the activity?

This further analysis work will often require additional investigation of the activities in order to clarify the gaps and problems.

Using gap analysis

Gap analysis compares the current and desired business systems. When examining these views, the following questions should be asked:

- Does this activity exist in the current business system? Sometimes, gap analysis exposes an absence of certain activities. Typical examples of this are where performance information is produced but it is not used to monitor performance, or where problems with performance are identified but not tackled. Another common issue is the lack of resources to carry out the work effectively. The 'plan', 'enable', 'monitor' and 'control' activities on a Business Activity Model (Technique 28) often highlight these problems during gap analysis.

- If the activity does exist currently, how well is it carried out, and are there problems acknowledged with this activity? Current system investigations often expose known problems that have not been tackled by the organisation. Gap analysis helps to show the impact of these problems on the other activities that are dependent upon the work being carried out correctly. The 'to be' business process models show how the work should be carried out in the desired system, so a comparison with the 'as is' business process models will help to identify where changes should be made. Some activities are performed perfectly well in the current business system, so it may not be necessary to change them. Given that budgets are usually limited, it is important to prioritise the work following gap analysis – so identifying areas that can be addressed with minimal effort, or even left as they are, is extremely helpful. Some activities will exist in the current situation but be performed poorly. These need to be the primary focus of any changes, since they are likely to be the areas where most benefits can result.

- If the activity does not exist, or only exists to a limited degree, is it an area that should be examined within the scope of the study? Some activities are not present in the current business system, and it is important to understand both why this is the case and whether the current business analysis study is required to address them. The scope defined in the terms of reference or project initiation document will be helpful in identifying where this is the case. It may be that an extension to the study will be required, because this area might not have been identified previously, or it may be that there is already work under way to address this gap. Where problems are highlighted with activities that are outside the scope of the study, it is still advisable to identify them as issues to be addressed. However, the focus of the gap analysis will be on the other areas.

As a result of this analysis, the gaps that will need to be bridged in order to implement the desired business system will be identified. In examining the gaps, it is important to consider the different aspects of the business system. One of the commonly used approaches is the four-view model (Technique 9, from Chapter 1), because it helps to ensure that all key aspects are considered. The areas to investigate using this model are:

Process: It is useful to begin by examining the 'as is' and 'to be' processes. Each process should be considered in turn in order to define the revised and the new tasks, and to identify the IT support required for them.

Technology: The IT requirements for each task can be identified from the process models. These requirements should be documented using a use case diagram (Technique 62), and they may also be added to a requirements catalogue. These techniques are described further in Chapter 6, 'Define requirements'.

People: Once the processes have been analysed, the new actor roles can be defined. This typically involves redefining the job descriptions and the competency requirements. Each 'to be' process shows the tasks and the actors who should carry them out. Collating these tasks for each actor helps to develop the new job descriptions and create an understanding of the competency requirements.

Organisation: The revised business processes may require changes to the structure of the organisation. Teams may be merged or split, and actor roles revised. This might require changes to the management and team structures, and these will need to be specified.

This analysis will result in a list of change actions that need to be made in order to bridge the gap between the current and the desired business system. The list of actions resulting from the gap analysis will form the basis for defining options for business change. These options are then developed and evaluated. This is discussed more fully in Chapter 5, 'Evaluate options'.

REFERENCES

Harmon, P. (2007) *Business Process Change*, 2nd edition. Morgan Kaufmann, Burlington, MA.

Porter, M. (1985) *Competitive Advantage*, Free Press, New York.

FURTHER READING

Arlow, J. and Neustadt, I. (2005) *UML 2 and the Unified Process*, 2nd edition. Addison Wesley, Upper Saddle River, NJ.

Paul, D. and Yeates, D. (eds) (2006) *Business Analysis*. BCS, London.

SSADM Foundation (2000) The *Business Context* volume of *Business Systems Development with SSADM*. TSO, London.

5 EVALUATE OPTIONS

INTRODUCTION

This part of the business analyst's (BA's) work is about considering and assessing the options that are available to address the business problem or issue, and presenting proposals for change to senior management in the form of a business case.

Figure 5.1 The process for evaluating options

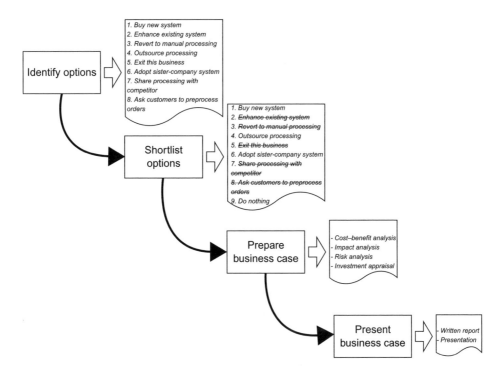

There are four main elements to this work, as illustrated in Figure 5.1.

- identifying the options available;
- reducing the possible options to a more manageable shortlist;
- preparing the elements of a business case;
- presenting the business case to management for decision-making.

Identify options (Technique 41)

This involves getting as comprehensive a list as possible of the options available, without eliminating any too early (before they have been properly considered).

Shortlist options (Techniques 42–43)

The initial 'longlist' of possible options needs to be whittled down to a more management set that can be considered more carefully. This can be done by using SWOT analysis (Technique 6) or PESTLE (Technique 1), both described earlier in the book, and also by employing feasibility analysis or force-field analysis, to be introduced in this section.

Prepare business case (Techniques 44–47)

For the selected option (and maybe for the key alternatives too), the business case now needs to be constructed. The issues to consider here are:

- cost–benefit analysis – contrasting the expected costs of the option with its predicted benefits;
- impact analysis – identifying and assessing any non-cost impacts of the proposed change, such as new ways of working;
- risk analysis – identifying the risks to success and possible countermeasures;
- investment appraisal – putting the (financial) costs and benefits together to see whether the project pays for itself.

Present business case (Techniques 48–49)

Finally, the various elements of the business case need to be presented to senior management for their decision. This can involve either, or usually both, of business case report creation (Technique 48) and business case presentation (Technique 49).

IDENTIFY OPTIONS

Technique 41: Options identification

The starting point for putting together a business case is the exploration of the options available for addressing the business problem or issue. And the starting point for *that* is generating a list of possibilities to be examined.

There are two kinds of potential solution to consider: the business options and the technical options. The first type are the different ways in which the organisation might tackle the issues, whereas the second are the various technical – which in practice usually means IT – possibilities. At one time it was recommended that these two aspects be considered separately, and, indeed, methods like SSADM

(Structured Systems Analysis and Design Method) explicitly separated them. The (reasonable) argument for this was that the business needs should be considered first and the IT possibilities second, in other words that the IT 'tail' should not be allowed to wag the business 'dog'. However, IT is now so intimately involved in the operation of modern organisations, and so often provides the stimulus for business change, that this distinction is no longer so valid. Here, therefore, we consider business and IT options as part of a continuum.

The important thing at this point is not to reject prematurely any idea that might offer possible benefits. Techniques such as brainstorming will probably be used, and these are discussed in more detail under 'Workshops' (Technique 14) in Chapter 2, 'Investigate situation'. In Figure 5.2 a company is considering what it can do about the impending obsolescence of the sales order processing system it uses for some of its products. At a workshop several ideas are put forward, including some quite radical ones like exiting this line of business, sharing the order processing with a competitor or asking customers to process the orders themselves. Although some of these might seem rather 'off the wall' at first, they should not be dismissed without more detailed consideration. For example, the company might only be continuing with this line of products because it has the capability to process orders for them, and would not be attempting to get into this business without such a capability. That being so, the obsolescence of the system might provide an opportunity to give up these products and concentrate on more profitable – and easier to service – lines. Also – and this is an important feature of brainstorming – one idea may well spark off another. In the example in Figure 5.2 someone might have suggested outsourcing the processing, and this could have led to someone else coming up with the idea of sharing processing with a competitor.

Figure 5.2 Options identification

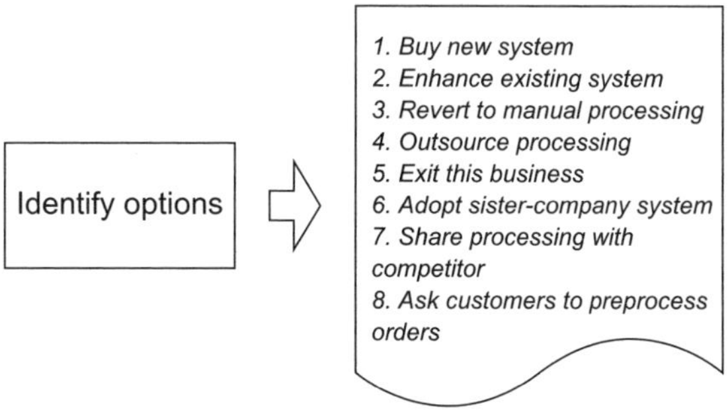

Identify options ⇨

1. Buy new system
2. Enhance existing system
3. Revert to manual processing
4. Outsource processing
5. Exit this business
6. Adopt sister-company system
7. Share processing with competitor
8. Ask customers to preprocess orders

SHORTLIST OPTIONS

Eight options, as listed in Figure 5.2, is too many for detailed consideration, so we need to get our initial 'longlist' down to a more manageable 'shortlist' of, say, three options, as shown in Figure 5.3. In addition, if it has not come up already,

Figure 5.3 Shortlisting options

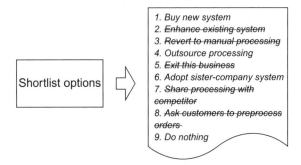

we must ensure that we at least consider the option of staying as we are now – the 'do nothing' option.

To whittle down the longlist, we could adopt any or all of the following techniques:

- SWOT analysis (Technique 6);

- PESTLE analysis (Technique 1);

- feasibility analysis (Technique 42);

- force-field analysis (Technique 43).

Whatever methods are used, the idea is to end up with two or three distinct options that we can present to the decision-makers. We would also have to decide which, if any, of these are going to be recommended, and here a basic decision is needed by the BA. Sometimes BAs just present the various options in as neutral a way as possible and leave the choice between them entirely to senior management. However, senior managers do not usually have time to evaluate the options in detail for themselves, and are often looking for a 'steer' as to which option would be best. In this situation the options presentation will not be neutral, and the various options must be explained in a way that shows why each is being recommended or rejected.

As Figure 5.4 illustrates, the choice is not always only between distinctly different options; the issue of **incremental** options also arises. The first option is the quickest and cheapest to implement but perhaps only satisfies the most pressing requirements; the second one includes some additional features, facilities or benefits; and the third provides the full 'bells and whistles'.

The 'do nothing' option must also be explored, even if only to show that, in the situation being considered, there isn't one. For example, if the 'do nothing' option is to keep on using a computer system that is both mission critical, on the one hand, and obsolete and unsupportable, on the other, the consequence could be that it would at some point become impossible to run the business. If that is the

Figure 5.4 Incremental options

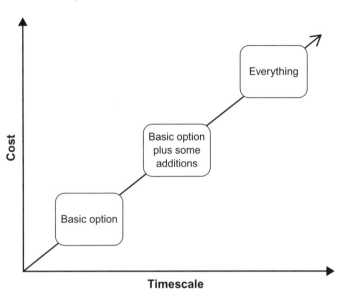

case, the facts need to be pointed out frankly to the decision-makers. In some cases, however, doing nothing might be a viable alternative that should be properly considered alongside other proposals.

SWOT analysis for evaluating options

SWOT analysis (Technique 6) was described in Chapter 1, 'Business strategy and objectives'. Here we are using it to identify the strengths and weaknesses of each of the ideas on our longlist, and also considering what opportunities each idea might enable us to seize, and what threats it might ward off.

PESTLE analysis for evaluating options

PESTLE analysis (Technique 1) was also described in Chapter 1, 'Business strategy and objectives'. Here we are using the six PESTLE factors in a slightly different way, to pose important questions about each of the proposed options:

Political: Is this option likely to be politically acceptable (both within and outside the organisation)?

Economic: Are the funds available, or can they be borrowed?

Socio-cultural: Does this option fit with the culture of the organisation?

Technological: Is the option technically possible, and is it compatible with the organisation's other technology?

Legal: Is this legal? Will the regulator allow us to do this?

Environmental: Are there any environmental impacts that might prove a problem?

Technique 42: Feasibility analysis

Description of the technique
In assessing the feasibility of each option on the longlist, it can be considered in three dimensions: business, technical and financial. The issues to be explored for each are illustrated in Figure 5.5.

Figure 5.5 Elements of feasibility

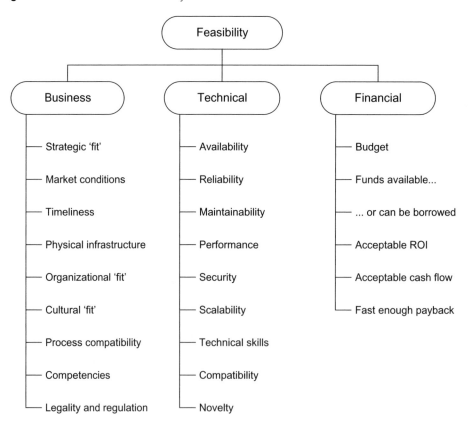

It should be borne in mind that the discovery of difficulties during the feasibility analysis of a proposed option does not necessarily mean that the option should be discarded. Rather, it means that there will be problems associated with that option that must be factored into the implementation plan; and, perhaps, some additional risks (with possible countermeasures) should be included in the business case.

The business issues highlighted in Figure 5.5 are as follows:

Strategic 'fit': Fairly obviously, any proposal should conform with, and ideally be designed to advance, the strategy of the organisation. Sometimes short-term measures are called for, which are not necessarily closely aligned with the longer-term strategy; but they should, at least, not be at variance with it.

Market conditions: Any solution must be suitable for the current market conditions an organisation finds itself in. For example, if the market is booming, the solution ought to contribute to that; if the emphasis is on restraining costs, the solution must take that into account.

Timeliness: There may be deadlines by which a solution must be available, perhaps because of some new regulation that will come into force or the expected launch of a new product or service by a competitor. It is irrelevant how brilliant a solution is in absolute terms if it cannot be delivered in time; sometimes a less elegant approach may have to be adopted instead.

Physical infrastructure: Sometimes the question of whether the physical infrastructure of the organisation is suitable for the proposed solution arises. Is there space, for example, to install new equipment, or might additional accommodation have to be sought?

Organisational 'fit': There are two things to consider here. One is whether the proposed solution involves changes to the organisational structure in some way (for example, if two 'swimlanes' are to be merged in a 'to be' process), and whether that reorganisation is acceptable. The other issue to think about is organisational politics: does the proposed solution impinge on anyone's empire or maybe reduce someone's importance, and how might people react to that?

Cultural 'fit': The proposed solution must fit with the culture of the organisation, or, if it does not, thought has to be given as to how to change the culture. For example, if managers have been used to supervising their people quite closely in the past and the proposed solution will empower those people and require them to make their own decisions, how do we prepare the managers for their new roles as coaches, mentors and 'sounding boards'? Indeed, are the managers capable of adjusting to this new reality?

Process compatibility: Most business analysis projects do not involve the total redesign of all of an organisation's processes. That being so, the question of whether the more limited changes that **are** proposed will fit in with other processes has to be considered.

Competencies: The question to be faced here is: does the organisation possess the capabilities required for the proposed solution? If it does not, then retraining of existing staff or the recruitment of people with the new skills may be required. Or, perhaps, short-term support can be obtained from consultants or the contract labour market.

Legality and regulation: Finally, many organisations are now subject to external regulation, and some thought needs to be given to whether the proposed solution accords with the current law, and what the attitude of the regulator is likely to be.

The technical issues in Figure 5.5 are:

Availability, reliability and maintainability: The so-called ARM requirements are very important, and sometimes they are in conflict. For example, the demand for 24/7 availability raises difficulties for maintainability: if a system is in operation all the time, how do the support people get at it for maintenance and upgrades? In very demanding situations – associated with on-line banking or national security for example – off-the-shelf solutions may simply not be good enough.

Performance: There is usually some sort of trade-off between performance and cost, and any solution must satisfy the performance requirements at an affordable cost.

Security: Sometimes packaged solutions developed for commercial applications might not be sufficiently secure for other purposes, for example if they are to be used in law enforcement.

Scalability: Some thought needs to be given to whether, in the future, the solution might be required to support additional users, or more transactions – in other words, is it capable of growing with the organisation's growth?

Technical skills: A computer system will need support and maintenance after implementation, and the organisation needs to consider whether it has the technical skills to do this. If it has not, then support might have to be outsourced, for example to a package vendor or IT services firm, and the cost of that has to be considered when thinking about the option. The development of the proposed solution may also have to be outsourced if the organisation lacks the required technical skills.

Compatibility: If the project does not involve the total replacement of all of an organisation's systems – as it usually does not – compatibility and interoperability with other systems becomes an issue. Sometimes the optimal solution to a specific problem may have to be set aside in favour of one that is compatible with other hardware and software used within the organisation.

Track record: Finally, an organisation may prefer a tried and tested, if unimaginative, solution to one that is 'better' but has not been attempted before. If an unproven solution is to be recommended, then the risks associated with this must be properly considered and included in the risk assessment for the project, together with any countermeasures that are available.

The financial issues to consider include:

Budget: The organisation may have set aside a budget for the proposed project. If a solution does not fall within that, it will be necessary to identify additional benefits to justify the higher cost. Failing that, it may be necessary to scale back the proposal and recommend a less ambitious, but less costly, solution instead.

Funds available or can be borrowed: Irrespective of the long-term justification for a project, the question has to be asked: can the organisation afford to undertake it at the moment? It may have funds available, or a good credit rating that will enable it to raise the finance. If funding is not available, then the proposed solution may have to be scaled back or the project postponed until the financial climate improves.

Acceptable return on investment: Most large organisations have targets for the return on investment (ROI) they expect from projects. It could be that a proposed solution does pay for itself, but does not do so by enough to meet these ROI targets.

Acceptable cash flow: Many projects involve short-term investment and recovery of the benefits over a longer period. However, en route to payback the project may show a deficit that is too large or goes on too long to be acceptable to the organisation. In that case, other approaches, maybe including other funding mechanisms (lease rather than purchase, for instance), might have to be considered.

Fast enough payback: Lastly, the BAs need to know how long a period the organisation mandates for projects achieving breakeven or payback. At one time, for example, major IT investments were assessed over seven or even ten years, but three years is now a more common interval.

Technique 43: Force-field analysis

Description of the technique
Force-field analysis is illustrated in Figure 5.6.

Figure 5.6 Force-field analysis

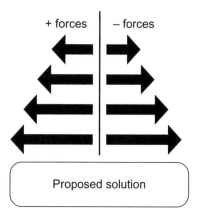

The idea with a force-field analysis is that we examine those forces within or outside an organisation that will tend towards the acceptance of a proposed option, and those that will tend towards its rejection. For example, a negative force might be a currently poor financial climate, with money hard to come by; but a positive force might be pressure from a regulator, or from customers, to do something.

The point is that if the negative forces are collectively more powerful than the positive forces, adoption of the proposed option will be very difficult. The BA must therefore give consideration to trying to weaken the negative forces in some way, or to finding more powerful positive forces to counteract the negatives – or both.

Very often, key stakeholders appear in a force-field analysis. Perhaps, for example, the chief financial officer has a track record of opposing this sort of project, and can be expected to do so this time. But we know that the chief executive is personally very keen on the project, so that should provide a strong enough positive counterforce.

Sometimes, however, the conclusion may be that the time is simply not right for the proposal to be accepted at the moment, and the best strategy might be to put the proposal on hold until a more propitious moment.

Using feasibility and force-field analysis
Options identification and assessment is not a wholly scientific process, and people's prejudices, obsessions and foibles get dragged into it. This does not matter very much at the identification stage, since we want to encourage as many ideas as possible, but more rigour does need to be applied when it comes

to sifting through those initial ideas to produce the shortlist to be presented in the business case.

Another problem is that sponsors often, when initiating a business analysis project, present not only the issue but also their preferred solution to the BAs. If that solution turns out to be the best one, the sponsor's preference is a powerful entry in the force-field analysis, but if it is not, the BA will have to be very careful in showing why and how it is not to be recommended. The sponsor's pet idea should probably make it to the shortlist, and then the reasons for not recommending it should be explained carefully and diplomatically. (Even better, of course, the issue should have been discussed and agreed with the sponsor before this point; then, perhaps, the idea could have been quietly dropped.)

It is often a mistake to go into too much detail on the options, particularly those that are not being recommended. Obviously, **some** detailed work will have to be done so that the shortlisted options can be properly defined, costed and described, but the emphasis should be on getting **just enough** information to enable an informed decision to be made.

PREPARE BUSINESS CASE

Once the shortlist of options has been developed, a business case needs to be prepared for the one that is to be recommended. Sometimes detailed work is also done on the other options, but we consider this to be a waste of time and effort. It is certainly necessary to be able to justify why a particular option is not being recommended, but this should be done at the level of broad outline costs, benefits, impacts and risks. If too much detail is available on these rejected options it is apt to find its way into the business case report, where it will certainly take up space and waste the time of busy decision-makers in reading through it.

Technique 44: Cost–benefit analysis
Variants/Aliases
This is also known as **CBA** or **benefit–cost analysis (BCA).**

Description of the technique
Cost–benefit analysis (or, if you prefer, benefit–cost analysis) is central to options evaluation and business case development. It is where we investigate the costs of taking a particular course of action and the benefits of doing so. It is challenging but also interesting work, and requires both creativity and analytical skills from those involved.

CBA is – or should be – a cooperative venture between various people involved in business analysis work. For example:

- The project sponsor should be in overall control of the process.
- The business users or actors should have a say in identifying, and quantifying, the potential benefits.

- The BA often plays a coordinating or facilitating role in helping the other parties to work together and contribute their ideas; BAs may also, of course, inject their own ideas into the process and help sift through other possibilities.

- Software developers, and vendors of hardware and so on, may be involved in providing the detailed information that goes into the 'cost' side of the analysis.

Types of cost and benefit

Costs and benefits have this in common: they are either tangible or intangible, and they are incurred or enjoyed either immediately or over the longer term. Combining these two aspects gives us the four categories illustrated in Figure 5.7.

Figure 5.7 Types of cost and benefit

	Immediate	Longer term
Tangible	Tangible and immediate	Tangible and longer term
Intangible	Intangible and immediate	Intangible and longer term

The distinction between tangible and intangible is about whether a credible valuation can be put on the cost or benefit **in advance of undertaking the project**. It does not say whether the cost or benefit is inherently measurable, but rather whether it can be predicted with some accuracy in advance. For example, let us take 'increased sales', often claimed as a benefit in business cases. The organisation might have good, solid research evidence that shows clearly what the increased sales to be expected would be, such as:

- market research that shows what the pent-up demand is for a product not yet launched (as often happens with new products from Sony or Apple);

- study of a competitor that might have revealed their sales from a particular product, and reasonable assumptions that could be made about the share of those sales that this organisation's product might take from them.

In either of these cases, justifiable predictions could be made for 'increased sales', and it could be claimed as a tangible benefit (with the evidence cited in support). However, in other situations 'increased sales' might only be a hope or a reasonable expectation, in which case it is better classified as an intangible benefit.

There are schools of thought that say either (i) that there is no such thing as an intangible benefit or (ii) that intangibles have no place in a business case at all.

We would probably agree, in theory, with assertion (i), but the real problem is that often there is not the time or the specialist statistical expertise available to quantify a benefit properly. For example, a value could probably be established for 'reduced staff turnover' by finding the total recruitment and training costs for replacement staff over a period but, frequently, such information is hard to come by. In any case, how can we **prove**, in advance of doing something, that it will actually reduce staff turnover? As to assertion (ii), surely if all decisions were based on tangible information, we would not need bosses at all – just spreadsheets to make decisions? Jack Welch, former CEO of General Electric, put it this way in his book *Winning* (Welch and Welch 2005): '... the world is filled with gray. Anyone can look at an issue from every different angle. Some smart people can – and will – analyze those angles indefinitely. But effective people know when to stop assessing and make a tough call, even without total information.' It is, sadly, true, however, that in many organisations, and particularly those that have to account for spending public money, managers are reluctant to make decisions except on the basis of tangibles.

The other issue is that some costs and benefits appear immediately and others over time. In fact, in most business cases we are faced with a mixture of immediate and longer-term tangible costs which need to be compared with both tangible and intangible benefits that accrue over time.

It is important, by the way, to distinguish between **features** and **benefits** in a business case, and the two are often confused. For example, sometimes something like a 'faster response time' is claimed as benefit, but, really, it is a feature; we need to say in what way it is beneficial or what benefit it leads to. A faster response time could, say, result in (i) requiring fewer people to do the same work (a cost saving) or (ii) enabling more orders to be taken per day (an increase in the value of sales).

In the sections that follow we identify some typical costs and benefits that arise from projects where information technology forms all or part of the solution, and we suggest ways in which the tangible ones might be quantified. The list is not comprehensive, but it should provide at least a starting point for a cost–benefit analysis.

Tangible costs – one-off or initial

Hardware: This is the most obvious cost associated with introducing a new IT system, and could involve processors, terminals, printers and so forth. Some idea of the number of items required must be obtained, and vendors can be asked for quotations for the supply of this equipment. Alternatively the hardware might be leased, in which case quotations are required from the manufacturers or their finance arm.

Infrastructure: This includes things like networks and cabling for new systems, and again possible suppliers must be identified and asked for quotations or estimates for the work involved.

Packaged software:
Licences for software are generally sold on the basis of the number of users, so some calculation of this is needed, and again vendors must be approached for quotations.

Development staff costs:
Where software is to be developed from scratch, or maybe a package is to be customised or enhanced, the work involved in doing so must be estimated. This can be tricky at the business case stage, because the full requirements have probably not been defined. One approach is to estimate very roughly the size of team required and make some assumptions about its composition (project managers, BAs, designers, software engineers and so forth). The HR department should then be able to supply approximate per day costs for each grade, and the costing can be based on these. It should be borne in mind that a proper per day cost should include not only salaries but also overheads such as national insurance, pension schemes, private medical cover, company cars and other benefits; it might also include accommodation and infrastructure costs. If it is proposed that the development work be outsourced, then possible vendors must be approached for estimates, though they may be rather guarded at giving estimates at this stage before the scope of the proposed work is properly defined.

User staff costs:
Sometimes these are included in business cases, sometimes not; the policy varies from one organisation to another. We think they should be included, to get a true picture of the cost of the project, but some organisations exclude user time on the basis that the people are there and are being paid anyway. If they are to be included, then costs can be arrived at in a similar way to development staff costs – get an estimate of their involvement, and use day rates provided by HR to work out what their time is worth.

Training and retraining of users:
There are two aspects to this – the cost of developing the training courses and materials, and the time of the trainers (and users) spent on the courses. A very rough rule of thumb says that the time to develop a course is about 10 times that of delivering it, so a one-day event would take 10 days to create. The trainer and user time (if the latter is included – see above) can be calculated by working out how many courses are required, and how many people there will be per course, and using the usual HR day rate information.

Redundancy:
If one of the claimed benefits is to be staff savings (see later), then it may be necessary to make people redundant, which incurs costs. In discussions with HR, a view will be needed of how many people are to be let go and their grades, salaries, length of service and so forth. It is unlikely that specific individuals will be identified at this stage, and, needless to

say, discussions like this must be handled with the utmost sensitivity and discretion.

Relocation: If part of the business solution involves people moving to new offices, then relocation costs may be involved. Again, the HR department should understand the terms and conditions, and any union agreements involved, and can provide information on the costs expected.

Data creation, cleanup and migration: If a totally new IT system is being implemented, work will be needed to create the initial data. If the system replaces an existing one, data will need to be migrated from the old system to the new one. In either case, work may also be needed to clean up the data for the new system. This area of expenditure is often overlooked and nearly always under-estimated, and, in fact, it can be difficult to get an idea of the effort involved. Sampling the existing data can give some idea of what will be needed.

Tangible costs – ongoing

Hardware maintenance: Once the new systems are in place, regular maintenance of the hardware will be needed, and vendors can be asked to quote for this.

Software support: If a packaged solution is being implemented, the vendors usually have standard support packages available. For a bespoke solution, an estimate will be needed of the work expected for support and routine upgrades. As a **very rough** guide, perhaps 10 per cent of the initial development cost could be expected per annum.

Salaries of new and additional staff: If extra people, maybe with different skills, are to be recruited to operate the new business processes and systems, then their ongoing salaries will have to be included as costs. As usual, the HR department are the people to ask for information here.

Intangible costs

Recruitment: The costs of recruiting new people, if they are needed to operate the new processes or support the new systems, **ought** to be tangible, but many organisations do not seem to keep this information, which is why we have classified it as intangible. Of course, if the HR department does have data on recruitment costs, then they can be included with the tangible costs.

Disruption and short-term loss of productivity: It is obvious that, however careful the preparation and thorough the training, the introduction of new processes and systems will cause some short-term disruption as the organisation's own people, and perhaps their customers and suppliers too, get used to the new ways of working. However, it is very difficult, if not impossible, to put a credible value on this, so it is better just to identify it in the business case and let the decision-makers put their own valuation on it. Disruption and short-term loss of productivity may also be included in the impacts section of the business case and in the risk assessment.

Tangible benefits

Staff savings: This is the most obvious benefit and the one that, often, senior management is seeking. The amount of money saved – which is the real benefit in this case – can be arrived at in consultation with the HR department. Beware, though, of what we might call the 'FTE fallacy'. This occurs in large organisations, where the time saved in each department is small but is aggregated to equate to a saving of a certain number of 'full-time equivalent' posts. The fallacy arises because in practice one cannot really save one-tenth of a clerk, so no real saving in salary costs will result – although it might be possible to take on additional work with the existing staffing, and to claim that as the benefit instead.

Reduced effort or improved speed of working: We have included this as a tangible benefit, because it ought to be possible to measure how much effort and time it takes to perform various operations now, and to carry out simulations or experiments to assess what the improvement will be with the new processes and systems. The time savings can be converted into cash terms (if required) by using staff costs supplied by HR. In some cases, however, measurements of the 'as is' situation are lacking and it is not practical to assess the 'to be' situation. In that case, it is far better to explain why and how the improvement ought to come about, and to allow the decision-makers to judge how much that is worth to them, than to make spurious and unsupportable claims about time and cost savings.

Faster response times: Strictly, this is not a benefit but a feature. However, it can be connected to benefits by, for example, showing how a faster response time will save costs internally (through less effort being expended on each transaction) or perhaps improve the customers' perception of the service. There is a practical difficulty in that, although measuring current response times ought to be fairly easy, estimating what they will be with the new process or system is rather trickier. In particular, response times measured on 'test' or pilot systems tend to be abnormally fast compared with those from live systems handling large volumes of transactions, so some allowance must be made for this to avoid raising expectations that will not be met later.

Reduced accommodation costs:	If the work can be done with fewer people, this may result in a reduction in the office or workshop space required, which can be claimed as a cost saving. However, sometimes accommodation costs are factored into staff day rates, so claiming accommodation savings as well would amount to double counting; a check needs to be made with HR to see if this is the case. Also, the question of whether the accommodation really will be released altogether has to be faced. Will people just expand their workplaces to use up the surplus?
Avoided costs:	This is a special, and sometimes extremely useful, tangible benefit. Let us suppose that an organisation has an obsolete computer system that will shortly run out of support from its vendors, and that these vendors have quoted, say, £100,000 to move the systems onto a new platform without any other improvements or increases in functionality. Let us say, too, that the organisation has budgeted for this expenditure. The BA may, instead, propose spending £200,000 on an entirely new system that will offer significant advantages in terms of speed of operation, functionality, ease of use and so forth. In this case the £100,000 could be claimed as an avoided cost, in that the organisation would not be obliged to spend this money in order to get precisely nowhere, and the project would only be seeking the additional £100,000 for the new system. In the run up to the year 2000 many projects were partly justified in this way, where organisations had already budgeted for work to make their systems millennium compliant and these budgets were used as avoided costs to offset against new, better and already compliant systems.

Intangible benefits

As we have already mentioned, these are benefits that, though real enough, are difficult or impossible to quantify convincingly in advance of undertaking the project.

Increased job satisfaction:	Introducing new processes and systems may reduce the routine work associated with a job and hence make it more interesting. Or it might enable the jobholder to spend more time dealing with people and less with paperwork (for example, giving a nurse more time for patient contact). This should increase job satisfaction, a worthwhile benefit, and it might even reduce attrition or 'churn' in the workforce, as people stay in the job for longer.
Improved customer satisfaction:	Better designed processes and systems should result in a better customer experience; if they do not, the question may be asked, why introduce them? The likely improved customer satisfaction will be difficult to assess, however, unless there is evidence (a fat file of complaints, for instance) that suggests specific customer dissatisfaction with things as they are now.

Better management information:	Managers often complain that they have to make decisions based on imperfect information – though it can be argued that this is part of the challenge and fascination of management (see the quotation from Jack Welch given earlier). Nevertheless, better management information – not to be confused with merely more management information – is usually regarded as a benefit, though its precise value cannot really be quantified. The decision-makers must judge how much it is worth to them. An exception might be where the BAs can point to a specific business error, with costs attached, that resulted from inadequate information and might have been avoided had the proposed new processes and systems been in place.
Greater organisational flexibility:	The modern world is in a constant state of flux, and organisations have to reconfigure themselves all the time in order to adapt to changing circumstances. Such things as legacy IT systems are sometimes a positive barrier to change, so replacing them can make an organisation more flexible and adaptable. Exactly what this is worth is very hard to say, however.
More creative thinking time:	Managers, in particular, often complain that too much of their day is taken up with routine matters, leaving them insufficient time to consider longer-term strategic issues. If a proposal will liberate them from much of the routine, this will be seen as useful and can be presented as a benefit.
Improved presentation:	Sometimes new systems will enable an organisation to present itself more effectively. For example, a well-designed website, attractive and easy to navigate, is now a considerable asset to any organisation. If the website is designed to take orders the increased volume of business can be measured after its introduction, but the point is that assessing this increase beforehand is more or less impossible, which is why such a benefit must be presented as intangible.
Better market image:	This is really an extension of the previous benefit. The introduction of a good website, for example, might change the image of an organisation in the eyes of its customers or of the public at large. For example, one of the authors recently developed a website for a local gardening club, part of the idea being to make the organisation more attractive to a younger, web-savvy generation of gardeners.

Using cost–benefit analysis

The terms tangible and intangible do cause confusion, and, in particular, many people associate tangible with 'measurable'. However, although a tangible benefit is measurable, it does not follow that a measurable benefit is tangible! As we have shown, the real issue is whether the value can be estimated credibly in advance of undertaking the project. As we have also shown, a valuation can probably be placed on anything, given time and the right expertise, but both are usually lacking in real business analysis projects. Nothing undermines a business case more than the claiming of intangible benefits as tangible; when this is challenged, and found not to be supportable, the whole viability of the business case begins to unravel.

Even if a benefit has to be shown as intangible in a business case, it may still be measurable – or at least assessable – after the project has been implemented, as part of the benefits management and realisation process. For example, let us suppose we had said that staff morale should improve as a result of the project. Certain individuals – managers as well as members of the workforce – could be identified for the purpose of seeking their opinion later as to whether morale had, in fact, improved. We would have to be careful in this case that the chosen individuals were not biased, for example by having their own bonuses tied to an improvement in morale! As an alternative in this case we could carry out staff attitude surveys before and after the project to see whether morale had improved or not, although we would then face the difficulty of factoring in other changes not related to the project that might have affected the outcome.

With regard to tangible benefits, although they are usually related to money in some way, they might not necessarily be. For example, a saving of two minutes per transaction for passengers using a new automated ticket machine at a station is measurable (both before and after implementing the machine), even if we cannot say what that two minutes is worth to each passenger.

Finally, we have used in this discussion a fairly simple classification scheme, treating benefits as either tangible or intangible. Ward and Daniel (2006) and Gerald Bradley (2006) use some more complex schemes in their books, which we believe have potential value for organisations; interested readers are directed to their publications for more information.

Technique 45: Impact analysis

Description of the technique

Impact analysis is the identification and presentation of those effects of a potential project or other business decision that need to be considered as part of the decision as to whether or not the investment should be authorised. It is needed so that the managers assessing the proposal have the most complete information on which to base their decision.

Some impacts may have costs associated with them, and so will already have been considered in the cost–benefit analysis (Technique 44). Others may give rise to risks, so they are reviewed in the risk analysis (Technique 46). This leaves various other things, usually associated with the way an organisation thinks and acts, that need to be considered. The list below is far from exhaustive, but it does indicate the sorts of things that might be included in an impact analysis.

Organisational structure:	Implementing a proposal may involve some, or a lot of, restructuring in the organisation – or the introduction of

new types of structure. For example, an organisation might decide to set up project teams in future to manage major programmes or product launches, and this may not be a method of working with which its people are familiar. They would thus need training, and perhaps the accounting systems would need to be altered to capture information at a project (rather than departmental) level.

Interdepartmental relations: Part of the proposal may involve changing the relationships between departments, or perhaps formalising them through the use of service level agreements. This might be novel and unnerving to people in the organisation, and so would need sensitive handling and support for the people affected.

Working practices: The introduction of new business or computer systems may require changes to working practices. If the existing practices are long standing or ingrained, getting people to change might prove difficult and require a combination of management pressure, training, support from HR and so forth. If the workforce is unionised, extensive consultation and perhaps protracted negotiations with trade union officials might also be required.

Management style: The adoption of a different management style may be required. For example, if a changed business system results in the removal of layers of 'middle management' and the empowerment of front-line staff, the role of the managers could become that of coaches, mentors or 'sounding boards'. The transition to this changed role might be difficult for managers used to operating in a command and control mode.

Recruitment policy and methods: The way people are recruited may have to change, for example if customer facing or IT skills are needed in the future. The organisation might also try to recruit people who better match its 'target market', for example in terms of age group, gender or ethnicity (although care has to be taken not to infringe antidiscrimination legislation in so doing). The methods of recruitment may also have to change: for example, the ability to work in teams is better judged using something like an assessment centre rather than in a traditional job interview.

Promotion criteria: Similarly, the way people are selected for promotion may have to be changed. For example, the criteria might traditionally have included things like speed and accuracy of working, whereas now the ability to work with colleagues and interface with customers might be just as important.

Customer focus and other attitudinal issues:	Some people, particularly those with 'back room' or support jobs, often see the effective operation of internal processes as their key drivers, and actual customers may even be seen as a bit of a nuisance, disrupting the smooth flow of these processes. In introducing new business and IT systems designed to improve customer service, therefore, there may have to be a major campaign to change the attitudes and behaviours of these support staff to see customers as the real *raison d'être* of their work.
Supplier relations:	Relationships with suppliers are often adversarial by nature, with the customer's procurement people and vendors' sales staff trying to secure advantages over each other. In modern, complex customer–supplier relationships, though, particularly those where part of an organisation's work has been outsourced, such behaviours are often unhelpful and lead to underachievement of the expectations of the deal. Contracts may therefore have to be renegotiated, and perhaps procurement staff re-educated to operate in a more collaborative, less confrontational way.

In the business case it is important that not just the impacts but also the things that can be done about them are presented for the decision-makers. Only in this way can they properly assess whether the proposal should be accepted or not.

Using impact analysis

Many of the issues identified above may have costs associated with them. Changing behaviours, for instance, may involve re-education and retraining of staff, or, possibly, recruiting new staff with different attitudes. However, even if no costs are involved, or if the costs cannot be assessed with any accuracy, the decision-makers need to be made aware of the issues, since they highlight the problems likely to be encountered in implementing the proposal, and may lead to its rejection as being too difficult in the existing situation.

Technique 46: Risk analysis
Variants/Aliases

The terms 'risk management' and 'risk identification' are sometimes erroneously used for risk analysis. As we describe it here, risk identification is the first stage of risk analysis, while risk management includes the processes of actively managing risk during the lifecycle of a project. What this means, in short, is that risk analysis is actually part of the larger process of risk management; and risk identification, in turn, is a part of risk analysis.

Description of the technique

All projects and most investments involve risk of some sort, and a business case is strengthened immeasurably if it can be shown that the risks have been considered and convincing countermeasures have been devised. We are not talking here about the full risk analysis that should be performed during the detailed planning of the project; rather, we are looking for the main, or most serious, risks to achieving the objectives of the proposed investment.

Conventionally there are three stages to risk assessment:

- identifying what the risks are;
- assessing the significance of each risk in terms of its possible impact(s) and probability;
- devising the responses to the risks, and identifying risk 'owners' who will carry these out.

In full-scale risk management there are also stages involving the constant reassessment of risk as the project or investment proceeds, but we shall not cover these here, since we are thinking about risks in the context of the initial business case. However, bearing in mind that a business case should be a living document throughout the lifecycle of a project, there will be a need to revisit the pattern of risk each time the business case is reviewed.

Risk identification

Risk assessment starts by identifying what the risks are, and the BA could consider some fairly standard approaches to this:

- interviewing the key project stakeholders to find out what they believe the risks are;
- holding workshops of stakeholders to uncover the risks;
- using a checklist or 'risk breakdown structure' of common risk areas to see if any of those is applicable to the proposed project.

With regard to the checklist approach, bear in mind that any such list can only be generic in nature, and may not help identify the risks that are specific to this project because of its unique features.

Having identified a risk, the BA also has to determine what would be its likely impact on the proposed project. For example, if a software package is being sought, one clear risk is the selection of the wrong package; the impact is that the features and benefits expected by the organisation, whatever they are, might not be fully realised.

Risk assessment

Next, the risks must be assessed along two dimensions – scale of impact and probability. Various numeric scales can be used for this purpose, but, in our opinion, many of these offer a rather spurious accuracy. We prefer the following simple scales:

Impact: Large, moderate or small. If it is thought useful, these could be assigned notional values: for example, a large impact could be one that extends the timescale, increases the budget or degrades the product by more than 10 per cent; for a moderate impact this could be 5–10 per cent; and for a small impact, less than 10 per cent.

Probability: High, medium or low. These could possibly be equated numerically with more than 30 per cent for high, 10–30 per cent for medium, and less than 10 per cent for low.

Having thus assessed the risks, we may choose to edit them somewhat for inclusion in the business case. Probably only those with a large impact and a high probability would make it into the main body of the report, others being reviewed in an appendix.

Actions and owners

Identifying and assessing risks is pretty useless unless the business case also contains some convincing ideas about what can be done to deal with them. There are four main possibilities:

Avoidance: Avoidance actions are aimed at lessening the probability of hazard occurring, ideally to zero. For our example of the risk of selecting the wrong software package, one avoidance action might be to build a bespoke solution, but that would probably prove too costly. A more realistic option would be to mandate a rigorous requirements specification and a procurement exercise using objective selection criteria, in order to make sure that the wrong package is not chosen.

Mitigation: Avoidance actions are not always available and sometimes they fail, so we also need actions that will reduce the scale of impact if the hazard occurs. In the package selection situation, a mitigation action might be to build bail-out clauses into the contract with the vendor, such that the purchase can be cancelled if the system proves unsuitable. Obviously costs would be incurred here, not least in carrying out a new tendering exercise, but that would still be cheaper and better than soldiering on with entirely the wrong solution.

Transference: Transference actions aim to shift the impact of a hazard, if it occurs, to someone else – as happens, for instance, with insurance. With our package selection project, a possible transference action might be to ask the vendor to underwrite the suitability of their solution to our needs. In practice, though, they might be unwilling to do that; packages tend to be sold 'as seen', and it is usually up to the purchasers to make sure they have bought the right thing.

Acceptance: Finally, it could be that all of the available avoidance, mitigation or transference actions would actually prove more costly, or more damaging, than allowing the hazard to occur; or there might, in fact, not be much that can realistically be done about the risk. In these cases the decision-makers need to be made aware of the situation so that the acceptance of the possible impact can be factored into their decision-making.

Assuming that realistic actions can be identified, we also need a 'risk owner' for each of them: that is, someone who will be tasked with making these actions happen. To function effectively as a risk owner, a person must have both a good understanding of the risk and its possible impact and the authority to get the required actions taken. It may not, in fact, be possible to assign ownership finally at this early stage of the project; this might have to wait until the business case is approved and work starts in earnest.

Using risk analysis

There can be a reluctance to mention risks, or a tendency to play them down, in a business case because of a fear that the decision-makers will be put off by a more rigorous and realistic assessment. Such fears are probably misplaced, since what is really worrying to decision-makers is being invited to approve a business case without having the full picture in front of them.

Another rather insidious problem is that highlighting risks is sometimes seen as somewhat negative behaviour, especially when someone senior is rather keen on a business case being approved. This can put BAs in an awkward situation, because if they do **not** identify the major risks and the associated hazards later occur, they will probably be blamed for not doing a thorough enough analysis. There is no simple solution to this, and whether it is a problem or not is probably a reflection of the organisation's culture and values; but in general we would counsel BAs to err on the side of caution – or perhaps realism is the word – in presenting risks for consideration.

Identifying the risks initially is also fraught with difficulty, since by definition each project has some unique features, and risk often results from this uniqueness. We have mentioned earlier how interviews, workshops and checklists can help in spotting the possible risks, but so can discussions with other BAs or project managers who may have experience of similar projects in the past on which they can draw. If available, post-project reviews can also be a mine of information about what has gone wrong in the past.

Finally, assessing the risks realistically can be difficult, since people will differ in their assessments of how serious a threat might be posed by a risk and what its likelihood is. Here it is usually a good idea to try to get a collective view from as many 'SQEPs' (suitably qualified and experienced personnel – a term used within, for instance, the British Ministry of Defence) as possible. We are not, after all, aiming for perfect mathematical accuracy here, just a broad-brush estimate that will enable us to rank the risks and identify those that pose the greatest threat to the proposed project or investment.

Technique 47: Investment appraisal

Description of the technique

Investment appraisal is the process of comparing the financial benefits expected to flow from a proposal or project with the predicted costs, to see if it is worth undertaking. Investment appraisal is the province of accountants, specifically management accountants, but BAs need to have at least a working knowledge of the concepts and techniques for two main reasons: BAs are often asked to contribute to the construction of investment appraisals, so it is useful to understand how the information they provide is going to be used; and BAs have to communicate with accountants in putting business cases together, so, again, a working knowledge of their approach makes this easier.

The three most commonly used methods of presenting an investment appraisal are discussed here. They are:

- payback or breakeven analysis;
- discounted cash flow leading to a net present value for the investment;
- internal rate of return.

Readers interested in a more in-depth understanding of these topics are directed to the 'Further reading' section at the end of this chapter.

Payback (breakeven) analysis

A payback or breakeven analysis is, essentially, a cash flow forecast or projection for the proposed investment. We compare the expected financial benefits year-by-year with the predicted costs and find out when the cumulative benefits exceed the cumulative costs – in other words when payback or breakeven occurs. An example of a payback analysis is shown in Table 5.1.

In Table 5.1 an initial one-off investment is made in new computer hardware (£200,000) and software (£150,000). In addition, maintenance of the hardware is expected to cost £30,000 per annum and support of the software £30,000 per annum. The accounting convention is that this investment is said to have been made in Year 0.

Benefits will begin to flow from the project in Year 1, in other words the year after the investment is made. These benefits take the form of staff savings, valued at £80,000 per annum, and increased sales, expected to be £100,000 per annum (based on detailed market research).

In Year 0, then, a total of £410,000 will be paid out with no benefits in exchange, and so the cash flow for the year (and carried forward for the project as a whole) is minus £410,000.

In each of Years 1–4 the total benefits (£180,000 per annum) need to be set against the total ongoing costs (£60,000 per annum), so the yearly net cash flow is plus £120,000. That means that the cumulative position after Year 1 is minus £290,000, after Year 2 it is minus £170,000 and after Year 3 it is minus £50,000. At the end of Year 4 (in other words, the fifth year of the project), it achieves payback, or breaks even, as the cumulative balance is now plus £70,000.

The great advantage of a payback calculation is that it is simple and straightforward for anyone, not just accountants, to understand. And, if interest rates are low, it provides a reasonable prediction of the outcome of the project.

Table 5.1 Payback or breakeven analysis

	Year 0	Year 1	Year 2	Year 3	Year 4
Cumulative cash flow for project brought forward		*–410,000*	*–290,000*	*–170,000*	*–50,000*
Hardware purchase	200,000				
Software purchase	150,000				
Hardware maintenance	30,000	30,000	30,000	30,000	30,000
Software support	30,000	30,000	30,000	30,000	30,000
Total costs for year	*410,000*	*60,000*	*60,000*	*60,000*	*60,000*
Staff savings		80,000	80,000	80,000	80,000
Increased sales		100,000	100,000	100,000	100,000
Total benefits for year	*Nil*	*180,000*	*180,000*	*180,000*	*180,000*
Cash flow for year (benefits less costs)	*–410,000*	*120,000*	*120,000*	*120,000*	*120,000*
Cumulative cash flow for project carried forward	*–410,000*	*–290,000*	*–170,000*	*–50,000*	*70,000*

Discounted cash flow / net present value (DCF/NPV)

However, a simple payback calculation does not factor in what the accountants refer to as the 'time value of money'. The concept here is that a pound (or dollar, or Euro) spent or saved today does not have the same value as the same amount spent or saved next year or in five years' time. People often think this has to do with inflation, but, though that can affect the calculations indirectly through its influence on interest rates, this is not actually the case. The issue is more to do with the 'cost of money' to the organisation, or with what else it could do with the money instead.

Consider the situation of an organisation wholly funded by debt capital – by loans from the bank – on which it is paying 10 per cent interest per annum. Over five years the organisation would spend roughly 61 pence in compound interest for every pound borrowed (interested readers are invited to do the sums on a calculator!). So if it is to get £1 back in five years' time, it will need to 'discount' that £1 by 1/1.61 – that is, to 62 pence – to find its value after that period.

On the other hand, if the organisation had put its £1 into the bank at 5 per cent interest, it would have earned over 27 pence in interest over that period of time. If it were to invest the pound in a project instead, it would be foregoing this interest, and would have to discount the £1 by 1/1.27 – or to roughly 79 pence – to find the true value of its return.

A method of investment appraisal that takes into account this 'time value of money' is called **discounted cash flow** (DCF). We discount the net cash flows for each year after Year 0 to adjust for the declining value of money; then we add up all these discounted cash flows to find the **net present value** (NPV) of the project – the overall value of the project after taking this decline in value into account. Table 5.2 presents a DCF/NPV for the same project that we considered by using payback in Table 5.1.

Table 5.2 Discounted cash flow / net present value calculation

	Benefits less costs	Net cash flow	Discount factor at 10% interest	Discounted cash flow or present value
Year 0	(0 – 410,000)	–410,000	1.000	–410,000
Year 1	(180,000 – 60,000)	120,000	0.909	109,080
Year 2	(180,000 – 60,000)	120,000	0.826	99,120
Year 3	(180,000 – 60,000)	120,000	0.751	90,120
Year 4	(180,000 – 60,000)	120,000	0.683	81,960
Net present value of project				*–29,720*

Working out the interest rates, and thus the discount factors, to use is a highly complex subject, the province of management accountants; in principle, they take the 'cost of money' to the organisation and make informed judgements about the movement of interest rates in the future. Interested readers can learn more about the mechanisms used by studying some of the texts listed in this chapter's 'Further reading' section, or perhaps by talking to some management accountants. Let us suppose, though, that the accountants have settled on an interest rate of 10 per cent. Then we can find the relevant 'discount factors' as shown in Table 5.2 by using any of three methods:

- We could work them out. The discount rate in Year 1, for instance, could be arrived at by calculating 1/1.1. That for Year 2 would be $1/(1.1)^2$; for Year 3 it would be $1/(1.1)^3$, and so on.

- Textbooks on management accounting often contain tables of discount factors, so we can just look them up.
- Spreadsheets like Microsoft Office Excel have the discount factors built in as functions.

By whichever means we choose, we will discover that the discount factor for Year 1 is 0.909, that for Year 2 is 0.826, and so forth.

We now take the net cash flow for each year in isolation (that is, ignoring any amounts either carried forward or brought forward), and discount it by the appropriate factor. Thus, the £120,000 in Year 1 becomes £109,080, the £120,000 in Year 2 becomes £99,120, and so on. Notice that we did not discount the minus £410,000 in Year 0, since this money is being spent now and so is given its full value.

The result in Table 5.2 is rather interesting. Whereas the payback calculation in Table 5.1 suggested that the project would pay for itself in Year 4, Table 5.2 shows a net present value of minus £29,720, so the project does not pay for itself.

Accountants may also perform a **sensitivity analysis** on these calculations, to see how affected they would be by changes in interest rates. For example, if in Table 5.2 we had used an interest rate of 5 per cent, the net present value of the project would have come out as £1,869. This is not much of a return on a £350,000 investment over five years, so, even if interest rates dropped a lot, the project would probably not be authorised on the basis of tangible financial benefits alone. (It might, however, still go ahead on the basis of intangible benefits like better market image or compliance with regulations.)

Internal rate of return
A third method of presenting the results of an investment appraisal is to calculate what it is called the **internal rate of return** (IRR) of the project. The is, in effect, a simulation of the return on the project, which can be used to compare projects with each other and with other investment opportunities, such as leaving the money in the bank to earn interest.

The IRR is worked out by standing the DCF/NPV calculation on its head. In Table 5.2, for instance, we ask what interest rate we would have to use to get an NPV of zero after Year 4 – in other words, for costs and benefits precisely to balance. The snag is that there is no formula for IRR, and it has to be arrived at by trial and error. So we might set up a spreadsheet and try out various interest rates until we find one that makes the NPV zero. In the case of our example project the result works out at roughly 6.6 per cent. So if the project were being compared with one with an IRR of, say, 5 per cent, this one would be a more attractive proposition. However, if the current interest rate being earned in the bank were 7 per cent (or if the organisation was having to pay 7 per cent to borrow money to finance its projects), it would be better to undertake neither project.

Using investment appraisal
As we have seen, the various methods of investment appraisal are used to determine whether a project is worth undertaking at all, and also to choose

between competing projects if, as is usual, an organisation cannot afford to carry them all out.

IRR gives a single 'headline' number, but it does not take into account the size of the projects being compared. So an IRR of 3 per cent on an investment of £20 million would produce more actual pounds in the end than an IRR of 6 per cent on a £100,000 project. This is why the various accountancy textbooks seem to agree that DCF/NPV is the most reliable method of evaluating potential investments.

In the various examples above we have not taken inflation into account, except indirectly in the choice of interest rates and discount factors. In practice, management accountants would take it into account, even with a payback calculation. For example, in Table 5.1 we might decide that the different elements of the costing could be subject to differing inflationary pressures, for example:

- Hardware maintenance and software support might be inflated at 3 per cent per annum.

- The staff costs might be inflated by 2 per cent per annum (reflecting expected increases in the wage bill).

- Sales might be expected to inflate by 5 per cent per annum.

This is just one reason why actual investment appraisals are quite complicated, and why the professional advice of management accountants is usually used in their preparation. In many large organisations the accountants issue a standard spreadsheet, which has all the assumed interest rates and inflationary pressures built in to its formulas; users of the spreadsheet then simply 'plug in' their estimates to complete the calculation. BAs, though, need to understand at least the principles underpinning these calculations, so that they can discourse knowledgeably with the business managers and management accountants.

PRESENT BUSINESS CASE

Once the elements of the business case have been developed, as described earlier, these can be assembled together and presented to management for a decision. Usually a written business case is required, and, often, the BA is also asked to present the main parts in a face to face meeting with the managers.

Technique 48: Business case report creation

Description of the technique
In a way, writing a business case is much like writing any other report, and the usual rules of good report writing are relevant here – keep it short, make it succinct and lead clearly to the conclusions. The format of a business case varies between different organisations, and in some cases the business case has to be distilled into one or two A4 pages – the argument being that the senior people who make the decisions do not have time to read anything longer. The following, however, represents a fairly typical structure for a business case:

Introduction:	This 'sets the scene' for the document and explains why it has been prepared. The methods used to conduct the business analysis study may also be outlined here, together with thanks for those in the business community who have contributed to the work.
Management summary (or executive summary):	This part of the business case is in many ways the most important, since it is probably the main (or perhaps the only) part that the senior decision-makers will read fully. It should be created after the rest of the business case has been prepared, and should summarise the whole thing concisely, ideally in three paragraphs:

1. what the business analysis study was for, and what its principal findings were;
2. what options were considered, and what their main advantages and disadvantages were;
3. a recommendation as to what should be done, and a clear statement of the decision required.

The three-paragraph format is an ideal, and, realistically, cannot always be achieved. Even so, the management summary should be kept as brief and focused as possible so that the managers can understand the issues quickly and see clearly what decision they are required to make.

Background or description of the current situation:	This is a more detailed discussion of the situation now, and what problems or opportunities have been discovered for the organisation during the study. Again, this part of the document should be kept as brief as possible, commensurate with explaining the issues properly. A particular difficulty sometimes arises where the 'problem', as originally defined by the management or the project sponsor, turns out not to be the real issue. In this case a more detailed explanation of what the real issue is may be required, so as to show why the later recommendations are as they are.
Options considered:	Each of the options on the shortlist should be presented briefly, and an explanation given as to why some are not being recommended. As we mentioned when discussing force-field analysis (Technique 43), special care may have to be taken when dismissing an option that is the 'pet idea' of an important stakeholder such as the project sponsor. The 'do nothing' option should also be set out here, maybe to show that the organisation will suffer from doing nothing, or perhaps because it is a realistic possibility.
Description of benefits and costs:	The costs and benefits of the proposed solution are now analysed in more detail, but, psychologically, it is better to present them the other way round – benefits and

then costs. This way the decision-makers are focused first on what they will get from the proposal, so they can then put the inevitable costs into a proper perspective.

Investment appraisal: The financial costs and benefits are now presented, as a payback/breakeven, DCF/NPV or IRR calculation, as described in Technique 47, 'Investment appraisal'. If the calculations are complex it is better to put the detail into an appendix and just summarise the final results here.

Impact analysis: The non-cost impacts go here, so that management can consider properly the difficulties and advantages of accepting the recommendation.

Risk analysis: Only the main risks (to the business and to the proposed project) should be presented here, and it is important that convincing countermeasures are offered too. If required, a more detailed risk assessment can be put into an appendix.

Conclusions and recommendations: Finally, the recommendation (if there is one) should be set out clearly, and the decision-makers also need to be advised if there are any external time pressures – like a regulatory deadline or an expected move by a competitor – on making a decision.

Supporting appendices: In order to keep the main document as concise as possible, the detailed information should be placed in appendices. It will be available for examination there without disturbing the main flow of the document and the thrust of its arguments.

Practical points about writing business cases

Many business case documents are far too long. Sometimes this is unavoidable, if the organisation has a detailed template that writers are obliged to follow. But sometimes it results from the desire of the writers to show just how much work and research has gone into the document. Although this does indeed emphasise the writers' thoroughness, the decision-makers are liable to become frustrated by the amount of reading they are required to do and the difficulty of 'seeing the wood for the trees'. In extreme cases this may just result in the document languishing in an 'in tray' forever. As we have suggested, the detailed information should instead be placed in appendices, where it is accessible but does not detain the decision-makers unless they specifically go looking for it.

Similarly, many business cases are written in a hard to read, passive third-party style, using phrases such as 'It is recommended that …', 'It is not understood why …' and so forth. Although this is a perfectly sound technique for academic writing (and, in fact, is often advocated for that), it is not really appropriate in business, where a more direct style is more likely to gain attention: 'We recommend that …', 'We cannot understand why …' Sometimes business case writers are unwilling to insert themselves into the document in this way, but, after all, they are putting forward their recommendations, so why not?

Finally, the decision-makers have to be induced to read the document in the first place. Tactics for success here include these:

- Consider who the decision-makers are and what interests them. Are they, for instance, 'big picture' people or interested in detail? The business case should be tailored to the demands of the audience.

- Make the document easy to access and follow. Again, a preset template may restrict the writer's freedom here, but otherwise lots of white space, illustrations (ideally in colour), graphs rather than tables, and bullet points rather than long paragraphs all aid accessibility.

- Have the document properly proofread! Nothing so undermines the credibility of any document than avoidable typos and grammatical errors. These give the reader an impression of sloppiness, which, subconsciously at least, also reflects on the content of the document.

Technique 49: Business case presentation

This is not a book about presentation skills; there are lots of excellent books and training videos on that subject. However, the presentation of a business case is an opportunity for BAs to 'sell' their ideas (and to an extent themselves) to senior management, and should be prepared for thoroughly.

Description of the technique

The main thing to bear in mind is that the presentation should add value to the written report and not just be a read-out version of it! Senior managers are busy people and a BA will most likely only get a small slice of their time – a 20-minute slot in the middle of a board meeting, for example. So the presentation needs to be short, sharp and to the point, and to get the main issues over quickly and succinctly.

The old formula for any presentation holds good here:

- Tell 'em what you're going to tell 'em.
- Tell 'em.
- Tell 'em what you've told 'em.

What this means in practice is:

Start with a bang!	An opening statement such as 'This presentation will explain how our organisation can save £12 million a year from its operating expenses' is more likely to get attention than 'I am here to explain in detail our proposal for the new stock requisitioning system'. Stakeholder analysis (Techniques 26–29) and understanding the audience are important here, in order to know what will engage the interest of the participants.

Present the issues and solutions:	Now the main issues found should be presented succinctly using the minimum number of slides. Detail is not needed on the slides, but presenters should have it at their fingertips so as to be able to field questions.
End on a high:	At the end of the presentation summarise the issues, and clearly restate the decision the managers are being invited to make.

Practical points about presenting business cases

The reason why you are being invited to present your ideas in person is probably that the decision-makers want to hear what you have to say, and to have the arguments summarised. So it is a mistake to turn up and, in effect, simply read the report to them!

Another error is to take along too many slides, so that the complaint of 'death by PowerPoint' is made. If, say, 15 minutes is available for the presentation, that implies a maximum of five slides if sufficient time is to be spent speaking to each of them. Those slides should not be endless sets of bullet points, since it is very difficult not to just read these to the audience. Instead they should contain the main points of the presentation, and present, in pictures, things that are difficult to explain in words – such as the shape of a new organisation chart, the configuration of a network, or a bar chart showing expected increased sales.

One way of improving the chances of staging a successful presentation is to hold rehearsals. At its simplest this could involve delivering the presentation a few times to the mirror, but by far the best idea is to have a fuller practice session, with colleagues taking the roles of the real audience and asking difficult questions at various points. That way, the presenter gets experience of handling these situations, and is much more relaxed, comfortable and confident when the real thing comes around.

REFERENCES

Bradley, G. (2006) *Benefit Realisation Management: A Practical Guide to Achieving Benefits Through Change*. Gower Publishing, Aldershot.

Ward, J. and Daniel, E. (2006) *Benefits Management: Delivering Value from IS and IT Investments*. Wiley, Chichester.

Welch, J. and Welch, S. (2005) *Winning*. HarperCollins, New York.

FURTHER READING

Blackstaff, M. (2006) *Finance for IT Decision Makers*, 2nd edition. British Computer Society, Swindon.

Cadle, J. and Yeates, D. (2008) *Project Management for Information Systems*, 5th edition. FT Prentice Hall, Harlow.

Gambles, I. (2009) *Making the Business Case: Proposals that Succeed for Projects that Work.* Gower, Farnham.

Jay, R. (2003) *How to Write Proposals and Reports that Get Results*, Financial Times/Prentice Hall, Harlow.

Jay, R. and Jay, A. (2004) *Effective Presentation.* 3rd edition, Prentice Hall Business, Harlow.

Lucey, T. (2003) *Management Accounting*, 2nd edition. Thomson Learning, London.

Schmidt, M.J. (2002) *The Business Case Guide*, 2nd edition. Solution Matrix, Boston.

6 DEFINE REQUIREMENTS

INTRODUCTION

Requirements definition is a significant part of the business analyst's role, no matter which lifecycle approach is used and no matter whether the focus is on business or IT requirements. Standard investigation techniques such as interviewing, workshops and observation (Techniques 13–15 – see Chapter 2) can help in the elicitation of such requirements, but additional techniques can be applied to improve the quality of this elicitation, the definition of the requirements themselves, and more importantly the quality of any resulting solutions. This stage of the business analysis process model focuses on a selection of such techniques, which serve to bring the requirements to life. It also covers some of the additional aspects to consider when using traditional investigation techniques with the specific objective of documenting, analysing, validating and managing requirements. By the very nature of requirements they focus on some future state, and as a result analysts need to support any approach to requirements elicitation with a balance of creativity and innovation if they are to add real value. The techniques described here can be used in isolation, but are likely to be most effective when they act in combination with each other.

When interviewing stakeholders it is easy to get entrenched in the detail of the current situation and existing issues, and hence not focus on what will really be needed in the future. For example, when trying to identify an initial set of requirements by the use of interviewing, the analyst will often be faced with two extreme responses, both of which need to be carefully handled:

'I don't know what I want, or even what is possible, so it's your job to find out.'

or:

'I know (or think I know) what I want, and here it is, so all you have to do is make sure I get it.'

The skill in requirements definition is to look beyond what is being said by individual stakeholders, and try to identify and define requirements that will ultimately result in a solution delivering features and behaviours that meet the true business objectives, in a way that satisfies individual needs while exploiting the 'art of the possible'. A key characteristic of the business analyst's role when defining requirements is to 'question the norm'.

If you take the time to consider any systems or devices that you enjoy interacting with, such as a smart phone or a particular internet site, you will soon realise that the best solutions are driven out from requirements that have really got inside the potential user's mind, and are delivered accordingly. When was the last time you enjoyed interacting with a call centre? This is a classic example that shows how important it is to integrate business and system requirements, coordinating them in a way that is focused on the end user.

Traditional analysis and investigation techniques have an important role to play in eliciting and defining requirements, but only if the analyst is clear that they are a means to an end and not an end in themselves. This is why they are most effective, and lead to better quality solutions, when used in conjunction with additional techniques such as those discussed in the rest of this section.

The set of techniques described here are presented in a sequence of groups, showing how each contributes to the overall 'Define requirements' stage of business analysis. The groupings are:

- requirements elicitation;
- requirements analysis;
- requirements development;
- requirements modelling.

Requirements elicitation (Techniques 50–53)
This section introduces:

- scenarios;
- storyboarding;
- prototyping;
- hothousing.

This is a set of techniques that help to enhance traditional investigation methods in order to maximise the quality of the requirements gathered.

The techniques described here can be utilised throughout the lifecycle, but they have their main focus wherever requirements are being identified and discussed with business representatives and subject matter experts. In the case of prototyping, specifically, the application of the technique will change fundamentally when an Agile or evolutionary development approach is employed, and this is also discussed within this section. Techniques such as scenarios, storyboarding and prototyping will usually be most effective in conjunction with other approaches such as interviewing (Technique 13) or workshops (Technique 14), or in combination with others from this group.

Requirements analysis (Techniques 54–56)
This section introduces:

- timeboxing;
- MoSCoW prioritisation;
- requirements organisation.

The techniques in this set work together to ensure that the requirements are well organised, both in terms of when they should be delivered and how they should be arranged into groups, in order to maintain control and assist with subsequent development and management.

Requirements development (Techniques 57–61)
This is a collection of techniques which ensure that standard and complete documentation is produced and maintained, both for the full set of requirements and for the individual requirements themselves. They are:

- requirements documentation;
- acceptance criteria definition;
- requirements validation;
- requirements management;
- requirements traceability matrix.

Requirements modelling (Techniques 62–65)
This is a collection of conceptual modelling techniques, which support the textual descriptions of requirements and any prototypes produced. The focus here is on process and static data models, and on the way these cross reference with each other to support the definition of requirements. The techniques introduced in this section are:

- use case diagrams and use case descriptions;
- entity relationship models;
- class models;
- the CRUD matrix.

Used carefully, these techniques can serve not only to demonstrate the business analyst's understanding of the problem situation to the business user, but also to ensure completeness and consistency within the set of requirements, and encourage creative thinking, which will help identify useful additional requirements.

REQUIREMENTS ELICITATION

Technique 50: Scenarios

Description of the technique

Scenarios can be used to bring to life either business situations or IT situations (usually described via use case specifications – see Technique 62), but are most powerful when used to describe both of these and the interactions between them. In addition to helping validate requirements for completeness of coverage, they also provide a solid base for prototyping, testing and subsequent training for business users. A scenario describes a specific situation that the user will recognise, which works through a single instance to a logical (although not always successful) conclusion. Each individual scenario is specific in that it does not deal in generalities; instead, it homes in on a particular set of circumstances and 'walks through' the task that needs to be performed, in a thread that has a start point and a stop point.

Each individual scenario can be used to validate the business requirement, and the development of the scenarios is also likely to identify additions or enhancements to the requirements during elicitation, analysis and subsequent definition. Thus the requirements and their supporting scenarios are developed together in an iterative way.

To develop a scenario, the business analyst starts by writing down descriptions of examples of a variety of situations that a range of users might encounter. These help to ground the analysis in reality and allow all concerned to understand the detailed steps that typical users go through, and the information they will need to perform these. This selected set of scenarios should be reviewed with users and used to refine the initial requirements definition. Later they can be used as the basis for the development of prototypes and acceptance test plans.

It is important when developing scenarios to ensure that there is sufficient coverage of both normal and critical conditions, as well as considering some of the more unusual and less important situations. There is often a temptation to focus scenarios only on the interesting cases, and ignore more mundane and common cases.

We recommend that the set of scenarios considered should cover:

- common tasks and the responses to important business events;
- situations involving a selection of users;
- critical events which happen occasionally;
- situations that are difficult to deal with;
- situations where users are likely to make mistakes;
- different working environments;
- both current and future situations;
- how any new technology might be used;

- boundaries between tasks and handoffs between users;
- interleaving of tasks, showing their likely sequences.

However, scenarios should **not**:

- try to cover every possible condition;
- provide cases that users think are not worth considering;
- only cover correct usage of the system.

The documentation of a scenario has two main components to it: a **situation** or set of circumstances for a specific task, and a detailed **script** describing how a user (in the case of the example shown below, a garage attendant) performs the task in this particular situation. The scenario is expressed in terms of a sequence of steps, perhaps demonstrated via a textual narrative, a dialogue or a storyboard.

Each scenario should be described from a user's point of view, and should include actions involving all of the actors who have a part to play in undertaking the task, including any decisions that need to be made. Exceptions which may occur at various points of the scenario are best shown separately in the description, at the point at which they might occur.

Example scenario

Scenario:	Customer buying petrol (paying at kiosk)
User role:	Garage attendant
Frequency:	65 per cent of all customers buy something from the shop in addition to fuel; 40 per cent of customers pay by credit card; 5 per cent of customers require a separate (VAT) receipt for their fuel.
Background (situation):	A customer walks into the garage to pay for fuel, and also wants to buy some items from the shop. The customer wishes to pay by credit card but needs a separate receipt for the fuel part of the transaction.
Description (script):	A customer walks into the garage shop and states which pump they have used. The customer has also selected some items from the shop. The attendant checks the pump details and adds the payment amount to the bill. The attendant scans the shop items and asks the customer whether they have a loyalty card and how they wish to pay. The customer does not have a loyalty card but hands over a credit card, and the attendant swipes this, requesting a PIN or signature from the customer. The system contacts the credit card system for verification. Once the transaction has been completed the attendant returns the credit card to the customer and asks whether a separate receipt is required; this receipt is then issued. (The payment component of the scenario could simply invoke another task called 'take payment', which would have its own set of scenarios

and exceptions). The attendant clears the screen ready for the next customer who is standing in line, and wishes the customer a good day.

Scenarios should always be written from the user's perspective, and should consider any decision-making undertaken during the task. This often leads to the description of the scenario in the form of an interaction between the user and other actors (both people and systems), perhaps even using the storyboarding technique discussed later.

In order to try and assess whether the set of scenarios that has been developed has sufficient breadth and coverage, it is useful to develop a model that describes various properties of the scenarios and compares them with the mix of circumstances found within the organisation. Where there is a mismatch, this is likely to highlight the need for additional scenarios to be considered. This comparison will also help the business analyst to decide when enough scenarios have been written to cover a particular area.

A scenario coverage model can be used to set targets and review the number of scenarios that are written in each area, and will help in the clarification of non-functional requirements and support the estimating process. It is developed after the first few scenarios have been written and when the important scenario properties are understood, based on an understanding of what is important to the various users within the organisation.

Factors to consider when developing a scenario coverage model include:

- an appreciation of the major problems in the current situation that will need to be resolved in the future situation;
- the range of users (this is needed to determine how many users there are within each user role);
- frequencies of different types of business events;
- a selection of example scenarios;
- an appreciation of the properties and coverage of each scenario.

Each scenario has a number of characteristics that can be assessed to evaluate its coverage. These can vary depending upon what is required. The three main questions that are considered here are:

- How many users does this scenario involve?
- Which organisational units are included in this scenario?
- How frequently are the tasks that are included in the scenario performed?

The examples in Tables 6.1 to 6.3 show the way a number of scenarios are assessed under these three headings, and compare the scenario coverage with the expected percentages in the set of business situations.

Table 6.1 Scenario analysis by user population

User population	Garage attendant	Garage supervisor	Customer at kiosk	Garage manager
Expected use	50%	20%	28%	2%
Scenario coverage	30%	18%	15%	5%
Evaluation of discrepancy	More scenarios required	Reasonable match	May need more scenarios	No more scenarios required

Table 6.2 Scenario analysis by environment

Environment	Front office	Back office	Maintenance
Expected use	50%	25%	25%
Scenario coverage	30%	23%	1%
Evaluation of discrepancy	More scenarios required	scenario coverage sufficient	More scenarios required

Table 6.3 Scenario analysis by frequency of use

Frequent tasks	Walk-in fuel payment	Sell lottery ticket	Issue loyalty card
Expected use	40%	23%	10%
Scenario coverage	90%	0%	0%
Evaluation of discrepancy	Enough scenarios covering this area	Some scenarios required here	Some scenarios required here

In the examples shown here, the factors chosen when undertaking the comparison are:

User population: Is each section of the user population covered by at least one scenario? Are the roles of users who will be expected to have a greater involvement in the use of the system covered by a greater proportion of the scenarios?

Environment: Access will be given to the IT system in various different locations – do the scenarios defined cover each of these different locations?

Frequent tasks: There are certain tasks that are key to the business, and the expectation is that these will be performed most often – do the scenarios cover these frequent tasks more than the others?

In building the scenario coverage model, the focus should be on developing a minimum set of scenarios that cover all the areas that are important to users, and emphasis should be given to ensuring that coverage of these areas is in proportion to their occurrence within the business environment.

Using scenarios

Scenarios should be written to show what working with the new system is anticipated to be like. They can be considered as the first prototype of the new system; this prototype might subsequently be disposed of, or it might form the basis of an evolutionary development of the solution. Initially they may be written to abstract out the details of how the system will actually work, but later versions will be described in sufficient detail to drive the creation of a more comprehensive prototype if appropriate. Scenarios can also be written to summarise cases that the current system has to deal with, as a way into understanding the current system (if this is required).

The key uses of scenarios include:

- to help elicit and clarify requirements;
- as a validation technique;
- to identify and investigate boundaries between tasks;
- to identify areas of potential IT support;
- as the basis of prototyping and modelling;
- as the basis of test criteria and acceptance testing;
- for subsequent user training or as inputs to any Model Office (i.e. setting up a mock-up of the live environment for testing purposes prior to final implantation).

Scenarios should be considered as concrete examples of specific paths through a task, which provide a complete story. The additional technique of storyboarding (described later in this section) can be used to support their development, acting as a key input to subsequent prototyping. In some extreme cases, alternatively, the use of 'hothousing' (also described later in this section) may even be appropriate.

Once scenarios have been described they should be validated, to assess whether they represent the actual interactions between actors. The script should be analysed for possible usability problems, by asking questions such as:

- Is this a scenario which people find difficult to complete successfully?
- Do errors occur frequently when undertaking this?
- To what information does the user need access during this scenario?
- Could the task be rationalised or simplified in some way?
- What use could be made IT to automate some parts of the scenario?

Technique 51: Storyboarding

Description of the technique

A storyboard, which may be used in conjunction with scenario definition, is a low-fidelity prototype usually consisting of a series of diagrams or screen sketches showing navigation routes through a task or a series of screenshots. Storyboards are often used by designers to illustrate the structure and navigation through scenarios, but are also particularly useful for discussing requirements with user groups. An initial demonstration storyboard may be a throwaway or could be used as input to subsequent evolutionary prototyping, depending on circumstances. Storyboards are used by both business analysts and solution designers to help illustrate and organise their ideas and obtain feedback from other interested parties. They are particularly useful for multimedia presentations and website designs, or where there is significant interaction between people and systems.

It is part of the business analyst's role to try to see the bigger picture and to try to communicate this to others involved. Storyboards can assist in getting this right. The technique of storyboarding also helps the business analyst to break this bigger picture into smaller components in order to focus on one at a time. In addition to enhancing communication and organisation of ideas, this helps the business analyst to identify specific areas where more analysis or research is needed. Storyboards therefore provide not only a visual representation of the bigger picture but also a mechanism for zooming in on the various aspects of the detail as required.

Storyboarding usually starts as a pencil and paper technique for designing and testing ideas, particularly those related to user interfaces. Although a storyboard is not as realistic as a full prototype, it has the advantage that it can be done quickly without the use of technology. Thus its application does not involve the need for any particular technical expertise.

A storyboard shows the sequence of events, and specifies the user actions that often interact with them, for a range of situations. A further possible refinement of storyboards is to use index cards or Post-it notes to permit rapid changes in the design. These permit users to evaluate several possible sequences in a single session.

Using storyboarding

The following additional guidance may make the use of the storyboarding technique more successful.

- Use context definition and scenarios as input.

- Brainstorm ideas: this might include the use of lists, charts, doodles and quick notes.

- Select the best ideas. Reconsider the project requirements, time and resource constraints, the target audience and the end users. Choose the top ideas and try to get feedback from others involved.

- Sketch each screen, and describe any pictures, images, animations, sound, music, video or text.

It is useful to create the storyboard on a whiteboard or a brown paper wall in conjunction with coloured Post-it notes (and perhaps standard magnetic icons). Using this approach before diving into formal process modelling or prototyping can make a massive difference when working with users to show them how a potential solution will help them with their work. Collaboration with appropriate stakeholders is important when storyboarding, as is making sure that business users are given sufficient opportunity to contribute their ideas and experience to the stories being told. In is interesting to note that Google used storyboards as part of the beta release of its new Chrome browser, to explain why the product would be so useful to customers.

Figure 6.1 Storyboard for a travel agent

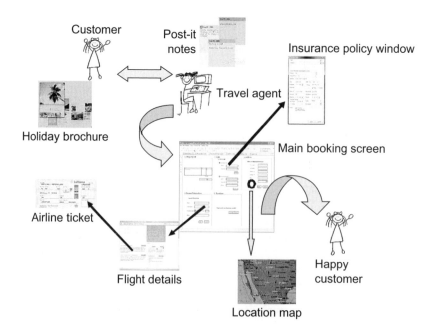

The storyboard in Figure 6.1 shows the interaction between a customer and a travel agent's representative, and the various screens navigated during the booking of a holiday. It helps to emphasise the importance of the holiday brochure, the physical flight tickets and the visual map, as well as showing the possible screenshots themselves.

Storyboards can change a lot as you are working on them. When you feel you have a good first attempt, with lots of detail and a reasonable sequence, you can move to using software to log all the information agreed so far and to support a very visual way of doing things, while allowing everyone in the team to have a shared copy for subsequent use. Presentation software such as PowerPoint works well for this. Each individual slide can be used as a frame in the storyboard, and it is easy to insert images, text, tables, charts and screenshots as required. Most presentation software also allows you to add notes at the bottom of the slide, which can be printed off separately from the slides and will provide additional support when talking through the storyboard with users.

The main benefits of storyboards are that they:

- provide an overview of a system (both the manual and the automated parts);
- demonstrate the functionality of the various storyboard elements;
- demonstrate the navigation sequence;
- check whether the presentation is accurate and complete;
- can be evaluated by users early in the requirements gathering process.

Technique 52: Prototyping
Overview
Many industries benefit from the use of mock-ups, models, visual designs and prototypes to establish requirements, confirm expectations and test the achievability of objectives. These can range from simple storyboards through scale models to fully working prototypes. They can be temporary, transient, or disposable – here called throwaway prototypes. Some, however, may be evolutionary prototypes, for example working models, which will ultimately evolve into the eventual solution (usually as part of some Agile or iterative development lifecycle). For instance, in a software-related project, screens may be prototyped and refined before the detailed logic is written to make them fully functional. Once reviewed and agreed, these then become the basis of the design of the final product.

The benefits of building prototypes are significant. Prototyping is one of the many techniques that Agile approaches such as DSDM/Atern (DSDM Consortium 2007) and Scrum (Schwaber 2004) adopt to ensure effective communication between stakeholders, whether from different parts of the business, different organisations or different cultures. The Agile approach advocates the use of such models to improve communication and to bring ideas to life by making products more visible early in the lifecycle. As discussed previously, prototyping may involve diagrammatic representations such as storyboards, often driven by the definition of a range of scenarios. The intention is to produce something visible, valuable and in a working state as soon as possible, in order to clarify understanding and minimise subsequent reworking. Only then is it possible for users to say whether what has been produced is what they actually need, and thereby improve the quality both of the definition of requirements and of the ultimate solution delivered.

Prototyping can help improve the effectiveness of solution development, when it is used carefully and in appropriate circumstances. It enhances communication between business users, business analysts and solution developers. It is a technique which helps all parties involved to understand the relationship between business process and IT support, and helps to identify additional requirements and scenarios.

Description of the technique

A **prototype** is a model which forms an exemplar or pattern, on which a more detailed design can be based or formed: something that serves to illustrate the typical qualities and characteristics of the potential solution. It may evolve into the eventual solution (an evolutionary prototype) or it might always have been intended to be an experimental model (a disposable prototype).

Throwaway or rapid prototyping refers to the creation of a working model that will eventually be discarded rather than becoming part of the finally delivered software. After preliminary requirements gathering is accomplished, a simple working model of the system is constructed to show the users what their requirements might look like when they are implemented into a finished system.

Evolutionary prototyping is quite different from throwaway prototyping. The main goal when using evolutionary prototyping is to build a very robust prototype in a structured manner, and then constantly refine it in an iterative way. The reason for this is that the evolutionary prototype, when built, forms the heart of the new system, on which any improvements and further enhancements will be built. Evolutionary prototyping is usually at the core of any Agile development approach.

There are three key aspects that should be considered when undertaking prototyping, regardless of whether the prototype is disposable or evolutionary. They are determined by the following questions:

- What is the **scope** to be covered by the prototypes? This can range from one specific task to the whole system, or simply be a subset of the scenarios.

- Will the prototypes be high or low **fidelity?** The prototypes may range from sketches drawn on paper (similar to storyboards) to well-defined real screens developed using the target technical environment.

- How extensive will the **functionality** of the prototypes be? They may use simulated data, or they could access fully working system data complete with business rules and testable functionality.

Early in the requirements elicitation process, it may be useful to produce low fidelity, limited scope prototypes to demonstrate to the users the result of their requests. At a later point in the process of eliciting requirements, a prototype that is more extensive might be more applicable.

Once the prototyping sessions have been completed it is important to ensure that appropriate documentation is updated to incorporate any new or amended requirements. In addition, the impact of any agreed changes needs to be assessed, to check for effects on other requirements and supporting documentation. It is possible that conflicts with other requirements may have been raised as a result of the prototyping exercise.

One of the main issues with the whole prototyping process is that of managing the users' expectations. This is because:

- simple prototypes may create a negative impression within the target community;
- high fidelity prototypes may cause users to expect immediate delivery of the full solution;
- impressive response times of prototypes may raise users' expectations of the new system's performance to an unrealistic level.

Categories of Prototype
Prototypes of the solution are the basis on which tests can be planned and performed. Prototypes can be designed to test both the functional features and non-functional aspects of the solution such as usability and the levels of performance required. Three main categories of prototype cover these very different purposes and objectives:

business or requirements prototypes – used to elicit requirements and an understanding of the features or functionality required;

usability prototypes – used to define, refine, and demonstrate user interface design, usability, accessibility, look and feel, and perhaps such aspects as security and availability (non-functional requirements);

performance or capacity prototypes – used to define, demonstrate, predict and test how systems will perform under peak loads, as well as to demonstrate and evaluate, for example, volume handling, response times and availability (i.e. other non-functional aspects of the system).

One physical prototype could cover more than one of these categories, but it is often confusing to mix the categories within a single prototyping session with a user. The greatest benefit of considering these categories is to ensure that no aspect of demonstration or testing has been missed. For example, a business prototype may be constructed early in the project, while a performance or capacity prototype will only be able to allow testing of actual performance during subsequent stages, once a working product with sufficient volumes of test data is available. The same components of the prototype are thus tested more than once, for different reasons each time.

Using prototyping

When defining the scope of the individual prototyping sessions it is useful to distinguish between vertical and horizontal prototyping. Evolutionary prototyping may evolve vertically, where each feature of the proposed solution is developed prior to moving on to the next feature. Each feature may be a complete increment or part of an increment.

A horizontal approach, where the breadth of the solution is developed before the depth is considered, could be used as an alternative. The benefit of this approach is to demonstrate clearly to all stakeholders the overall scope of the system, and to establish areas where conformity to a standard or style is required, for example in the user interface to an IT system.

It is possible to combine both vertical and horizontal prototyping by adopting a T-shaped prototype, where the breadth is developed along with a finished slice of the proposed solution.

Failure to manage the users' expectations during the application of the prototyping technique may lead to dissatisfaction within the project and with the delivered system. It is important to manage these user expectations actively, and this involves:

- setting out the objectives of the prototyping exercise up front, including:

  - agreeing levels of scope, functionality and fidelity,

  - deciding whether the prototype being demonstrated is vertical, horizontal or a combination of these,

  - categorising the objective of the prototyping session (business, capacity or usability);

- informing the users of the extent of the prototype, and clearly defining any impact this may have on performance, usability, and so forth;

- keeping the users up to date with the progress of the development process;

- not promising that the finished system will achieve the performance (and other non-functional requirements) of the prototype if it is not certain that it can be achieved.

Advantages of prototyping

There are many advantages to using prototyping as the basis of requirements definition and demonstration. These include:

Reduced time and costs:	Prototyping can improve the quality of requirements and the specifications provided to solution developers. Because changes cost exponentially more to implement the later in development they are detected, the early determination of what the user really wants can result in faster and less expensive delivery.

Improved and increased user involvement:	Prototyping requires active user participation and allows users to see and interact with a prototype, enabling them to provide better and more complete feedback and input to specifications. User examination of the prototype prevents many of the misunderstandings and miscommunications that occur when each side believes the other understands what they said. Since users know the problem domain better than anyone in the solution development team does, increased interaction can result in a final product that has greater tangible and intangible quality. The final product is also more likely to satisfy the user's desire for functionality, look, feel and performance.

Disadvantages and risks of prototyping

Despite being an excellent technique for requirements clarification and evolutionary solution development, prototyping carries with it a number of drawbacks and risks which should be considered carefully before embarking on its use. These include:

Poor documentation:	The prototyping replaces any formal analysis and documentation, leading to difficulties later, particularly when the finished system is in a maintenance situation.
Changes to user expectations:	Poor prototyping reduces credibility, while good prototypes may raise user expectations to an unachievable level.
Unmanageability:	Large prototypes may become unmanageable and lead to 'skeleton' systems.
Exclusion of some users:	Involving insufficient people in the prototyping sessions may lead either to 'personalised' solutions (ones that just reflect certain people's ideas) or to 'historic' solutions (those that just perpetuate what has been done in the past).
Poor system performance:	Untested or insufficiently tested prototypes may result in unacceptable performance once the system is in live operation.
Over-optimistic estimates:	Optimistic estimates based on prototypes may upset overall delivery timescales for the final system.

Technique 53: Hothousing

Description of the technique

Hothousing is an Agile development technique that can be used to clarify and enhance the quality of requirements and delivered solutions. Hothouses are intense face-to-face workshops (often held over three days) that bring together people from the IT development and delivery communities along with their customers, business partners and key users.

Working in small teams at an off-site location, the participants create and demonstrate prototype solutions to business problems, which are judged by their peers each day. Sometimes this may involve different teams competing with each other to produce the best overall solution. In this case, a winning prototype is chosen to be taken forward into full development at the end of the event.

Hothouses are effectively Agile prototyping workshops that closely map development to customer needs, significantly increasing the quality of solutions while shortening delivery timescales.

Hothousing is used to ensure a shared understanding of the business problems and define working solutions that will be delivered in a subsequent fixed release cycle (timebox) of, say, 90 days, with business benefits quantifiable in customer terms. The outcome of the initial hothouse session itself is a mixture of prototypes, processes, priorities, cost–benefit analyses and metrics. It is common for this three-day period to involve a number of teams producing competing prototypes, with one of these being selected to progress forward to full delivery.

While the actual structure of this three-day hothousing session will vary, the general approach is as follows.

- Day One focuses on presenting and understanding the business problem, with each team developing a high-level outline of how they would solve it. At the end of the day each team summarises its proposed approach. Some form of scoring and ranking takes place, and the teams are left to reflect on their efforts overnight, ready to begin Day Two with a modified approach if appropriate.

- On Day Two each team develops a prototype version of their solution to the problem, based on the approach outlined on Day One. For this to work successfully they will need access to business users and domain experts as appropriate. By the end of Day Two each team should have produced a working prototype that can be demonstrated to all concerned. Again, feedback and scoring is undertaken.

- Day Three is primarily a fine-tuning exercise, and after this is completed the final evaluation takes place and the 'winning' team is given the opportunity to turn its prototype into a fully specified and documented working product ready for release.

Each hothouse session establishes a post-implementation review (PIR) 'handshake'. This PIR handshake ensures that all participants (IT and its customer) have identified what must be done to achieve customer and commercial success over the next 90-day period (timebox), and that there are clearly measurable targets and objectives. The handshake can then be formalised and captured in a 90-day measures and targets document, which forms the basis by which the programme's achievements can be assessed at the end of the subsequent timebox cycle.

Figure 6.2 Hothousing process

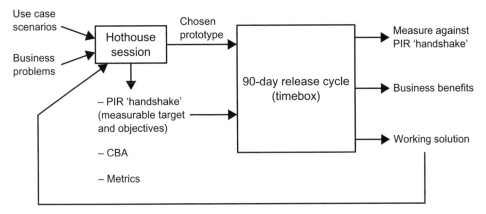

The technique of hothousing can be summarised as:

Transport a group of IT staff and business users to an off-site location. Have them stay overnight. Provide accommodation, laptops, a network, a handful of servers, flipcharts, a presentation room – and unlimited food and drink. Have teams compete over the course of three days to build a real IT system specified by the business. Reward the winning team.

Hothouses are about bringing together the delivery community, and focusing on the understanding of a business problem. Hothousing can be used as the first stage of an Agile development approach. It emphasises:

- common understanding;
- building a realisation of the solution;
- using competition (between teams) and intensity (long hours, frequent deliveries) to instil a sense of urgency.

Hothousing was first proven in retail environments, and has since been deployed successfully across a range of sectors and organisation types. The secret of using it successfully is to unleash the creative powers of those who know the business best, supported by experienced coaches, skilled facilitators and motivated implementers. With effective hothousing, teams get swiftly into their creative stride, implement ideas quickly, evaluate effectively, prove concepts and identify areas for improvement – and then iterate. The result is fast-paced, highly productive, high-speed evolution leading to optimal business solutions.

REQUIREMENTS ANALYSIS

Technique 54: Timeboxing
Overview
Timeboxing is one of the most important and yet most misunderstood techniques available to the business analyst (and anyone else who has anything to do in a

fixed or tight timescale). It does, however, have the advantage of being particularly simple to perform, if it is approached in the right way and with the right mindset. In many ways its success is as much about having the right mindset as it is to do with using the technique itself. All involved stakeholders need to buy into the concept of timeboxing and into an agreement about the proposed timescale of the timebox itself.

This section provides guidance on how to use the technique in an effective way. Without effective timeboxing, focus can be lost and things will run out control. Much of what is discussed here is to do with planning, control and keeping a clear focus on what actually has to be delivered at the end of the timebox. It is for this reason that there is a very close relationship between timeboxing and the clear prioritisation of deliverables. In addition to this, there is also an important reliance on an ability to estimate the complexity and duration of the tasks to be undertaken. It is also vital that whoever is actually undertaking the work within the timebox should be involved in the development of these estimates.

Description of the technique
There are many definitions of a timebox. Here we will distinguish between two main types.

An **outer** or **overall** timebox is the time between the start and end dates of a project, or a major stage, or the date on which a major set of deliverables are due. As a technique, timeboxing is most significant when the end date is not movable.

Inner or **lower-level** timeboxes are nested, like Russian dolls (quite appropriate when used in conjunction with the MoSCoW approach to prioritisation, Technique 55) or wheels within wheels within the overall timebox, to provide a series of fixed times by which interim products are to be delivered or partially produced. This leads us to consider carefully the interrelationships between the various inner timeboxes in terms of their dependencies and overlaps.

Figure 6.3 Outer and inner timeboxes

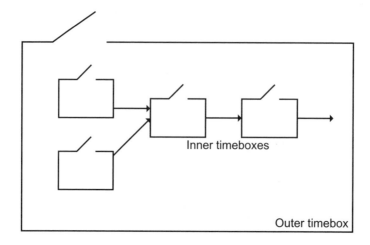

Timeboxing (of both the outer and the inner types) means setting a deadline[1] or agreeing a time by which an objective can be met or specific products be delivered, rather than describing when a task must be completed.

This approach allows us to refocus our efforts on the development of the required deliverables rather that constantly watching the clock or calendar. Any timebox, at any level, must therefore have an agreed scope and clear objectives based on a high-level definition of what needs to be delivered. It is also important to be aware (particularly for inner timeboxes) that the focus should be to produce something, leaving the details of how that thing is actually made to the people doing the work – assuming that standards and procedures are followed. This makes timeboxing a product – rather than activity-based technique.

Using timeboxing

The timeboxing technique can be used for the production of any time-critical deliverables, and is particularly useful where the timescale itself is a critical aspect of the delivery.

Sometimes people use the phrase 'Let's timebox this now' when they are running out of time to do something. This usually means they ignore the key aspects of the technique such as objective setting, estimating, planning, obtaining consensus and prioritisation. That approach should always be avoided.

Each of the inner timeboxes, which may themselves be nested, will produce a visible set of deliverables. At the end of the timebox these can be assessed for completeness and quality before being used as input to the subsequent timebox, and used to decide whether any of the future timeboxes will need to be replanned. Inner timeboxes should be kept reasonably short, to make it easier to calculate what is likely to be capable of being achieved within the specified time with the resources available. This means that the technique of timeboxing is not only good for controlling various components of the business analysis process, but can also be useful in estimating the resources that will be required to deliver specific products such as a requirement document or a business case.

On completion of a timebox, whatever has been delivered usually undergoes an additional review by those who are going to use the product. If at some point it becomes apparent that the agreed completion time may be missed, then the deliverable set should be reduced in scope rather than letting this happen, otherwise the knock-on effect on other timeboxes may be problematic. The technique of prioritisation will usually help significantly in ensuring that this can be handled successfully, and may lead to replanning of subsequent timeboxes. For the effective use of this technique, it is always better to stop the timebox at the agreed time, review the actual progress, and then perhaps instigate a new timebox or move some things from one into another, rather that letting any individual one slip without action beyond its agreed time. In other words, the philosophy is that scope slips but timing never does. This approach ensures

---

[1]Some proponents of timeboxing prefer to avoid the word 'deadline' when describing the technique: this can create the wrong impression, since a timebox is often an agreed or negotiated delivery date rather than one that has been imposed without discussion.

timely and frequent delivery of individual products, and ultimately results in the successful delivery of the final products of the outer timebox. However, although it provides greater control, it is worth being aware that this does result in more intense working patterns.

While with careful planning it is possible to undertake parallel timeboxes, it is important to note that a subsequent timebox which involves dependent work cannot normally be started before any previous ones are complete. This is because, until an individual timebox has actually been completed, there will be no guarantee as to the actual coverage of what is delivered. This is particularly true when this technique is used in conjunction with a formal approach to prioritisation such as MoSCoW (Technique 55).

All timeboxes, outer ones and inner ones at all levels, should follow certain general principles in terms of structure, content and resourcing. These include:

Structure and content: All timeboxes should begin with a planning or kick-off component and end with a timeboxed review or close-out component. In between it is good practice to nest inner timeboxes covering initial investigation, refinement and consolidation activities. Each of these three activities should also have their own individual planning and review elements.

Resourcing: When a timebox commences, all the required resources to achieve the objective should be in place. These include people, any appropriate technology required, inputs from previous timeboxes, a prioritised list of what need to be achieved in the timebox (using MoSCoW, Technique 55), a clear definition of the objectives and timescale imposed, and any other facilities needed. This should enable, whenever possible, the timebox to be self contained. It sometimes helps to envisage the timebox as having a lid, which closes when it kicks off and doesn't open again until it is completed except when exceptional circumstances occur (such as the delivery of the 'Must haves' being in jeopardy).

By keeping each individual inner timebox reasonably short, it is possible to let it take place relatively undisturbed until completion, and only then to assess the impact on subsequent timeboxes in the light of what has actually been delivered.

Technique 55: MoSCoW prioritisation

Description of the technique
Usually there is a constraint on the time or budget available to undertake a piece of work, and not everything can be done at once or even at all. As a result some form of prioritisation is vital. The problem is that, despite these facts, prioritisation is not always done well. This is partly because consensus on what is most important is not always easy to achieve. Because there are interrelationships and dependencies between discrete requirements, and because things change constantly throughout projects, a re-evaluation of priorities already agreed on is required. However, the

Figure 6.4 Example of the structure of a typical timebox

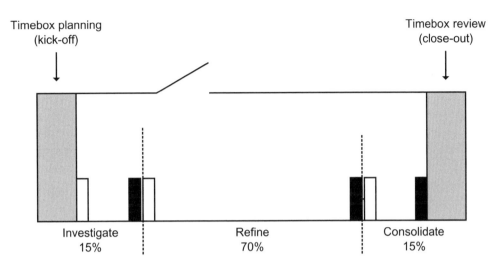

Timebox planning
(kick-off)

Timebox review
(close-out)

Investigate
15%

Refine
70%

Consolidate
15%

main reason for problems with prioritisation is the lack of agreed standard definitions as to what various priorities mean, and of clear procedures as to what to do when these priorities change.

This section uses an approach to prioritisation based on a concept called 'MoSCoW'. It proposes some specific meanings for the terms used in this approach, and identifies some guidance that overcomes some of the most common difficulties that occur with its application in practice. The technique described here is of particular use when timeboxes are fixed and when it is possible to deliver products incrementally rather than in a one-off release covering everything. In all cases it is vital to ensure that all essential work is done first, with less critical work being delayed until later or omitted altogether if appropriate.

The MoSCoW rules are employed to help achieve clear prioritisation of requirements. The 'o's in the acronym have no meaning. The remaining components of 'MoSCoW' as used in this chapter are defined here.

Must have: These are requirements that are fundamental (they are sometimes also referred to as the 'Minimum usable subset'). Without them, the deliverable will be unworkable and useless. Their delivery at the end of the appropriate timebox is guaranteed (it is specifically because of this guarantee that much effort should be employed to ensure that the list of Ms is kept as small as possible, and that sensible estimates of the time at which they can be ready are agreed). If any one of these 'Must haves' is not ready then nothing can be released: if it could be, then they were not really 'Must haves' in the first place. As a result of this, it is important to be aware that the term 'Must have' covers the functionality itself, its legality and its level of quality. It is for this reason that things can usually only be prioritised properly once a certain level of decomposition and definition of the requirements has been achieved.

Should have: These are important requirements for which there is a work-around in the short term, or where expectations can be managed. They are things that would have normally have been classified as 'Must haves' in a less time-constrained situation, but the deliverable will still be useful and usable without them initially. The mindset of good MoSCoW prioritisation is that one would normally expect to deliver, in addition to all the 'Must haves', a large proportion of the 'Should haves' (but this delivery is not guaranteed). The 'Should haves' are often described as those things that you would expect to be included within a product of this type, but whose non-inclusion would not necessarily delay the release. They would, however, be expected to be delivered soon afterwards, since the work-around is not usually a long term solution.

Could have: These are requirements that can more easily be left out at this point. They may well be included in this delivery if their inclusion is easy to achieve without jeopardising the delivery of the 'Must haves' and 'Should haves'. A 'Could have' may be differentiated from a 'Should have' by considering the degree of pain caused by its non-inclusion in terms of business value or number of people affected.

Want to have but won't have this time round (or won't get yet): This refers to those valuable requirements that can wait until later. It is often useful to keep these in the initial priority list, since, although they are not due for delivery yet, knowledge that they will be coming later may influence design decisions and the approach taken to the planning of subsequent deliveries. Remember, however, that although something is a 'W' initially it will almost certainly get a different priority in subsequent increments (perhaps even an 'M' in the next one), and knowing when it is due to be delivered can be very useful for planning purposes.

This clear definition of terms with precise meanings is significantly better than any prioritisation approach that uses numerical values for priorities, or, even worse, words such as high, medium or low, which do not have a precise meaning outside a specific context.

All of the items in the prioritised requirements list (the MoSCoW list) are due for delivery at some point, although the total delivery may be spread over a number of increments. The MoSCoW rules provide the basis on which decisions can be made regarding the whole project, and during any timeboxes included within the project. It is for this reason that the techniques of prioritisation and timeboxing are so useful when applied together. The MoSCoW list is likely to change throughout the project, in terms both of changes to requirements and of changes to the priorities themselves. For this reason it is vital that they are subject to well-defined change- and version-control procedures.

As new requirements arise, or as existing requirements are defined in more detail, decisions must be made as to how critical they are to success by using these MoSCoW rules. All priorities should be reviewed throughout to ensure that they are still valid. It is not appropriate to wait until time is running out, resources are transferred or conflicts occur before starting the prioritisation exercise.

Using MoSCoW prioritisation

It is essential that not everything proposed in a given timebox or project is a 'Must have'. It is the existence of lower-level priority requirements that allows for flexibility and agility in dealing with problems that arrive and with the inevitable change of scope. In fact, experience suggests that if more that 60 per cent of the estimated time for a piece of work is taken up by 'Must have' requirements then the proposed timescales are unlikely to be met.

Once all stakeholders are clear about the meaning of each of the MoSCoW priority levels, and there is a published procedure specifying who is allowed to change priorities, it is much easier to make rapid progress through a project and to reduce delays when decisions are needed. For example, some organisations empower team members to adjust the scope of delivery as long as there is no effect on the delivery of the 'Must haves' within their work package, only referring to a higher authority when the delivery of 'Must haves' is at risk or when a decision is required to drop a 'Must have' to a lower priority level. As new requirements are identified they can be allocated a priority themselves and take their rightful place in the stack of requirements, sometimes causing existing requirements to move further down this list.

When undertaking a prioritisation exercise it is not unusual for there to be heated discussions as to what priorities should be allocated to various requirements, and it is particularly common for there to be a very large list of 'Must haves'. It is important that this situation is addressed early. This can involve spending some time explaining the specific meaning of the MoSCoW levels. People often say 'M' when they mean 'S', and 'S' when they mean 'C'. (It is also common for the 'C's and 'W's to be mixed up). Remember, if a 'Must have' is not delivered on time then neither is anything else! A very good tip to help avoid this happening is to allocate everything initially as a 'W' and work backwards towards 'M', justifying each move.

However, the main reason why there are usually so many 'M's is that the prioritisation is often carried out on requirements that are defined in insufficient detail. While the high-level definition of the requirement might suggest a priority of 'M', once decomposed or considered in terms of different scenarios it becomes apparent that there is much that can be categorised as 'S', 'C' or even 'W'. In fact it is this decomposition approach that provides even more flexibility, once various aspects of a requirement are considered separately in terms of priority.

Consider the following example:

Requirement: to be able to view a customer bank account balance.

For any reasonable banking system, this will be an 'M' for the first release of the system. However, if it were to be decomposed into its component parts and also considered from the perspective of various scenarios and extensions, it becomes clear that there is plenty of scope for some elements to be allocated a lower priority or left until later without jeopardising the delivery of the basic facility to customers. It is of course important not to overdo this, and to ensure that enough is initially offered to the customers for them to be comfortable while waiting for the remainder of the features to become available.

This approach is even more powerful when applied to the non-functional as well as the functional aspects of a requirement. So a more detailed definition of the requirement might lead to the following use of MoSCoW:

Functional requirement: to be able to view a bank account balance – priority M.

Related non-functional requirements:

- security – priority M;
- being up to date, to the latest transaction – priority S;
- availability in both pounds and Euros – priority C;
- availability in various languages – priority C.

This would allow us to deliver a system on time that allowed customers to check their bank balance; while we would initially expect it to produce totally up-to-date results, the first release might need to put out a message saying that transactions performed during the current day might not yet be shown. This approach would also allow the work on currency and language to be carried out with less urgency and released when it is completely ready and tested, without delaying the initial key features.

MoSCoW is particularly powerful as a prioritisation technique when used in conjunction with timeboxing (Technique 54). For example, a requirement that is an 'M' in the overall project might only be an 'S' in an early timebox, allowing it to slip out of that timebox and be delivered later (but still in time for the full release) rather than delay other early requirements, which may need to be in place quickly to allow other areas of development to get started. In fact, a MoSCoW priority for an item is only really meaningful in a specific timeframe; items may take on different values in other timeframes or lower-level inner timeboxes.

Technique 56: Requirements organisation

Description of the technique
At its simplest, a requirement is a service, feature or behaviour that the user wishes the ultimate solution to perform or exhibit. However, once a potential set of requirements has been identified, it is vital to organise these before validating

them and using them to derive solutions. This topic of requirements organisation can be further subdivided into requirements structuring, and requirements negotiation and conflict analysis.

Requirements structuring

Sets of requirements that analysts are dealing with are often big and complex. This makes the structuring process one of the most important activities in requirements engineering. How requirements are structured and presented has a direct impact on the requirements definition process and on their ultimate quality. In particular, the analyst should create a clear vision of the way requirements are being defined, built and presented. This organisation and structuring also helps with checking the completeness and consistency of the requirements and will support their subsequent review. In addition, most projects will involve more than one user and more than one business area. During analysis of the set of requirements that have been identified it is important to see if some of them overlap, or if in fact they form a single high-level requirement when taken together. Identifying this situation early will make any subsequent structuring of requirements easier.

When structuring them, it is important to consider both how the overall set of requirements is organised and how the individual requirements themselves are structured. Attention should be paid to:

- requirements sets and clusters;
- links and dependencies between requirements;
- levels and hierarchical decomposition of requirements.

Requirements sets and clusters

Within even the most trivial development the number of individual requirements can quickly become large and unmanageable, particularly when these requirements are supported by additional models and diagrams providing more detailed definitions of business rules and information usage. As a result it is good for organisations to agree a standard way of grouping similar types of requirements together within the requirements specification. Perhaps the simplest way to undertake this grouping initially is to cluster the requirements set into the following high-level groups:

- functional requirements (and non-functional requirements that relate only to specific individual functional requirements, which could remain here with their owning functional requirements rather that being kept separately);
- non-functional requirements;
- general requirements;
- technical requirements.

Some organisations may wish to extend this list of high-level categories by adding an additional category of 'data requirements', if this is deemed useful. However, such requirements can normally be incorporated into the other four categories.

Once this high-level clustering has been completed it is usual to regroup the requirements in each set further, into lower-level groupings. In this case the actual groupings chosen will depend not only on local standards, but also on considerations such as the type of project and the volume of requirements of each type.

Typical lower-levels groupings that could be considered include:

Functional requirements:

- by business area;
- by business process;
- by use case;
- by access type;

Non-functional requirements: by non-functional type, such as:

- performance;
- access;
- availability;
- backup;
- security;

General requirements:

- project constraints;
- legal matters;
- look and feel, and style;
- cultural aspects;

Technical requirements:

- hardware;
- software;
- telecommunications.

In addition to providing clear partitioning of the requirements specification, grouping into this standard set of types also provides a prompt to the business analyst to ensure that each type has been fully considered and analysed during the requirements engineering process. When this is not done it is easy to miss requirements, particularly non-functional and technical ones. Their omission will almost always lead to subsequent problems during testing or delivery, and ultimately when the final solution is implemented.

Links and dependencies between requirements

As well as clustering the set of requirements into groups, it is also useful to document the links, relationships and dependencies between individual ones. These links can support planning (at both the project and the timebox levels), prioritisation, traceability, and allocation into discrete work packages and implementation phases. The links may be between one functional requirement and other functional requirements, between functional requirements and a set of non-functional requirements, or between requirements and related supporting models (such as use cases and use case specifications, Technique 62) or even supporting prototypes (Technique 52). In addition to identifying the links of the requirements themselves, it is often useful to document these relationships separately, for example in a requirements traceability matrix (Technique 61).

Levels and hierarchical decomposition

When looking at the individual requirements within the set (particularly the functional ones), it is important to identify at what level it is appropriate to define each requirement. Is a high-level or coarse-grained definition sufficient, or is this too vague? This decision will depend on a number of considerations, including which models, more detailed supporting specifications and prototypes are being employed. However, it is usually necessary to decompose most high-level requirements hierarchically into more granular levels of detail in order to support clear communication, to facilitate scenario analysis and to allow for additional prioritisation at these lower levels.

Requirements negotiation and conflict analysis

It is often the case that, when analysing requirements, we find that some of them are mutually exclusive or represent opposing views as to what should be done. Sometimes this conflict relates to a disagreement regarding the priority of the requirement, where one stakeholder believes that it should be higher than that suggested by another. The process of requirements analysis cannot be completed successfully until such conflicts have been resolved and there is a clear, agreed way forward. In these cases the ideal way of resolving any conflict is via some form of negotiation. This may be carried out in a workshop or perhaps with a closed discussion between the relevant stakeholders. In both cases the analyst can perform the role of facilitator in order to gain consensus, while maintaining an awareness of the overall business objectives, priorities and dependencies between requirements.

When seeking to undertake requirements negotiation, it is useful to employ the following three-step approach.

1. **Requirements discussion.** All stakeholders involved should be alerted to the situation, and open discussions should be held to resolve the problem. In order to move interested parties towards an agreed position, this will normally involve a discussion as to the impact and contribution of each requirement in question.

2. **Requirements prioritisation.** When agreeing the priorities of requirements the use of a well-defined standard approach to prioritisation such as MoSCoW (must have, should have, could have, want to have but won't get this time

round – see Technique 55) is strongly recommended. It is particularly helpful at this point to investigate not just which requirements are critical for a particular stakeholder, but why. A workshop environment may enable stakeholders to appreciate other stakeholders' points of view.

3. **Requirements agreement.** This allows for the negotiation to move forward in a constructive way, gaining consensus without the need for a confrontation. Only when it turns out to be unsuccessful should the analyst revert to escalation or to seeking an imposed decision from the sponsor or executive committee.

Once this agreement has been achieved, it will be possible to complete the organisation and structuring of the set of requirements, ready to move on to more formal validation.

REQUIREMENTS DEVELOPMENT

Technique 57: Requirements documentation

Description of the technique
Requirements come in a number of forms from a wide range of sources. For consistency, communication and change-control purposes, it is important to document and store them in a standard way across the organisation. The level of detail and specific content of this standard documentation set will depend on a number of factors, including:

- local policy and standards;
- the lifecycle being used for solution delivery;
- the structure and roles of the development team;
- the level to which the requirements apply – they may be for part of a contract, as in the case of outsourcing or sending work offshore;
- the relationship between the requirements themselves and any related models and supporting documents.

In addition to these characteristics, it is also worth noting that the names of the various requirements documents produced within a given organisation will vary, as will the scope of what is covered within them. This is true both of the document containing the full set of requirements and supporting documentation (names include 'requirements specification', 'business requirements specification' and 'requirement document') and the document containing the detail of individual requirements (which might be called a 'requirements catalogue', 'requirements log' or 'prioritised requirements list'). For reasons of clarity, this chapter will use the terms 'requirements specification' and 'requirements catalogue' when referring to these and their possible content. A core set of requirements documentation is emerging, and is achieving overall consensus across the discipline of requirements engineering. It is this common core that is described here, although all organisations are likely to use a subset, adaptation or extension of it. There are also a number of proprietary approaches available, some of which are driven by the facilities and features available in requirements management software support tools such as RequisitePro and Doors. Whatever approach is adopted, all requirements need to be thoroughly and consistently documented, and this should include, ultimately, an agreed resolution of every requirement defined.

Using requirements documentation

First, let us consider the typical content of the **requirements specification,** which acts as an overall document for the full set of detailed requirements and any supporting material. Its structure is shown in Table 6.4.

Table 6.4 Content of a typical requirements specification

Introduction and background	Business context Business objectives Project context Definition of scope Drivers and constraints Assumptions Stakeholder list	This section is used to explain the background to the analysis project, and documents any constraints or assumptions on which it is based. It is useful, too, to identify the stakeholders in the project and explain what their interests are.
Functional model	Context diagram Use case diagram Use case descriptions Requirements traceability matrix	This illustrates what system processes are likely to be required. Use cases are ideal for this, but there are other similar techniques that may be used.
Data model	Class diagram Entity relationship diagram Data dictionary	An understanding of the data in a system helps enormously in understanding the system itself. We suggest using an object class model for this, as it fits with the UML approach, which is becoming very widespread, but a conventional relational data model (for example, an entity-relationship diagram) would serve the same purpose.

(Continued)

Table 6.4 *(Continued)*

Requirements catalogue	Functional requirements Non-functional requirements General requirements Technical requirements	This is the core of the document, and is explained in more detail later in this chapter.
Glossary of terms	Glossary Naming conventions	Any terms used within the document, and also any terminology specific to the organisation that might otherwise confuse or mislead readers, should be explained.

While the requirement specification provides a mechanism for documenting much of the information needed to support the requirements definition process, it is the detail that is provided for each individual requirement within the requirements catalogue that is most significant in ensuring an effective description of requirements, and therefore, ultimately, the delivery of a solution of the highest possible quality.

It is in the contents of the requirements catalogue that there is the most variation across organisations. While not all of the items listed below are always needed, it is difficult to see which ones could be sensibly omitted without causing subsequent problems during design, testing and implementation. The requirements catalogue establishes a common understanding between users and business analysts throughout the project, and supports the controlled management of any proposed change to requirements.

The descriptions listed below identify the key items needed within the requirements catalogue to document requirements adequately. In some cases these items will cross reference to other documents, models or specifications that provide more detailed definitions of specific aspects of the requirement, for example to supporting use cases, use case descriptions and the definitions of data items and elements.

Requirement identifier: This is a unique identifier for the requirement, usually structured in such a way as to show the type of requirement, with a number to show the decomposition of requirements, if applicable.

Requirement name:	This gives a one-line shorthand title for the requirement.
Business area/ domain:	This can be used to indicate to which area(s) of the organisation the requirement relates.
Requirement description:	This is a fuller description of the requirement, written in business terms.
Source:	The source of the requirement is usually the person or department who requested it, or, in some cases, the legislation, policy or other document that gave rise to it. This enables the business analyst to identify where to refer back for further clarification of the requirement.
Owner:	The owner is the person who can provide expertise and detailed advice about the requirement. The owner should also decide whether the requirement is complete and correct, and, later in the system development lifecycle, whether it has been satisfied by the solution or not. The owner is usually the senior business person or sponsor for a particular area of the business, and may also be the source of the requirement.
Priority:	This gives the degree of importance of the requirement in relation to others, usually by using some formal approach to prioritisation such as MoSCoW (Technique 55).
Stakeholders:	This names the person or persons who have an interest in the successful resolution of the requirement, along with details of their interest. Identifying stakeholders and their interests for each requirement provides a useful reminder to the business analyst to ensure that all relevant stakeholders' interests have been covered, and later, satisfied (see Technique 30).
Type of requirement:	Categorising each requirement by standard type provides one way of partitioning the catalogue, and assists with completeness checking.
Associated non-functional requirements:	This defines any non-functional requirements associated with a particular functional requirement. Alternatively it can be to create a separate entry in the requirements catalogue, used where a non-functional requirement applies to a number of functional requirements.
Acceptance criteria:	These are the measures (or benchmarks) that will determine whether this requirement has been met by the system. They specify how the system may be tested by the end users to prove that the requirement has been met. They are sometimes referred to as 'fit criteria'. This is an absolutely fundamental entry in the catalogue, and must be developed with great care.

Justification and benefits:	This gives the business reason why the requirement has been included, and/or the way its prioritisation has been determined.
Related documents and supporting material:	Cross references to source documents, or to documents where further information about the requirement may be obtained, are found here. An example would be documentary evidence of the requirement for audit purposes. It is very common to use this item to refer to any use cases related to the requirement (for functional requirements – Technique 62), hence in effect producing a useful requirements traceability matrix (Technique 61).
Related requirements:	This is for cross references to other requirements. These may be included because they have a connection with the same business issue, or because they depend upon the successful resolution of this requirement. This also shows where a non-functional requirement should be applied to a functional requirement, or where an individual requirement is further decomposed into more detailed ones.
Resolution:	This says how the requirement is to be included in the solution, or gives the reasons for its exclusion from the final solution, annotated with agreement from all appropriate stakeholders.
Comments:	This item lists other information useful in understanding the requirement, and/or for formulating possible solutions.

Some information, such as the requirement name and the source, will be available immediately, but other areas will only be completed as the definition of the requirements progresses. The resolution of the requirement, for example, is recorded once it has been decided which phase this specific requirement will be delivered in. By the end of the project this item should contain a resolution for each requirement, showing how it was delivered or why it was not included, with a note saying when this was agreed and by whom. In this way the requirements catalogue provides a useful audit trail of the requests from all stakeholders and how they were ultimately resolved.

Figure 6.5 is a typical example of a requirements catalogue entry, in this case relating to the introduction of an airline's internet booking system. No detailed resolution has been recorded at this point, since, although it has been agreed to deliver this feature in Phase 1 of the development, no decision has yet been taken on the way the requirement will actually be satisfied in the final system.

Technique 58: Acceptance criteria definition

Description of the technique
Once requirements have been identified, documented and validated they will be used to drive the development and subsequent delivery of solutions. The quality of this ultimate delivery depends on a wide range of factors, one of which is the quality of the requirements themselves.

Figure 6.5 Example requirements catalogue entry

Requirement ID:	F-073
Requirement name:	Book a flight
Business area/domain:	Airline reservation system
Source:	Customer focus group
Owner:	Head of Internet Booking Services
Priority:	Must have
Stakeholders:	Airline customers, airline staff
Type of requirement:	Functional
Requirement description:	Having identified themselves as registered, customers should be able to book themselves a flight via a secure web site.
Associated non-functional requirements:	1. Access should be limited to the specific customer themselves and any authorised airline staff. 2. Ensure timely response.
Acceptance criteria:	In addition to displaying the correct flight details, the system should confirm the booking by displaying a reservation reference code and take note of the date and time that the booking was made. Response time should be within 10 seconds for 95% of transactions.
Justification:	A customer focus group stated this to be a key requirement as the airline's competitors already offer this service.
Related documents:	Minutes of focus group meeting on 12th November.
Related requirements:	Take credit card payment.
Resolution:	Due for delivery in release one of the system.
Comments:	

One key aspect of the quality of a requirement is that it is 'testable'. In addition to being used as a communication channel between the business and the development communities, requirements must also provide testers with a clear definition of what is required from them in terms of the creation of test plans and expected results. To facilitate this, it is vital that, in addition to the description of the requirements themselves, the business analyst also defines detailed acceptance criteria for each requirement. Also known as 'fit criteria' or 'test completion criteria', these acceptance criteria are absolutely vital in ensuring that the correct solution is delivered. In fact, a requirement that does not contain a clear definition of its acceptance criteria will probably need to be clarified further during testing, resulting in unnecessary reworking and extra costs.

As we will see here, acceptance criteria need to be defined in quantifiable and measurable terms for all types and levels of requirement. It is important to note that a requirement's acceptance criteria are not the same thing as the resulting test scripts and test cases, which will be produced later and against which the delivery of the requirement will ultimately be tested. The responsibility for definition of the acceptance criteria lies with the business analyst in conjunction with the organisation, while the responsibility for the development of the test scripts lies with the testers, often with support from the end user community. This leads to a clear separation of concerns between the key roles that the business analyst needs to involve. They are:

- the customer – who provides the driver for requirements, and the domain knowledge and experience;

- the developer – who fulfils the requirements, using technical knowledge and experience;

- the tester – who verifies that the system does indeed do what the customer wants it to do, as defined via the requirements.

Requirements can only form the basis for testing if they are specific, objective and measurable. The careful definition of the acceptance criteria for a requirement should ensure that the last two of these are adequately achieved. The key consideration here is to attach some form of quantification and scale of measurement to each requirement. Without this, it will not be possible to know whether the requirement has been met. Testing is only complete when these specific measurable acceptance criteria have been met. If such a mechanism for measurement cannot be identified during the development of a requirement, this is usually an indication that the requirement is not specific enough, or does not represent a single discrete requirement. If you cannot write acceptance criteria for what you are about to build, you should not be building it. The requirement and its related acceptance criteria should therefore be redefined until it becomes possible to identify such a measurement mechanism. Often the problem is that the acceptance criteria for requirements are not defined in advance, but only during development or testing, or, even worse, once the work has been done.

Using acceptance criteria definition
The acceptance criteria for requirements, used subsequently to produce detailed test plans and test data, should quantify the behaviour, the performance or some other demonstrable quality of the final end product. In order for implementation of an individual requirement to be considered acceptable, it is often necessary to meet more that one measurable criterion; this is why we use the plural, 'criteria', here. Acceptance criteria must be defined for all types of requirements (particularly functional and non-functional ones), and at the same level of granularity as the definition of the requirements themselves.

The development of acceptance criteria can clearly be linked to scenarios and storyboards (Techniques 50 and 51), and, in the case of functional requirements, use cases and use case descriptions (Technique 62). The use of scenarios particularly helps in defining the scope of a requirement along with its respective acceptance criteria. Defining the requirements and their related acceptance tests together can force earlier conversations with the users to take place, and ensure that more relevant detail is described than would be the case if one were not considering the acceptance criteria.

Even when it is not possible to allocate specific objective measures to a requirement, it is still important to try and allocate some scale of measurement that will enable the testing community to decide whether an acceptable standard has been achieved. For example, different individuals may have different interpretations of what 'an intuitive system' would look like, and it will be necessary to define a range of acceptance criteria for different groups of potential users. In some cases, where any potential criteria chosen seem very subjective, a more objective assessment may be obtained and verified by some recognised domain expert, independent accreditation body or standard piece of legislation such as the Disability Discrimination Act.

It is also necessary sometimes to extend the definition of the acceptance criteria for a specific requirement with some tolerance to allow for fluctuations in the working environment. For example, consider the following acceptance criteria for the handling of customer enquires.

> The acceptable response time shall be no more than 3 seconds for 90 per cent of enquiries and no more than 5 seconds for the remainder.

The more detail provided and care taken where defining acceptance criteria, the more likely will be success in producing a quality implementation, and the less likely is confusion to occur during testing.

In addition to the clear definition of acceptance criteria for functional requirements, driven by discussions with business stakeholders and the use of scenarios, it is also important to define acceptance criteria for each individual non-functional requirement attached to the functional requirements, to ensure that the operation of the delivered solution achieves the required standard in terms of performance, availability, security, robustness and usability. In particular, definition of acceptance criteria in the tricky area of usability can be made more measurable by applying the acronym PLUME, which stands for measures of:

Productivity: how long various tasks take to accomplish in a given time;

Learnability: how much training is needed in order to achieve a specified level of proficiency when undertaking a task;

User satisfaction: subjective responses a user has to the system when asked;

Memorability: how robust the learning about the system use is, and how long ability to use it is retained without retraining;

Error rates: accuracy in carrying out the task (this measure is particularly useful in conjunction with the productivity measures set).

As discussed earlier, a requirement which is not supported by well-defined acceptance criteria is likely to cause problems of communication, resulting in delays, omissions and inaccuracies in the delivered solution – so much so that a school of thought is emerging that the acceptance criteria definition is even more important that the definition of the requirement itself. This has manifested itself in some of the Agile approaches to development by the replacement of requirements-based testing with test-driven requirements. In this situation the emphasis on communication with testers focuses on the detailed definition of the acceptance criteria that must be met, and it is these that are used to drive the development of test plans and test scripts, rather than the actual requirements themselves. While this approach certainly has many merits, the optimum strategy is to follow best practice both in the definition and documentation of requirements and in the development of their respective acceptance criteria. This builds an important bridge between the disciplines of requirements engineering and testing, resulting in the more effective delivery of quality solutions to business problems.

Technique 59: Requirements validation

Description of the technique

Once requirements have been documented various checks need to be made, to ensure that the quality of these requirements is as high as possible. This is true for the individual requirements as they are identified and developed, and also when the set of requirements is complete enough to be passed forward to later stages of development. This section focuses on a range of these checks that can be made on the requirements, rather than any subsequent testing of the solution that is derived from them.

Before looking at the range of techniques that can be employed to improve the quality of requirements, it is worth examining the difference between the terms 'verification' and 'validation'. We define them as follows.

Requirements verification:	ensures that the requirements definitions and any supporting models meet the standard necessary to allow them to be used effectively to guide further work. Verification ensures that the requirements have been defined correctly. It constitutes any checks undertaken by the business analyst and other key stakeholders that determine whether the requirements are ready for subsequent formal review by customers and end users, and provide all the information needed for any further work to be undertaken based on them. In other words, verification ensures that **things are done right**.
Requirements validation:	ensures that all requirements support the delivery of value to the business, fulfil its goals and objectives, and meet stakeholder needs. In other words, validation ensures that the **right things are done**.

Obviously it is as bad to build the wrong thing right as it is to build the right thing wrongly. The guidance provided here helps to ensure that the right thing is built right, not just in terms of the requirements themselves, but more importantly in term of the ultimate solutions delivered as a result of these requirements. Without this there is of course even the possibility that we end up building the wrong thing wrongly.

Using requirements validation

In order to achieve quality in requirements definition by the application of both verification and validation techniques we need to consider all of the points listed in Table 6.5.

Table 6.5 Considerations for verification and validation

	What to check against	Techniques for carrying out checks
Verification	Quality criteria for a good requirement	Static testing (peer group reviews, walkthroughs, technical reviews, inspections) Feasibility checking
Validation	Business objectives and stakeholder goals and measures that the solution is meant to deliver	Static testing (peer group reviews, walkthroughs, technical reviews, inspections) Necessity checking Metrics and KPIs Scenarios and prototyping Stakeholder sign-offs

As Table 6.5 suggests, before we can employ the various techniques for undertaking both verification and validation we should be aware of the criteria against which the requirements need to be evaluated. This includes not only an understanding in principle of what constitutes a well-defined requirement, but also a clear view on which customer objectives need to be met.

When looking at what makes a good requirement, it always worth keeping in mind that different stakeholder groups will have different perspectives on what is important in the definition of a requirement. For example, some stakeholders have more interest in whether the requirements are defined according to local standards, whereas others are more interested in consistency across the requirement set. Since all these different views need to be incorporated into any verification checks, we will describe them all here. Here are the main characteristics against which individual requirements and sets of requirements can be checked in order to achieve quality. They should be:

- unambiguous;
- clear and understandable;
- cohesive;
- consistent;
- conformant;
- current;
- modifiable;
- traceable;
- relevant;

- unique;
- categorised;
- complete;
- correct;
- concise;
- testable;
- implementation independent;
- owned;
- feasible.

In more detail, requirements should be:

Unambiguous:	Each of them should have just one possible interpretation. Ambiguity is very dangerous in requirements, since it leads, at the best, to confusion, and, at the worst, to the wrong thing being built. It is also a potent source of disputes between analysts, developers and business stakeholders as to what was really wanted.
Unique:	Is the requirement unique, or does it overlap with other requirements?
Clear and understandable:	Requirements are useless unless they can be understood by all those who have to read them, but this can include people from a variety of backgrounds with different types and levels of knowledge and experience. The end users of the proposed system will possess business knowledge but not necessarily technical expertise, whereas developers may be in the reverse situation.
Categorised:	Has the requirements catalogue been correctly partitioned by type of requirement, and has each type of requirement been addressed (in other words, has any key category of requirement been overlooked)?
Cohesive:	While a specific requirement should relate to only one thing, all requirements in a set should support the overall purpose and scope.
Complete:	In some ways this is the most difficult characteristic to satisfy, since omissions from requirements are hard to spot. The chances of finding omissions are improved by getting several 'pairs of eyes' to examine the requirements. Techniques such as the development of a CRUD matrix (create, read, update and delete – Technique 65) can be particularly helpful in ensuring completeness.

Consistent: Consistency has a number of aspects in relation to requirements:

- Individual requirements must be internally consistent, or in other words must not have inherent contradictions (for example, 'available to all' and 'restricted access').

- Requirements must not contradict each other.

- Terminology must be used consistently (for example, the term 'customer' means the same thing in all requirements).

Correct: In a way, if positive answers can be given to all of the above characteristics, then the requirements can be considered correct. However, there is another issue of correctness here – do the requirements capture the essence of the problem or issue to be addressed? One approach to checking this is to make sure that it is requirements and not specific solutions that have been captured.

Conformant: It is desirable to have a standard format for the way in which requirements are documented and presented. Although standard formats can sometimes be seen as a straitjacket and not exactly suitable for all requirements, the benefits of following a standard are considerable and usually outweigh any disadvantages. Advantages include:

- Individuals gathering requirements do not waste time devising their own formats.

- Reviewers of the requirements documentation know where to find things.

- Those charged with devising and delivering solutions based on the requirements have them presented in a standardised format, making them easier to understand.

Concise: Subject to the need to be as precise and accurate as possible, it is also desirable to express requirements as concisely as possible. Over-wordy requirements descriptions are hard to read, and make it difficult for readers to grasp the important and essential points.

As well as the need for conciseness in individual requirements, it is important that there is no redundancy when considering the set as a whole. Redundant requirements tend to obscure what is important, and may contradict what is written elsewhere about the same business issue. So some general characteristics to be observed include the need for them to be:

Current: The requirements should not have been made obsolete by the passage of time.

Testable: An important use of the set of requirements, once a system has been developed, is in testing the system. However, requirements can only form the basis for testing if they are specific, objective and measurable. There must be a clear definition of how it is to be proved that the requirement has been successfully fulfilled.

Modifiable: Related requirements must be uniquely identified and grouped together in a standard way, in order to be modifiable. This criterion can be satisfied by clustering requirements logically and keeping careful track of versions.

Implementation independent: The requirement should state what is required, not how it should be provided, and should not reflect a particular design or implementation. There may be exceptions to this rule, for instance in the area of interface requirements, or because of other constraints. This characteristic of requirements is perhaps the hardest to judge and to implement.

Traceable: It is often necessary for people studying a set of requirements to get more information about them by studying source documentation (such as interview notes or meeting minutes). This can be particularly useful when maintaining and supporting a system after implementation. Each atomic requirement should be identified unambiguously, sources of requirements must be recorded, and cross references between requirements must be in place.

Owned: Has a specific stakeholder been assigned ownership of the requirement for the purpose of sign-off (of both the requirement and the ultimate solution delivered in response to the requirement)?

Relevant: It is important that all requirements really are within the scope of the project, and that their inclusion does not lead to 'scope creep'. It is also possible that some requirements, though within scope, do not add to the overall understanding of the business need.

Feasible: Each requirement must be capable of being implemented within any defined constraints such as budget, timescales and resources available.

In addition to these checks, which are primarily for verification purposes, some form of necessity, priority and objective checking will needed when undertaking validation prior to any form of sign-off or agreement to move forward.

One of the most important kinds of check is that of necessity. This involves performing a critical appraisal of each requirement in order to determine whether it genuinely addresses a real business need, and is relevant to objectives of the current project or programme. As the name suggests, necessity checking focuses on determining the level of actual need for a requirement. This is different from feasibility checking, which is concerned with ascertaining whether a requirement can actually be achieved in business, financial and technical terms. Necessity can be assessed in terms of three key aspects of each individual requirement or aggregated set of requirements:

- contributing to defined business goals;
- addressing the cause rather than the symptoms of a problem;
- being a real need rather than just a wish.

Enterprises invest in IT in order to achieve some business advantage, and it is vital to examine requirements with respect to business goals and organisational objectives. Any requirements which do not contribute towards the achievement of these should be at least questioned if not removed.

Having a set of defined criteria against which to check quality is not enough. The business analyst needs to select the most appropriate technique to use when undertaking the actual verification or validation checks. There are four main types of static testing techniques (that is, excluding prototyping and actual testing of the ultimate solution) that can be employed to undertake these quality checks. They vary in terms of those involved in the process and their level of formality. They are:

- peer reviews and desk checking;
- walkthroughs;
- technical reviews;
- inspections.

Peer reviews and desk checking:	These are similar in execution, the difference being that an element of software code is desk checked, whereas a document or model is peer reviewed. The purpose of the peer review is to identify defects and omissions, not to provide solutions to the problems – although suggestions may be given. The desk check is used to identify logic errors or omissions in code, not to provide solutions to the problems – although, again, suggestions may be provided. The peer review is usually an informal review of a document or model. No formal documentation, fault log or analysis is produced. Usually the original document is just marked up and returned to the author. The effectiveness of such reviews depends upon the motivation of the reviewers and their willingness to find a significant number of faults. They should have a skill level appropriate to the document being reviewed. A person with programming skills would review code; a business analyst would review a requirements specification.

Walkthroughs: The main purpose of a walkthrough is to impart information to others. It can be used as part of the learning process for a team. Participants at the walkthrough may be able to offer some valuable input, but they are usually less familiar with the subject than the presenter is. Walkthroughs are led by the author, and the document under discussion may be marked up and reworked after the walkthrough has taken place. In some walkthroughs the document being discussed is circulated in advance. In others it is presented for the first time at the meeting, and only the presenter is familiar with its content and structure.

Technical reviews: A technical review is used to subject a document or model to intense scrutiny with the objective of improving its quality or solving the problem it is addressing. For example, the design of a website may be subject to a technical review in which the proposed design is circulated in advance, and participants are asked to find faults and omissions in the design as well as making suggestions for its improvement. The technical review is a relatively formal process, generating records of faults found and recording actions to be taken. It is usually led by a chairperson who attempts to build a solution out of the contributions made by the participants. It is not purely a fault-finding activity, and can therefore be used to develop solutions rather than just evaluate current proposals.

Inspections: An inspection is a more formal static testing method. It follows a defined process based on rules and checklists, which includes both entry and exit criteria. If a document does not meet these entry criteria then the inspection does not take place. The document will only be released when it passes the exit criteria. Metrics are collected and are used to improve the documents as well as the processes by which those documents are produced and reviewed. The main purpose of the inspection is to find defects. It is a true testing activity.

Once all of the various checking (both verification and validation) and reviewing techniques discussed here have been employed, the formality of sign-offs or quality gateways for requirements is likely to be a less arduous process, and the quality of the requirements defined and the solutions that are subsequently derived from them will be significantly higher.

Technique 60: Requirements management

Description of the technique
Requirements management is primarily concerned with the control of changes to requirements. Throughout the time when requirements are being defined, and

also the period after the requirements set has been baselined, it is important to have a formal mechanism for their control, authorisation and management. This can include managing their development, maintaining consistency with other documents and models, handling changes as they occur, communicating changes to those concerned, and ensuring that correct versions are referred to at all times. While this is true of any configuration item that needs to be managed, it is particularly true of requirements, due to the iterative nature of their development and the fact that changes to them are inevitable, given the volatile nature of business, financial and technical drivers. Organisations are not static; they undergo constant change in order to deal with new situations and to respond to new threats and opportunities. Change itself is not a bad thing, but uncontrolled change will be very detrimental to the delivery of quality solutions and will lead to unmanageable scope creep.

The changes in requirements that may need to be reflected in order to ensure a good quality of requirements definition include:

- new laws and regulations;
- the results of more detailed investigation;
- new ideas;
- new people and changes in stakeholder objectives;
- new technology;
- changes in other systems and processes.

Configuration management is concerned with identifying and distinguishing between different versions of the various requirements documents, controlling any changes made to these and managing the way the various versions are grouped together to form a particular set. This discipline applies direction and control to the definition of requirements for the purpose of controlling change, and hence maintaining their integrity and traceability throughout the development. If this level of requirements configuration management is not applied, various problems can occur, including:

- difficulties in identifying the most current version of requirements;
- difficulties in replicating any previously reviewed version of requirements;
- the reappearance of errors and omissions that had previously been dealt with;
- testing or even building a solution from a wrong or incomplete version of the requirements.

Without an effective approach to requirements management, all of these issues are likely to occur and to influence the ultimate quality of the solution. In addition to managing the requirements in this way, it is also essential to apply the same levels of control and management to any supporting documentation and models.

A number of elements of the technique of requirements management need to be considered, including:

- baselining;
- configuration identification;
- planning which configuration items should be used;
- naming conventions;
- version and issue numbering rules;
- configuration control;
- version control;
- problem and issue reporting;
- change control.

Baselining: Much of what has been discussed in this section on requirements definition has focused on eliciting, analysing and documenting requirements in an effective way. However, there will come a point at which the focus will start to move towards the delivery of solutions based on these. This may be from the full set of requirements in a waterfall approach, or on a prioritised subset when a more Agile development approach is being taken. In both cases, the focus now becomes more one of formalised control in reaction to change than one of actively searching for new requirements. At the point when this transition of focus takes place, the requirements need to be baselined. After this a different set of values will be used when evaluating what to do when new requirements are identified or existing ones extended or amended. Once this change has happened the main focus moves from elicitation, analysis and documentation towards configuration and change control, version control and ensuring traceability. It is vital, however, to ensure that new requirements agreed after this point are still analysed, documented, verified and validated as rigorously as those introduced before the baseline point had occurred. After baselining the level of formality attached to requirements management will vary greatly, depending on the approach taken to development, the culture of the organisation and the software tools available to evaluate the impact of proposed change.

Configuration identification: This component of requirements management is concerned with the initial planning undertaken before change control procedures are implemented. It involves a range of activities, including:

- Decisions as to which deliverables need to be the target of configuration and version control. These configuration items would normally include the individual requirements themselves, the overall requirements priority list and any supporting models and documentation. It is also important to ensure that some form of requirements traceability matrix or product breakdown structure is used to maintain consistency between individual configuration items.

- Agreement as to the naming and numbering conventions to be used for each configuration item, and as to who has the authority to change version numbers either forwards, or, perhaps more contentiously, backwards. This is particularly significant in an Agile development environment, where ideas may be tried out via prototypes but there will remain a need for all changes to be reversible. This is impossible to achieve if good configuration management procedures are not in place and adhered to.

- Decisions about the level at which version numbers and change control apply. Should this be at the level of the requirements specification itself, a subset of the requirements catalogue or each individual requirement within this?

- Decisions as to what level of history of changes needs to be maintained, and to whom this is to be circulated each time a change is made.

Configuration control:

Once the configuration items and their groupings have been agreed, the mechanisms for actual requirements configuration and control must be defined. This control is applied to all configuration items, to ensure that only the correct and current versions are used during the remainder of the development. This element of requirements management includes:

- The implementation of a controlled area to set up a library of configuration items, and the allocation of specific levels of responsibility to particular roles and individuals, with items only being accessible by the person responsible for their area, and any changes only permitted within the constraints of this defined procedure.

- Control of defects or error reporting. Any problems identified with configuration items will be reported to the librarian, so that each problem can be investigated, and appropriate action taken, in a controlled manner.

- The definition and implementation of a formal change control process. This includes impact analysis, decision-making and the change implementation itself.

- Ensuring that everyone is working on the correct version of any item. At all stages of any piece of work this is vital. To achieve it, any changes made must be controlled, so that it is always possible to identify the latest version. In turn, this means that any changes are only made to these latest versions (thereby avoiding the problem of reintroducing errors that have been corrected previously).

Using requirements management

Proposed changes should not be seen as problems, but rather as further opportunities to ensure that the best and most appropriate solution is delivered as often as possible. What gets projects into trouble is the making of change in an uncontrolled way. Once baselining has taken place, changes need to follow a formal change control process. While this process will vary from one organisation to another, it will normally be based on the following four-stage structure:

- As part of the requirements configuration management system, the responsibilities for reviewing and authorising changes must be established so that everyone concerned understands them. The change control process is documented in the requirements management plan produced at the start of the analysis. The level of rigour required in this may vary from project to project and should therefore be carefully considered, agreed and communicated from the outset.

- Whenever a change is proposed, it should be documented fully on a change request form of some sort. As a minimum, this should document who raised the change, a brief description of the change and a justification for requesting it.

- For each of these change requests, a full assessment should be made of the impact of the proposed change, particularly in terms of costs, benefits and effort.

- The change should be reviewed by the designated approval authority. There are then three possible outcomes to the request:

  - the proposed change is approved;

  - the proposed change is rejected;

  - final consideration of the change is deferred until later, perhaps until a later phase or perhaps within the current phase but with a lower priority.

If the change has been approved for implementation, the configuration item is then released by whoever is deemed responsible, and all interested parties are notified, so that the change can be applied.

Configuration management in an Agile environment

The issue of configuration management needs particular consideration when an Agile development approach such as DSDM/Atern or Scrum is being used. This is because, with the dynamic and fast-changing nature of these methods, it is too easy for the traditional configuration management regimes to be forgotten, resulting in much wasted effort, and, potentially, in the delivery of a solution that is hard to enhance and maintain.

DSDM/Atern offers some useful advice on how configuration management can be operated in an Agile environment, and the starting point is deciding on the frequency at which changes should be baselined. The possibilities include:

- baselining every prototype before demonstration – which has the virtue of clarity as regards what has actually been seen by the users;

- baselining daily, which is highly disciplined but can prove onerous, and does not necessarily add much value;

- baselining software items once they have been unit tested – which is perhaps the most practical and realistic approach;

- baselining at the end of a timebox. This is probably fine if the timeboxes themselves are very short (a few days, perhaps) but less sensible with longer ones, or, for example, the 30-day 'sprints' used within Scrum.

The selection of the level of items to choose as configuration items is also very relevant. With a lot of development going on in parallel it is probable that lower-level items will need to be managed individually, but this will naturally create an additional burden later when the whole system is brought together.

The obvious targets for the application of configuration management in this environment are the prioritised requirements list and the prototypes that are developed from this by users and developers jointly. At the end of each prototyping cycle the prototype is placed under configuration control; this is the equivalent of it being signed off in more traditional approaches. This control will consist of logging the version of the actual prototype, the tests run on it and the record of the users' feedback and comments. Thus, as the prototypes are developed and refined, a complete audit trail is created of the changes made, and, very importantly, the reasons why they were made.

The high-level requirements, which should be relatively stable compared with the ever-changing prototypes, should be baselined quite early in the development project. They too may change of course, since the very process of prototyping is likely to give rise to further requirements, which will ensure that the prototype evolves iteratively towards the final solution. But at least these changes will be handled in a managed way, and this will ensure that the Agile approach will not lead to a development that spirals out of control.

Technique 61: Requirements traceability matrix

Description of the technique
The Requirements Traceability Matrix is a document which helps ensure that a project's scope, requirements, and deliverables remain consistent with each other when compared with the baseline. Thus, it traces the deliverables by establishing a thread for each requirement, from the project's initiation through to the final implementation.

The requirements traceability matrix can be used to:

- enable backward tracking of requirements to identify the source of each of them, to support clarification, change control and adjustment of their priorities – particularly important when requirements are in conflict;

- track all requirements and whether or not they are being met by the subsequent solution – achieved by providing a forward trace to identify what happens to a requirement throughout the rest of the solution development lifecycle, including design, build and test;

- assist in the creation of the requirements management plan and test scripts;
- cross reference each requirement to supporting models such as use cases and use case descriptions;
- help ensure that all requirements have been met during verification;
- help evaluate impacts when changes are proposed.

Using the requirements traceability matrix

The requirements traceability matrix should be initiated at the very beginning of a project because it forms the basis of the project's scope and incorporates the specific requirements and deliverables that will be produced. It should always be bidirectional in that it tracks the requirements 'forwards' by examining the development of the solution deliverables and 'backwards' by looking at the business requirement that was specified for a particular feature of the solution. The matrix is also used to verify that all requirements are met, and to identify and evaluate changes to the scope as and when they occur. It can also be thought of as a technique for documenting the connection and interrelationships between the requirements themselves and the ultimate solution delivered.

A traceability matrix is created by documenting the association between the individual requirements (using the unique requirements identifier) and other work products, such as the requirements catalogue itself, elements of the developing solution, test plans and test scripts. In some instances the requirements traceability matrix can also display a cross reference between the various types of requirement and between requirements and the benefits actually realised.

Figure 6.6 Links between requirements and other development elements

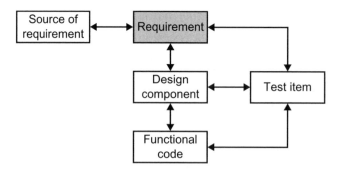

In practice a requirements traceability matrix can be as simple or as complex as required. The more complex its structure the more useful reporting may be possible, but the harder it will be to maintain throughout the lifecycle. In effect the matrix itself is a report generated from the requirements database or repository, driven by the elements contained in the requirements catalogue. The typical content of a requirements traceability matrix might be:

- requirement identifier;
- requirement description;
- use case;
- solution module;
- test type;
- test case reference;
- test result.

The following steps provide a simple approach to the development of a requirements traceability matrix:

1. Create a standard template for the content of the matrix. This ensures a consistent and logical format and will support sponsors and decision-makers.

2. Populate the template with data from the requirements catalogue and supporting documentation.

3. As requirements development and modelling progresses, cross reference the requirements in the matrix to other models and solution components as they are produced. This is particularly helpful when use cases are being employed. The matrix can then be used to demonstrate the many-to-many relationship between the business requirements and their respective use cases.

4. Insert a reference to test data into the requirements traceability matrix. The matrix can then be used to account for the different type of tests undertaken throughout the lifecycle. It should clearly indicate the specific test type, the date tests were undertaken and the outcome of each test.

REQUIREMENTS MODELLING

Technique 62: Use case diagrams and use case descriptions

Description of the technique
The concept of a use case
A use case is a unit of functionality in a system – a 'case of use', or something the users want to do with or through their system. In general this refers to an IT system, but use cases can also be developed at the business level, where they define something the business system (as opposed to the IT system) is required to do. However, since use cases are mainly employed to define IT systems, we shall concentrate on the IT system level here. If we think, for example, of a payroll system, then its users will probably want to do things like 'Add employee', 'Update employee', 'Update employee grade' or 'Uplift all salaries to reflect pay increase'. Each of these is a use case.

Depending on the amount of detail we need about the use cases, they can be defined as use case diagrams or as use case descriptions, or both – diagrams supported by use case descriptions. Some authorities, for example Alistair Cockburn (2001), are actually quite sniffy about use case diagrams and consider that only the detailed use case description actually properly defines a use case. We understand their point, but have found the diagrams to be too useful a tool for user communication to ignore; we will expand on this further under 'Using use cases and use case descriptions' later in this section.

Use case diagrams

Figure 6.7 illustrates the basic elements of a use case diagram.

Figure 6.7 Basic elements of a use case diagram

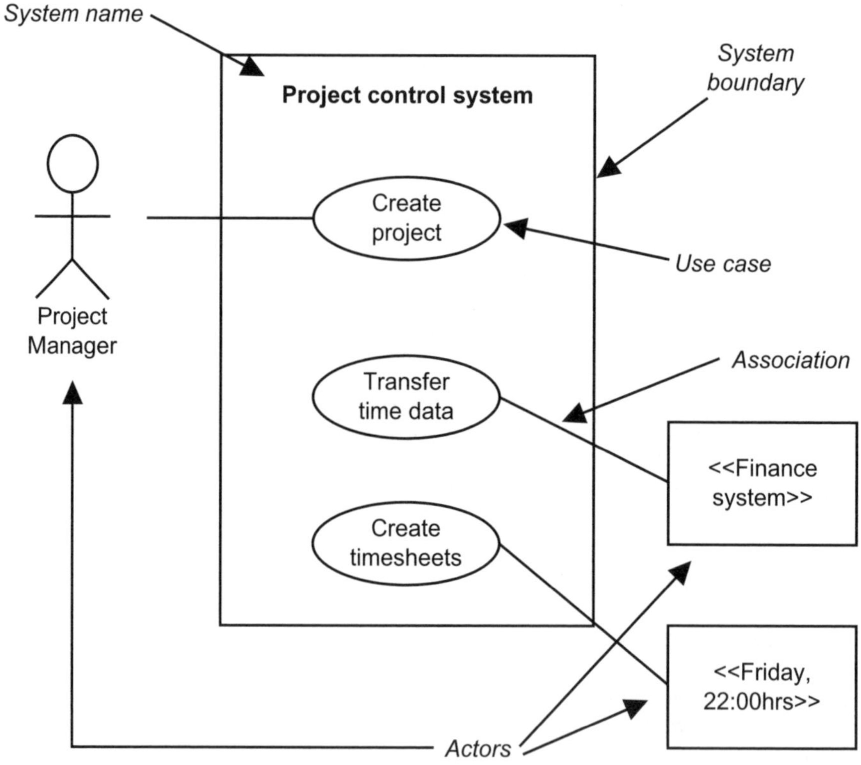

The six basic elements of a use case are:

System boundary: A box indicates the boundary of the system we are defining.

System name: This identifies the system we are defining.

Actor: An actor is someone – or something – that has an interaction with our system. The most obvious actors are people, and we define them in terms of user roles, like the project manager shown here. However, actors can also be other systems, and time can also be an actor, because some things a system does are triggered by time. User roles are usually shown using 'matchstick people', while other systems and time can be shown using a small box.

Use case: This is the piece of functionality, or system feature, that is used by an actor.

Association: The line between an actor and a use case shows that this actor has an interaction with this use case. Notice that the association line does not have an arrow head at either end, because it does not indicate a flow of data, merely that the actor interacts with the system via this use case.

Figure 6.8 is an extended model of the system shown in Figure 6.7. It contains more actors, use cases and associations and introduces some additional notation.

Figure 6.8 Additional use case notation

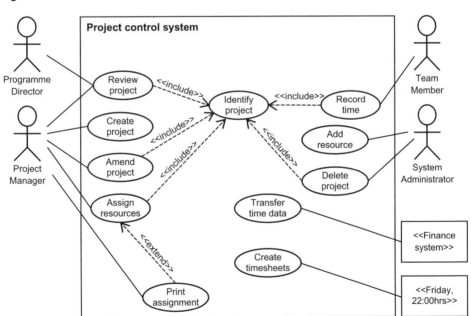

The additional concepts introduced in Figure 6.8 are:

<<include>>   Sometimes one use case can incorporate another, or, putting it another way, a particular system function can be incorporated into other functions. In Figure 6.8 the use cases 'Review project', 'Amend project', 'Delete project' and 'Record time' all start the same way – by identifying which project is involved. We have thus identified the existence of some common functionality, which we have called 'Identify project', and this is included within each of these use cases. The point of this is first to identify possible areas where functionality can be developed once and then reused within our system, and, later, to simplify the writing of use case descriptions. It is important to understand that an included use case is an essential part of the calling use case, which cannot operate without it. Note, too, that the arrowed dotted line points towards the use case that is included.

<<extend>>   After finishing the use case 'Assign resources', the Programme Director has the option of invoking the use case 'Print assignment'. 'Print assignment' is thus said to extend 'Assign resources'. Note that the arrowed dotted line points from the extending use case.

People are often initially confused by the <<include>> and <<extend>> concepts, but it is actually quite easy to distinguish between them – included use cases are mandatory, and extending use cases are optional as far as the calling use case is concerned.

Another thing to note about a use case diagram is that some business rules and non-functional requirements about system access can be deduced from it. In Figure 6.8, for example, it is clear that the ability to 'Delete project' is restricted to the System Administrator only.

Finally, in Figure 6.8 we have not shown an association between Project Manager and 'Record time'. This is because, when they are recording their time, Project Managers are acting in the **role** of team members, and it is roles that are represented by the actors on the use case diagram.

Use case descriptions
The use case diagram provides a simple, accessible visual representation of the interactions between actors and a proposed information system. But they lack detail and do not document how the interaction will work. For this detail we need to create use case descriptions, and, as we have mentioned before, authorities like Alistair Cockburn assert that these are the true use cases.

One way of understanding a use case description is to think of it as the record of a tennis match. On one side of the net is the actor and on the other is the system, and the use case description records how the ball passes backwards and forwards between them. Figure 6.9 is an example of a use case description; it describes 'Assign resources' from Figure 6.8.

The following are the entries in the use case description:

Use case, scope   These identify the use case, the system within which it
and primary   operates and the actors that will interact with it.
actors:

Preconditions:	These describe the state the system is in and what must have happened previously before this use case begins.
Trigger/event:	This states what causes the use case to be started.
Success guarantee:	Here is recorded what a fully successful outcome to the use case would be.
Minimal guarantee:	Optionally we may record here what we might settle for if a completely successful outcome cannot be achieved.
Stakeholders:	These are the people, or user roles, that have an interest in the outcome of the use case. We can, if we wish, also record what their interest is (the Accounts Department, for instance, might want accurate information about who is assigned to which projects.
Main success scenario:	Now we describe the tennis match – the inputs from the actor and the responses from the system. In this case we first list the 'happy day' scenario – what should normally happen. Notice in Figure 6.9 that the first thing the Project Manager does is to invoke the included use case 'Identify project'; this is indicated here by underlining the name of the included use case.
Extensions:	Here possible departures from the 'happy day' scenario, and what should be done in response to them, are described. 'Extensions' in a use case description are therefore actually exceptions to the normal situation. At the end of the use case in Figure 6.9 we have recorded the extension use case 'Print assignment', which the project manager can optionally invoke, and we again show that we are referring to another use case by underlining its name.

Obviously, real use case descriptions can get a lot more complex than this relatively simple example, and we have some observations about that below.

Using use cases and use case descriptions

While we would agree with authors such as Alistair Cockburn that use case diagrams are very simple (one might even say simplistic), that is one of the reasons we find them so useful. Diagrams have been used for years as a way of simplifying and clarifying discussions between business users and IT specialists, and use case diagrams fulfil this role very well. They do not show much detail, but they do allow business analysts and users to establish the scope of the system – what its main functions will be and who will have access to them. The use of the <<extend>> construct enables us to identify optional functions, but we are not so sure about the use of <<include>> in business analysis, since the decision to 'hive off' parts of a function into a common function is more likely to emerge during the technical design of the system. Still, if the business analysts do spot some reusable functionality at this stage, there is certainly no harm in recording it for later.

Figure 6.9 Use case description for 'Assign resources'

Use case	Assign resources
Scope	Project control system
Primary actor(s)	Project Manager
Preconditions	Project Manager has logged on to system; project has already been set up; no staff or some staff have already been assigned the project.
Trigger/event	Project Manager informed of staff assignment
Success guarantee	At least some staff assigned to the project
Minimal guarantee	Staff already assigned elsewhere and not available; no change to this project
Stakeholder(s)	Project Manager; Programme Director; Accounts Department

Main success scenario:

1. Project Manager(PM) uses Identify project.
2. System displays project details.
3. PM confirms project is correct.
4. PM enters surname of member of staff.
5. System displays staff details including employee number.
6. PM enters assignment start date.
7. System confirms that assignment start date is valid.
8. PM enters assignment end date.
9. System confirms that assignment end date is valid.
10. PM enters availability of staff member to project (% age or days per week).
11. System confirms that staff member is available as entered.
12. PM assigns staff member to specific task(s).
13. System confirms staff member's assignment to specific task(s).
14. PM confirms staff member's assignment.
15. Steps 4–14 repeated for further resources.

Extensions:

5a. System does not find staff name.
    5a1. 'No such name' message displayed. List of similarly-spelled names displayed.
    5a2. PM enters different name (possibly from list offered).
7a. System finds that assignment start date is invalid (completely invalid date or date over a weekend or before start of project).
    7a1. 'Date invalid' message displayed.
    7a2. PM enters revised assignment start date.
9a. System finds that assignment end date is invalid (complete invalid date or date over a weekend or before assignment start date).
    9a1. 'Date invalid' message displayed.
    9a2. PM enters revised assignment end date.
11a. System finds that proposed assignment, when added to existing commitments, exceeds staff member's available hours per week.
    11a1. Message 'Staff member overloaded', with %age or days per week overload displayed.
    11a2. PM revises assignment or overrides overload message.
15a. PM may Print assignment.

As to the use case description, the technique works fine as long as there are not too many extensions, and, particularly, no 'nested' extensions (in other words, extensions within extensions). The trouble with these complex use case descriptions is that they can become difficult for the business users to understand (and even for the business analysts to explain), and this difficulty rather defeats the objective of providing a clear and unambiguous means of communication between the parties.

It should be noted, though, that although this form of use case description has gained widespread acceptance in recent years, it is not the only way in which the details of a use case could be documented. For example, where there are lots of alternative paths through a use case, or complex combinations of circumstances to consider, an activity diagram (see business process modelling, Technique 37) or a decision table or decision tree (Technique 39) might prove more effective. Readers are directed to Chapter 4, where these techniques are described.

Technique 63: Entity relationship modelling
Variants/Aliases
Variant names include **entity relationship diagrams (ERDs)** and **logical data modelling/models (LDM)**.

Description of the technique
An entity relationship model (ERM) is a conceptual representation of the main data items (entities) used within an organisation and/or to be held in a computer system, and of the business rules that govern the relationships between these entities. Creating an ERM offers some significant benefits to a BA, including a better understanding of the data that is used within the organisation and may need to be stored and manipulated within a computer system, and a stronger grasp of the business rules that govern the creation, use and deletion of data by the organisation.

Some business analysts shy away from data modelling, thinking that it belongs more to the work of systems analysts and developers, but we do not think this attitude is correct. The BA is the person with the close relationship with the business, and so is in a much better position than developers to understand the data and how it is used.

(Various notations have been proposed and used over the years for building data models. In this book we have used a notation that has become more or less the default standard in the UK, and is derived from the Structured Systems Analysis and Design Method, SSADM.)

The concept of entities
As the name of this technique suggests, entity relationship models have two fundamental components – entities and relationships. An entity is 'something of interest to the system, about which data is to be held'. Entities can be:

- physical – a car, a room or a building, for example;
- conceptual – a car body type, a room's total capacity or a building's style;
- active – a car service, usage of a room or a council tax year.

211

Entities are represented by boxes ('soft' boxes in this notation) with nouns as names, as shown in Figure 6.10.

Figure 6.10 Examples of entities

We need to distinguish between the entity that is shown on an ERM and individual occurrences of that entity. For example, a garage will probably have many technicians and will look after many cars. The ERM is a **generalised** model that represents all occurrences of the entity.

Relationships between entities
Entities are related to (have connections or associations with) other entities, as shown for example in Figure 6.11.

Figure 6.11 One-to-many relationship between entities

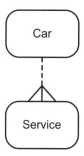

Figure 6.11 shows that one instance of Car can have a relationship with many instances of Service. The 'crow's foot' indicates the 'cardinality', or degree, of the relationship.

As well as cardinality, we can also indicate on our model whether the relationship is an optional one, as in Figure 6.12.

Figure 6.12 tells us that a Service must be associated with a Car but a Car does not have to have a Service associated with it; the relationship is said to be optional. If we think about this, it is obviously true, since a new car might not yet have been serviced.

Figure 6.12 Optional relationship

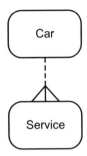

If we think about the relationship between Car and Service a bit more, though, we will realise that their relationship is actually more like a many-to-many one, as shown in Figure 6.13.

Figure 6.13 Many-to-many relationship

Figure 6.13 tells us that a particular Service (say the 20,000-mile major service) will be carried out on many Cars, whereas a particular Car will have many instances of Service over its life. Many-to-many relationships are not permitted on ERMs because they make it logically impossible to link a specific instance of one entity with a specific instance of the other one. So many-to-many relationships have to be 'resolved' into two one-to-many relationships through the insertion of what is called a 'link entity', as shown in Figure 6.14.

Figure 6.14 Resolved many-to-many relationship

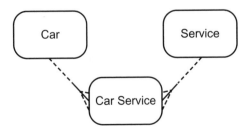

Figure 6.14 now shows a new entity, our 'link entity' called Car Service. If we read this small data model, we learn that it is possible for a Car to have many Car Services associated with it (as the relationship at the Car end is optional), and a Service may have been carried out on a specific car as a Car Service. The optional relationship here is caused by the fact that a particular Service may not yet have been performed on any car. Notice, though, that at the Car Service end of these relationships they are mandatory; after all, a Car Service cannot be carried out without a Car!

Figure 6.15 extends our model by considering how the entity Technician fits in.

Figure 6.15 Extended data model

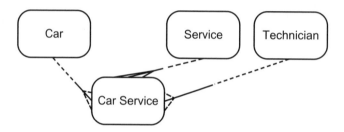

The relationship between Technician and Service and that between Technician and Car are also of the many-to-many type, and can be resolved through the link entity, Car Service, that already exists.

Sometimes a situation arises where an entity can have a relationship with itself. For example, in an HR system most employees (except the very top boss) will have a manager and many employees (except those at the bottom of the hierarchy) may have subordinates. Thus occurrences of the entity Employee will have a relationship with other occurrences. This is called a recursive relationship, and is shown in Figure 6.16.

Figure 6.16 Recursive relationship

The recursive relationship (also known, for obvious reasons, as a 'pig's ear'!) in Figure 6.16 is shown as fully optional because, as we have seen, the person at the top has no superior and the person at the bottom has no subordinates; and the ERM must cater for all possible occurrences of the entity.

The recursive relationship shown in Figure 6.16 is of the order one-to-many, but can many-to-many relationships also exist in this situation? The answer is 'yes'. Consider the situation where a component is made up of other components and is itself part of yet another component. This can be represented by what is known as a 'bill of materials' structure, shown in Figure 6.17.

Figure 6.17 Many-to-many recursive relationship

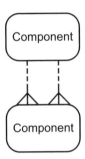

Finally, some relationships are 'exclusive': that is, an entity can participate in one or another but not both. Consider the situation modelled in Figure 6.18.

Figure 6.18 Exclusive relationship

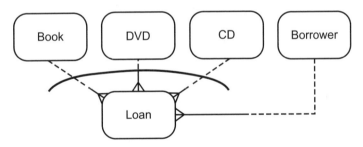

Figure 6.18 shows part of a library system, where a Loan can be for a Book, a DVD or a CD but not more than one of these. The arc across these three relationships with Loan indicates that they are mutually exclusive.

In Figure 6.18 the relationships that are mutually exclusive are handily next to one other, which makes drawing the arc easy. Figure 6.19 shows how we would handle the situation where an entity – in this case Borrower – is between the two exclusive relationships but is not itself part of the exclusivity. We show partial arcs and link them by the identifying letter 'a'.

215

Figure 6.19 Separated exclusive relationship

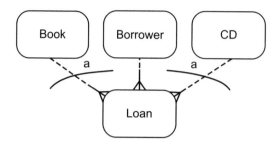

Finally, it is customary to name the relationships on the ERM in order to explain what they are about. An example of this is shown in Figure 6.20.

Figure 6.20 Named relationships

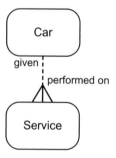

In the SSADM notation we have been using, relationships have a standard syntax, as follows:

Each   *[Entity 1]*   <u>may be</u>   *[link phrase]*   <u>one and only one</u>   *[Entity 2]*

                       must be   one or many

So, reading the relationships in Figure 6.20, we get:

- Each Car may be given one or many Service(s).
- Each Service must be performed on one and only one Car.

Notice that we name the relationship from both ends, to make the nature of the association as clear as possible. Some data modellers, however, omit relationship names where the nature of the association is obvious without them, so as to avoid cluttering the model too much.

Further notation – subtypes and super-types
One last piece of useful notation is that for subtypes and super-types, as shown in
Figure 6.21.

Figure 6.21 Subtypes and super-types

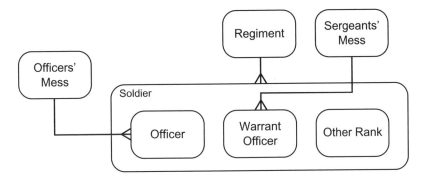

In Figure 6.21, Officer, Warrant Officer and Other Rank are subtypes of the
more general entity Soldier – a super-type. Most of the data items held about
all soldiers are the same – army number, name, address, date of birth and so
forth – but Officers, for example, will have additional data items such as the date
they were commissioned. As Figure 6.21 also shows, some relationships are true
of all Soldiers – that they belong to a Regiment, for example – whereas only an
Officer can belong to an Officers' Mess (dining club), and only a Warrant Officer
can belong to a Sergeants' Mess.

Example entity relationship model
Figure 6.22 shows a small data model that has most of the features
described here.

Readers may wish to compare this model with another model of the same business
in the description of Technique 64, 'Class modelling', below, to see how these two
techniques deal with what is essentially the same situation.

Supporting information
Strictly speaking, what we have been describing so far is an entity relationship
diagram. The entity relationship **model** consists of this diagram plus supporting
information. The supporting information gives more detail about the entities and
relationships in the model, and can include:

Entity descriptions:	These contain fuller details about the entities, including lists of the attributes – the data items – that they contain. Of particular importance is the key – the single attribute or group of attributes that will enable one occurrence of an entity to be distinguished from another. Car, for instance, would probably be identified by its registration number.

Figure 6.22 Example entity relationship model

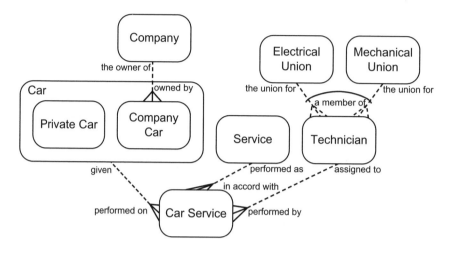

Attribute descriptions:	These give more detailed information about individual attributes.

Relationship descriptions:	More information on the nature of the relationships between the entities appears here.

All of this information – and indeed the data diagram too – is best kept within some form of CASE (computer-aided software engineering) tool that can automatically maintain the cross references between the different artefacts.

Using entity relationship modelling

The **principles** of building an entity relationship model are reasonably straightforward, but creating a real one is often quite difficult. This is because relationships that seem at first to be simple turn out, on proper investigation, to be less so. Consider, for example, the partial data model for a public library shown in Figure 6.23.

Figure 6.23 Partial library model

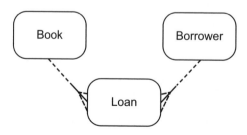

On the face of it, the situation in Figure 6.23 is straightforward. A book may have been the subject of a loan (or it might not, since it could be newly acquired), and a borrower might, or might not, have taken out a book on loan. If a loan exists, though, it must *ipso facto* be a loan of a book to a borrower. This much could probably be deduced from just thinking about the three entities, but, some years ago, one of the authors attempted to join his local public library. It emerged that, to do so, he was obliged to borrow at least one book – which, on our data model, would mean that the relationship between Borrower and Loan would have to be shown as fully mandatory.

However, we also have to consider the issue of time in constructing data models. If, in our library system, we learned that the librarians want to keep Loans on file for five years and then erase them, a fully mandatory relationship with Borrower would mean that if someone has not borrowed a book for five years then their entity would have to be erased also (since we have just said that we cannot have a Borrower with no Loans attached). This might be what the librarians want: if Borrowers have not borrowed a book for five years, they must rejoin the library. But if it is not what they want, then we will have to restore the optional quality of the relationship, so that we can remove a Loan without removing its associated Borrower.

This little scenario helps to explain why data modelling is the province of a business analyst, since what we have just explored are the business rules that cover the capture, storage and disposal of data. Such rules cannot be deduced by a developer sitting many kilometres away – or perhaps on the other side of the globe, in an offshore situation – but require careful discussion and analysis with business users.

Technique 64: Class modelling
(Before reading this section, readers are recommended to study the previous technique, 'entity relationship modelling', since many of the concepts explained there are also relevant to the understanding of class models.)

Variants/Aliases
This is also known as **object class modelling**.

Description of the technique
An object class model – often referred to as simply a class model – is the UML/object-oriented version of a data model. That is, it shows the data to be held within a system and the way the various data items are connected with each other. The concepts involved are similar to those in entity relationship models, but the UML notation has some additional features that enrich our understanding of the data.

As with an entity relationship model, a class model provides a better understanding of the data that is used within an organisation and that may need to be stored and manipulated within a computer system, together with a stronger grasp of the business rules that govern the creation, use and deletion of data by the organisation.

Objects and object classes

At the heart of an object class model are objects, and so we first need to define these. Objects are central to the object-oriented approach to software development, which sees systems as collections of interacting objects: in effect, very small subsystems. Each object has data within it and is capable of performing operations, that is to say doing something. Objects communicate by passing messages, so that, in a drawing system for instance, a Drawing Layout object might ask a Shape object to create a circle 5 cm in diameter. Within the Shape object there will be an operation capable of doing just that.

In UML, therefore, we are interested in knowing what these objects are and how they are related to each other.

In the previous technique, entity relationship modelling, we saw that the entities have to be sufficiently generalised to cover all occurrences of the things they represent. So a Car entity, for instance, has to be able to cater for the data for all cars. In the same way, objects can be grouped into classes and a class stands for all instances of the object. Thus, in UML, the data model is built at the level of classes and is called the object class model.

Classes can be:

- physical – a car, a room or a building, for example;

- conceptual – a car body type, a room's total capacity or a building's style;

- active – a car service, usage of a room or a council tax year.

Classes are represented by a three-box artefact, as illustrated in Figure 6.24.

Figure 6.24 An object class

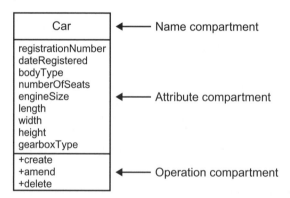

As Figure 6.24 shows, there are three compartments to our object class icon:

Name compartment: This is the name of the class, and usually relates to some real-world thing about which we wish to hold information.

In the example in Figure 6.24 we have a one-word name; where there are additional words, the convention is to concatenate them together, for example 'VehicleType'. This – we think – rather off-putting notation is known as 'UpperCamelCase'.

Attribute compartment: Here the principal data items or attributes to be stored about the class are recorded, using, this time, 'lowerCamelCase'. More details than just the name can be recorded here. To learn more about these, we recommend looking into one of the books listed in the 'Further reading' section at the end of this chapter, particularly that by Arlow and Neustadt.

Operation compartment: Operations are functions that are specific to a particular class. We have just shown the name of the operation in Figure 6.24, with the prefix '+', which shows that the operation is visible to other classes.

Having explained the three compartments of a class, in the rest of this section we shall mainly concentrate on the class as a whole, and ignore the attribute and operation compartments.

Associations between classes

In an entity relationship model, entities have relationships with each other; in a class model these are called 'associations', and a simple one is shown in Figure 6.25.

Figure 6.25 Association between classes

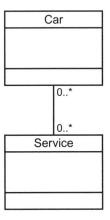

The association line shows both the cardinality of the relationship (its 'many-ness'), referred to in class models as **multiplicity**. We also show the extent to which the association is optional, through the numbers next to the line; these document the maximum and minimum numbers, separated by the two dots. We read these associations as follows:

A Car may have no Services associated with it (perhaps it is new and has not been serviced yet), and it can, over time, have any number of Services (this is represented by the asterisk).

A Service may be associated with no Cars (it has not yet been carried out), and, over time, there is no upper limit to the number of Cars on which it has been performed.

This is, in fact, a many-to-many association. These were not permitted in an entity relationship model, but they are allowed in a class model. (The reasoning here is that the class model is representing a business situation, rather than being a technical model for software engineers.) However, there may be information about the nature of the association that we would wish to record: for example, in this case, the date the Service was carried out and the recorded mileage of the Car at the time. We cannot very well hold this information within either Car or Service, so we can create an association class for the purpose, as shown in Figure 6.26.

Figure 6.26 Association class

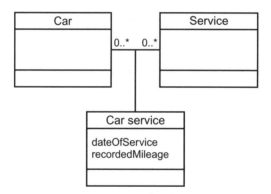

Just as we did with the entity relationship model, we can link other classes to our association class, as shown in Figure 6.27.

In Figure 6.27 we have also shown an additional piece of notation at the Technician end of the association. There seems to be a business rule here that a maximum of four Technicians can be assigned to a CarService. There is a minimum of zero, because, presumably, at some point in time the CarService will have been scheduled but no-one will yet have been assigned to carry it out.

In entity relationship modelling we had the concept of a recursive relationship, where one instance of an entity has a relationship with other instances of the same entity. The same concept is supported in UML, where it is called a **reflexive association**. It is illustrated in Figure 6.28.

Figure 6.27 Additional linked classes

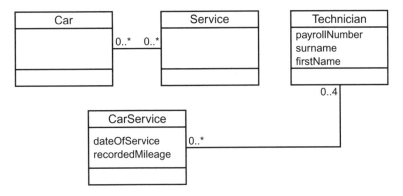

Figure 6.28 Reflexive relationship

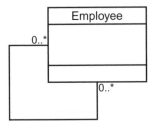

In Figure 6.28 an Employee may report to no-one (because he or she is the chief executive) but may, over time, report to any number of people (the asterisk). Similarly, they may have no other Employees reporting to them, or, over time, any number. Notice the importance here of taking the time element into account, since, otherwise, we might argue that someone can only have one boss at a time (thus ignoring some forms of matrix organisational structure). This is an illustration, by the way, of how the associations in a class model are richer in detail than the relationships in an entity relationship model.

Generalisation
When discussing entity relationship modelling we introduced the concept of subtypes and super-types. These ideas are very much supported in UML, and, indeed, one might argue that this is a very strong feature of UML.

The UML concept that underpins this is called generalisation. What this means is that a class can represent a generalised version of other classes; for example, Car, Bus and Truck can all be generalised as Vehicle. Much of the data held will be the same for all Vehicles – weight, engineSize, dimensions, numberOfWheels and so forth. But some data will be required only for cars, for example bodyType (saloon, hatchback, estate and so on). Figure 6.29 illustrates the notation used to show generalisation.

223

Figure 6.29 Generalisation

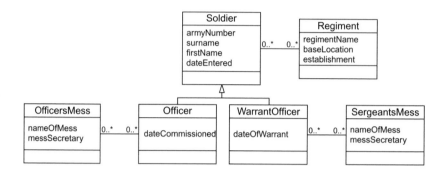

In Figure 6.29, Officer and WarrantOfficer are both specific variants on the generalised class of Soldier. For all Soldiers – including the other ranks who are neither Officers nor WarrantOfficers – we hold their armyNumber and other identifying data. For Officers we hold additionally the dateCommissioned, and for WarrantOfficers the dateOfWarrant. As you can see from Figure 6.29, all Soldiers have an association with a Regiment but only Officers are associated with an OfficersMess and only WarrantOfficers with a SergeantsMess. Notice that in this structure (unlike the supertypes and sub-types of the entity relationship model) we do not have to show other ranks specifically, since they are implied in the generalised class of Soldier.

Example class model

Figure 6.30 shows a small example of a class model constructed using the principles explained here. It models the same business as that shown in the entity relationship model that we used to illustrate the previous technique, entity relationship modelling, and readers may find it instructive to compare the two models to see how each would render the situation.

Using class modelling

Class modelling provides a method of analysing and representing the groups of data to be held within a system – and of understanding the relationships between the data. The nature of the associations – their multiplicity – represents a set of business rules that govern the creation, amendment and deletion of data, and these rules should properly be investigated by business analysts, rather than being left to software developers. However, it is less clear that the operations, which are documented in the bottom compartment of each class, are the province of business analysts, since to some extent they represent issues of design, which are better left to others.

As compared with entity relationship modelling, the detail of the multiplicities provides additional richness, which is valuable in understanding the data.

One possibility we would suggest to business analysts is to adopt a simplified approach to class modelling that uses just the top two compartments – or maybe

Figure 6.30 Example class model

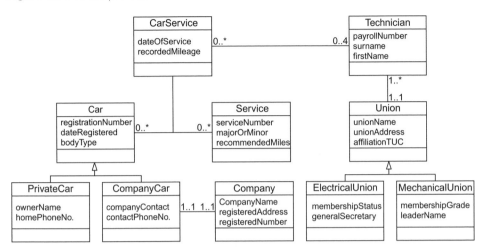

only the top one – of the classes, and leaves the detail of the attributes and operations to be investigated and documented by systems analysts, designers, software architects or software developers.

Technique 65: CRUD matrix

Description of the technique
Once the main elements of functionality (use cases, Technique 62) and categories of data (either entities in an entity relationship model – Technique 63 – or classes in a class model – Technique 64) have been identified, it is useful to develop a matrix, cross referencing these to each other and showing the specific interactions between them. This matrix is often referred to as a CRUD matrix, due to its coverage of create, read, update and delete actions. It can be a very powerful tool for the business analyst, because it will allow for a rigorous investigation of the relationships between the processes and data within a system, without the need to drill down using more detailed techniques, or to document these dynamic interactions with more precise modelling methods. The CRUD matrix can later be continuously extended, as more detail is obtained about the definition of the individual use cases and the data that supports the system under development.

Using the CRUD Matrix
A CRUD matrix is developed by listing the classes from the class diagram (or the entities if entity relationship modelling is being used) along the side of the matrix, and the use cases from the use case diagram along the top. Then for each use case we establish which classes will be affected and in what way, completing the relevant intersections between use cases and classes with a combination of C(reate), R(ead), U(pdate) and D(elete), depending on whether the use case needs to create, read, update or delete one or more instances of the class.

An example of a CRUD matrix for a simple library system is shown in Table 6.6.

Table 6.6 Example of a CRUD matrix (partial)

		Class			
Use Case	Borrower	Book copy	Book title	Reservation	Loan
New borrower	C				
Borrow book	U	U	R		C
Reserve book	R		U	C	
Maintain borrower	U				
Return book	U	U			U
Delete borrower	D	R		D	R/D

The CRUD matrix can be used for a wide range of purposes, including the following.

Completeness checking of models

The development of a CRUD matrix will help in the identification of omissions, both in the range of necessary use cases and in the set of classes in the class model. For example, in the case of the library CRUD matrix there no Cs or Ds in the column for Book title. It may of course be that these are created and deleted outside this system, but it certainly makes us ask whether we have missed vital use cases such as New book or Remove book.

Identification of dependencies

When considering the development of the system from the use cases, the CRUD matrix helps decide which ones should be handled first. For example, development of a specific use case that uses a certain class of data needs to take place after that of the use cases that create these classes of data. For example, for the library system the use case New borrower will need to be developed first, since all of the other use cases identified need the data that it creates in order to work.

Identification of discrete work packages for development

The CRUD matrix can be explored in order to note patterns in the use of classes, and where similar patterns are identified the use cases that relate to these may be candidates for development within the same timebox.

Estimation of the time needed for development

The CRUD matrix provides us with a simple mechanism for estimating the time needed to develop and test a specific piece of functionality. One approach would be to allocate an estimate for each type of access (for instance, $C = 2$ units, $R = 1$ unit, $U = 3$ units and $D = 4$ units), and total these up for a particular use case, giving an idea of the relative complexity of each element of the development. Ideally the actual values used should have been determined from statistical analysis of previous development times from previous projects, although these may not be recorded at this level of granularity. However, over time, especially if actual development times are recorded and monitored, the base values used can be refined to provide more realistic estimates for the future.

Consistency checking
The use of the CRUD technique will ensure a consistency between the models produced. For example, there may be some classes of data of which no use is made by the identified use cases. Alternatively, use cases may have been proposed that seem to have no impact on any of the classes identified. The iterative nature of the development of the CRUD matrix will ensure consistency across the various models defined, before they are used as input to further elaboration as the basis of development and delivery of the solution.

Identification of subsequent work and of increments
By looking at a particular row of the CRUD matrix, a developer will be able to see all the actions needed by the system in response to a particular event. This can then be used as the basis for subsequent development of such models as sequence or collaboration diagrams, if these are to be produced by designers or solution architects.

By looking at a particular column of the CRUD matrix, a developer will be able to see all the actions that can act upon a specific class during its existence. This can then be used as the basis of any subsequent development of dynamic models, such as state transition or life history models.

Use in prioritisation for development and delivery
It will sometimes be the case that the business users will try to lower the priority of certain aspects of functionality, or even move them to later delivery. In this case the CRUD matrix can quickly be used to see if there are any subsequent use cases that can no longer be implemented, because aspects of the classes on which they need to perform are no longer being created or updated to the required state.

REFERENCES

Cockburn, A. (2001) *Writing Effective Use Cases.* Addison-Wesley, Upper Saddle River, NJ.

DSDM Consortium (2007) *DSDM Atern Reference Manual.* www.dsdm.org

Schwaber, K. (2004) *Agile Project Management with Scrum.* Microsoft Press.

FURTHER READING

Arlow, J. and Neustadt, I. (2005) *UML and the Unified Process,* 2nd edition. Addison-Wesley, Upper Saddle River, NJ.

International Institute of Business Analysis (2009) *Business Analysis Body of Knowledge (Version 2.0).* International Institute of Business Analysis, Toronto.

Paul, D. and Yeates, D. (2006) *Business Analysis.* British Computer Society, Swindon.

Robertson, S. and Robertson, J. (1999) *Mastering the Requirements Process.* Addison-Wesley, Harlow.

Skidmore, S. and Eva, M. (2004) *Introducing Systems Development.* Palgrave Macmillan, London.

SSADM Foundation (2000) The *Data Modelling* volume of *Business Systems Development with SSADM.* TSO, London.

Yeates, D. and Wakefield, T. (2004) *Systems Analysis and Design,* 2nd edition. FT Prentice Hall, Harlow.

7 MANAGE CHANGE

INTRODUCTION

The last stage of a business analysis project is often to assist in actually introducing the change to the organisation. Business analysts are intimately involved in this because it is probably they who have the closest relationship with the business users. It is also the BAs who have developed a good understanding of the structure, climate and culture of the organisation, knowledge which is essential to the smooth introduction of change. Finally, since projects are undertaken to achieve business benefits of some sort, BAs are often involved in finding out whether, in fact, those benefits have been attained; and, if not, what else needs to be done to secure them.

In this chapter we cover three main topics:

- organisational changes;
- people changes;
- benefits management and benefits realisation.

Some of the concepts we examine in this chapter are, it could be argued, more **models** than techniques. Certainly, many of them have originated in academia, which has a passion to analyse and classify things. However, we have concentrated here not so much on the models themselves, but rather on the practical ways in which BAs can put them to use in their projects.

Organisational change (Techniques 66–67)
Here we consider some important issues to do with the introduction of change into an organisation. Specifically we discuss cultural analysis and Kurt Lewin's model of organisational change.

People change (Techniques 68–70)
Here we examine three useful concepts that help BAs to understand the human dimensions of change and to help implement the change in a way that takes these dimensions into account. They are:

- the SARAH model of business change;
- the learning cycle;
- the conscious competence model.

Benefits management and realisation (Techniques 71–72)

Benefits management and benefits realisation are, in fact, separate activities, though they are closely connected. Benefits management involves managing the whole project with one eye very firmly on the expected benefits, and in such a way that the chance of achieving these benefits is maximised. Benefits realisation involves checking, after the project has completed, whether the benefits were gained or not – and, if not, what else could yet be done to secure them.

A benefits review also helps an organisation, over time, become better at choosing which projects to undertake – just as a post-project review (a different thing) enables an organisation to get better at the execution of projects.

ORGANISATIONAL CHANGE

Technique 66: Cultural analysis

Description of the technique

Many of the techniques employed by the BA are inherently portable, in that they can be used across a wide variety of sectors and types of enterprise, in the public as well as the private sector, in large concerns and in small ones. However, the role of the BA is such that consideration also needs to be given to the less tangible cultural characteristics that differentiate organisations from one other. These characteristics are often overlooked, but the success of any proposed business change is often dependent on understanding these differences and adapting the business analysis approach to them. Guidance in this area focuses on techniques related to the study of organisational and corporate culture. While sometimes these two are seen as interchangeable, organisational culture is in fact wider in scope than corporate culture, and focuses on the social glue that binds the organisation together; it is sometimes described as a company's 'DNA'. Corporate culture, which is more likely to be capable of being 'imported' (for instance, by bringing in external specialists with their own inherent culture), is more holistic, usually historically determined and difficult to change. Corporate culture can be considered as further subdivided into two main areas: subjective aspects – based on an understanding of heroes, myths and rituals, which are often unique to a specific organisation; and objective aspects – based on a study of elements such as office decor, location and amenities, and rarely company specific.

A study of the various cultural aspects, both corporate and organisational, leads to an understanding of the identity of the organisation, and helps when deciding what needs to go and what needs to stay for the organisation to achieve its strategic goals. Theoretical studies on this topic are plentiful, with some excellent guidance provided to support their use in practice. Here we give a summary of the main published work, and suggest which of it is most likely to add specific value to the role of the BA, thereby maximising the chance of successfully implementing change.

In terms of corporate culture, Deal and Kennedy (on behalf of the McKinsey organisation) originally coined the phrase 'The way we do things around here' as a way of expressing simply what the entire topic of culture is all about (Deal and Kennedy 1988). Their model of corporate or business cultural types is based on classifying organisations into four different categories, based on how quickly feedback and reward are received after people have done something and the level of risks they take. They defined the following four cultures, which result from combinations of different levels of feedback and reward with different levels of risk:

- rapid feedback and reward, low risk – leading to a 'work hard, play hard' culture;

- rapid feedback and reward, high risk – leading to a 'tough-guy macho' culture;

- slow feedback and reward, low risk – leading to a process-based culture;

- slow feedback and reward, high risk – leading to a 'bet your company' culture.

Subsequently, Charles Handy popularised a method of looking at organisational culture by considering it in relation to various possible organisation structures, and, as such, this approach is of particular use to BAs who are involved with the implementation of organisational change (Handy 1993). He describes four main types of culture:

- A **Power Culture** concentrates power in a few pairs of hands. Control radiates from the centre rather in the manner of a spider's web (with the boss, or bosses, sitting in the centre). Power Cultures have few rules and little bureaucracy, which means that swift decisions can ensue; however, management style can be rather capricious, and success is rather dependent on the person at the top getting things right.

- In a **Role Culture** people have clearly delegated authority within a highly defined structure. Typically these organisations are hierarchical bureaucracies. Power derives from a person's position, and little scope exists for expert power to be exerted or for personal initiative. Such organisations are very effective in relatively stable conditions, but can get into difficulties in periods of rapid change, to which they are slow to adapt.

- By contrast, in a **Task Culture** teams are formed to solve particular problems. Power derives from expertise so long as a team requires that expertise. These cultures often feature the multiple reporting lines of a matrix organisational structure. Task cultures are good for bringing about specific change, but are perhaps less useful in more stable or ongoing operational conditions.

- A **Person Culture** exists where all individuals believe themselves to be superior to the organisation. Survival can become difficult for such groups, since the very concept of an organisation suggests a group of like-minded individuals pursuing the corporate goals. This is the classic 'herding cats' situation described by other writers such as Warren Bennis (1998).

Rather than focus on the structural or decision-making aspects of an organisation in order to explore its culture, Geert Hofstede (1991) identified the following five additional dimensions of culture in his study, which was based on understanding aspects of national influence:

Power distance:	This is the degree to which the less powerful members of society expect there to be differences in the levels of power. A high score suggests an expectation that some individuals wield larger amounts of power than others, and that everyone accepts that this is the situation.
Individualism versus collectivism:	This refers to the extent to which people are expected to stand up for themselves, or alternatively to act predominantly as members of the group or organisation.
Masculinity versus femininity:	This refers to the value placed on traditionally male or female values. Masculine cultures value competitiveness, assertiveness, ambition and the accumulation of wealth and material possessions, whereas feminine cultures place more value on relationships and quality of life.
Uncertainty avoidance:	This considers the extent to which a society attempts to cope with anxiety by minimising uncertainty. Cultures that score highly in uncertainty avoidance prefer rules (for example, about religion and food) and structured circumstances, and employees in this kind of society tend to remain longer with their employers.
Long- versus short-term orientation:	This describes a society's 'time horizon', or the importance attached to the future compared with the past and present. In long-term oriented societies, thrift and perseverance are valued more; in short-term oriented societies, respect for tradition and reciprocation of gifts and favours are valued more.

Hofstede added the fifth dimension after conducting an additional international study using a survey instrument developed with Chinese employees and managers. This survey resulted in the addition of Confucian dynamism. Subsequently Hofstede described this dimension as a culture's long-term orientation.

Much of this work was consolidated and extended by Johnson and Scholes (1999) when they defined what has become known as the 'cultural web', which provides a useful summary of characteristics for BAs to use when considering the cultural aspects of the organisation they are working with. The ideas demonstrated by the cultural web are particularly useful when aligning an organisation's culture with its strategy in order to provide support in the planning of business change. The cultural web identifies seven interrelated elements that, together, constitute an organisation's culture. These seven overlapping elements are illustrated in Figure 7.1. In the description that follows, we use examples based on Virgin Atlantic Airlines.

Figure 7.1 Johnson and Scholes's cultural web

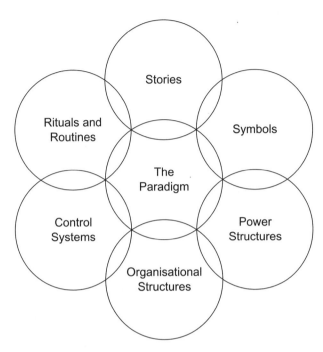

The elements of the cultural web are:

Paradigm: At the heart of the culture of any organisation are some assumptions about why it exists and what it is for. Ideally this paradigm would be reflected in its mission statement. In the case of Virgin Atlantic, in July 2009 this was 'to grow a profitable airline where people love to fly and where people love to work'.

Stories: These are past events and personalities that are talked about both inside and outside the organisation. Most stories regarding Virgin Atlantic, both internal and external, involve its founder, Sir Richard Branson, in some way. These usually relate to displays of his personality and management style and place him in the role of an anti-corporate and innovative hero. As a result, customers feel they are dealing with a small, friendly business rather than a large international organisation.

Rituals and values: These are the daily actions of individuals that are seen as acceptable behaviour within the organisation and are valued by management. Virgin Atlantic's offices are generally spacious, with many relaxed break-out areas creating a pleasant work environment, an impression that is felt also by visitors to the organisation. When staff have completed a major training programme they and their families are invited to an award event, which Sir Richard Branson himself likes to attend.

Symbols: These are visual representations of the organisation, including such matters as logos, the lushness of offices and policy on dress code. In addition to the obvious branding of a Virgin company, the dress code for staff is very informal, and the offices are very smart with slick procedures, indicating an attention to detail.

Organisational structures: These reflect the ways the organisation is managed and controlled, and the informal lines of power and influence. Virgin Atlantic's structure involves small, focused teams that still maintain a global perspective. This, again, creates a small company mentality within a large company.

Control systems: These are the ways in which the organisation is controlled, including governance, financial systems and performance rewards. In Virgin Atlantic, targets such as customer satisfaction and flight punctuality are not just measured; their ongoing results are displayed on large screens in the main office reception area for all to see.

Power structure: This reflects where the pockets of real power in the organisation lie, with particular respect to decisions, operations and strategic direction. While Virgin Atlantic's staff are encouraged to be empowered and innovative, real control and vision is driven from a small and closely knit group of senior executives.

The example here has used the cultural web to identify and analyse some aspects of an important company within the Virgin Group. It reveals a specific set of values and beliefs, and how these affect the way of working. While this particular culture creates many advantages for the organisation, it can also easily be seen that bringing a new company into the group would potentially involve major culture clashes, and that any such integration would need to focus carefully on resolving these in order to ensure success.

Using cultural analysis

By examining these individual elements and their interrelationships the BA can explore the gap in terms of cultural change between where the organisation is now (by studying the culture as it is) and where it needs to be (by considering it as they would like it to be), and hence support any proposed changes to processes and systems. The holistic nature of the BA's role is therefore enhanced by the application of the ideas gained from the cultural web and similar concepts. By taking time to understand these various elements the BA can avoid a situation in which aspects of the existing culture are likely to restrict progress, which would, if not addressed, potentially lead to such impacts as low morale, absenteeism and high employee turnover.

If we think about the seven elements of the cultural web, it can be seen that even a relatively limited (in scope) business analysis project will have an impact on at least some of them. If, for example, the BA recommends changes to the organisational structures (by merging swimlanes to improve processes), effective negotiation of the power structures will be needed in order to get ideas accepted; and the changes to the business processes may well affect the control systems.

In gaining acceptance for their ideas, Handy's and Hofstede's insights into culture can provide valuable insights to BAs. In Handy's power culture, for instance, the key is to get senior sponsorship and drive behind a proposal; in a role culture, a lot of appeal to committees can be expected; and in a person culture, a thorough understanding of all the stakeholders is needed since each of them may have to be brought 'onside' individually. In Hofstede's world, a diagnosis that the culture is one of high uncertainty avoidance suggests that there will be very little appetite for decisions based on intangibles, and more concrete benefits will have to be found.

Technique 67: Kurt Lewin's model of organisational change

Description of the technique
As far back as 1947, Kurt Lewin proposed a simple model to demonstrate a process for ensuring successful change in support of his force field analysis technique. While many consider this model over simplistic, and too mechanistic to be of use in our modern world, it is in fact its simplicity and clarity that makes it such a powerful tool for BAs wishing to make change happen and to address the emotions of change.

The essence of the technique is that if change is to be successfully implemented, then the process of enabling this must pass through three distinct stages; these stages should always happen, and always in the sequence defined. Planning the duration and content of each of these stages is therefore of key importance if all the hard work undertaken by the BA is to result in the delivery of the planned benefits. The three stages of the change process (Lewin 1947) are illustrated in Figure 7.2, and are:

- unfreeze – changing the balance of forces;
- transition (make the change) – 'moving' the organisation as a result of this balance of more powerful forces;
- freeze (often misquoted as refreeze) – creating a new balance.

The unfreeze stage involves focusing on overcoming inertia (one of the key negative forces for change identified in force field analysis) and dismantling the current mindset.

The transition stage is where the change itself actually takes place. It often involves confusion and uncertainty, as, during this period, the old ways of

Figure 7.2 Kurt Lewin's model of organisational change

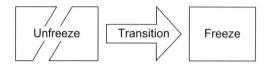

working are being challenged while the new ways, which have yet to form a clear picture, are still finding their way in.

The freeze stage takes place as the new ways set in and comfort levels begin to return to normal. It is only on the successful completion of this stage that the change can actually be said to have happened.

Using Lewin's change model

It is easy when implementing new systems, processes and organisational structures to focus on the mechanics of getting these delivered on time and on budget, while ignoring, or simply overlooking, the softer, more behavioural aspects of change. By keeping Lewin's three-stage model in mind, and being aware at all times of where we are in the overall process, the BA can really offer significant benefits. It is not sufficient simply to communicate to people what the future will look like, since this is seldom enough to move them from their current comfort zone. Often significant effort will be required to unfreeze their attitudes and get them into a position ready to move forward. The term 'readiness' comes to mind here, and some people will take longer to reach this state than others. In most cases, undertaking this unfreezing exercise will involve a combination of push and pull techniques to ensure the readiness to move in the desired direction.

The unfreezing stage is the one that is most relevant and important in the modern, ever-changing world, as it helps the organisation get to the point where the reasons for the proposed change are properly understood. Unfreezing is primarily about preparing people before the change itself occurs, and, if possible, creating a situation where they actively embrace the change. Without this acceptance the organisation will be just like a block of ice, resistant to change and impossible to reshape into another more appropriate form in the future.

Part of the unfreezing stage could be setting up an investigation to collate data that could be fed back to people to show the importance of a change. For example, the implementation of smoking bans in public places in various parts of the UK were preceded by large volumes of evidence and surveys explaining the reasoning behind the change. As a result the ban was accepted by most people, including most smokers, who might have been expected to oppose it. In fact, the subsequent freezing has been so accepted in this case that it would probably now involve another significant change programme in order to revert to the previous state. Surely this is a clear sign of a successful change initiative? The unfreezing stage is often missed in training programmes, with people being sent on courses to learn new processes or ways of working, with little or no effort being put into explaining to them the need for change. Individuals might perceive that the change is being implemented because they personally were doing things wrongly in the past, and it is hardly surprising, in this situation, if they resist the proposed change.

Transition is about actually making the change. By its very nature this is often a specific point in time, after which the new ways become the current ways. This second stage takes place as we make the changes that are needed. It is not an easy time for people involved in the change, and support and sensitivity towards mistakes needs to be available during this period as we move to the point where we have the confidence to refreeze the situation in the third stage. A classic problem here is that those who have been planning the change have been thinking about it for some time, whereas they expect everyone else to accept it at short notice as it is imposed on them.

The end of the change journey is the freezing stage, where we establish a new place of stability (albeit only temporarily until the next change comes along). The changes are accepted and become the new norm, as with the ban on smoking in public places. It is during this period that people become comfortable with their new routines and form new working relationships. In the modern world there is a school of thought that says there is no point in fully freezing, since this just makes it more difficult to get the next unfreezing stage started next time. This view would seem to suggest a constant world of slushiness where nothing ever stabilises. The idea is potentially valid, but it is worth considering Lewin's actual words in his original groundbreaking article:

> A change towards a higher level of group performance is frequently short-lived. After a 'shot in the arm', group life soon reverts to the previous level. This indicates that it does not suffice to define the objective of planned change in group performance as the reaching of a different level. Permanency of the new level, or permanency for a desired period, should be included in the objective. (Lewin 1947)

Lewin's concern was a very real one: that without a sufficient level of freezing, people tend to go back to doing what they are used to doing. This negates any benefits that were to be achieved by implementing the change in the first place. Often the simplest models are the best, and we omit any stage of Lewin's change model in any significant change initiative at our peril.

PEOPLE CHANGE

Technique 68: The SARAH model

Description of the technique
The SARAH model reflects the reactions of many people when they are faced with significant change in their lives. It shows the stages they go through, from their initial dismay on learning about the change to re-establishment of optimism once they begin to see the possibilities the change brings. The model is illustrated in Figure 7.3.

Figure 7.3 The SARAH model of change

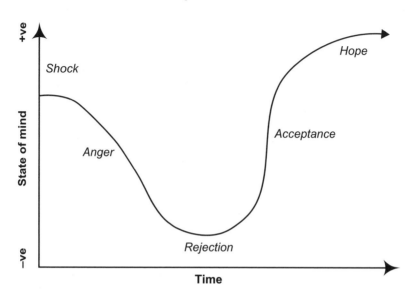

The stages of the SARAH model are as follows:

Shock: Initially people are often shocked when they hear about a change initiative. They may well not have understood the forces (for example, more aggressive competition or impending legislation) that have made the change imperative for the organisation. They have become used to their existing ways of working, including their IT systems (however much they might moan about them).

Anger: Shock then gives way to anger as people begin to understand what the change may mean. They are angry at the outside forces that have caused the change and also, often, at their own leaders, either for identifying the change or perhaps for initiating it. This anger can also be directed at others, for example BAs, whom people see as responsible for the change.

Rejection: The anger then shades into rejection of the whole idea of change. People just want to be left alone and to carry on with things as they were (however much they might realise inside that this is not really an option).

Acceptance: Eventually, though, people come to accept, even if not really to embrace, the idea that change is going to happen and that they had better get used to it. They are getting used to the new processes and IT systems and are not afraid of them any more.

Hope: Finally people may begin to see the positive benefits that the change has brought about, and to gain in hope that the future will be better and brighter. With regard to processes and systems, they start to think of ways in which these could be made even better, and begin to suggest improvements to the BAs and systems support personnel.

Using the SARAH model

The SARAH reactions to change are perfectly normal, and so should be expected. The issue for the team implementing the changes is to be aware of them, and to devise strategies to assist people through this emotional curve. The implementation plan will need to include these actions, and ensure that time and resource are allocated to carry them out. The actions identified should be added to the benefits map as additional enabling changes.

In the first three stages of SARAH, it is important that the BAs, who may be bearing some of the ire of the business users, does not overreact. Simply reiterating the reasons for making the change is useless, since the users know these perfectly well at a rational level; what we are dealing with are their deeper-seated emotional reactions. However difficult it may be, the only things the BAs can do are to empathise with the users' feelings (without agreeing with their rejection) and be patient until the benefits of the new arrangements finally become apparent.

It is also worth bearing in mind that where people are within the SARAH model is closely related to where they are in the process of acquiring any new skills they need in order to work in the changed world. Thus, the support they receive during training and initial implementation can have a material effect on the speed with which they progress through the SARAH model. This is explored more fully in our discussion of the 'conscious competence' model (Technique 70).

Technique 69: The learning cycle

Variants/Aliases

Variants include the Kolb cycle and the theory of learning styles (Honey and Mumford 1982).

Description of the technique

Various people have, over the years, developed theories about the way people learn a new skill. David A. Kolb developed his model (often referred to as the 'Kolb cycle') in the 1970s, and Peter Honey and Alan Mumford published their *Manual of Learning Styles* in 1982. Both present a cycle of the stages that people go through in learning a new skill, and they have been much used by educational and training professionals to inform the design of their programmes and to tailor them to the different 'learning styles' of their audiences. They are also useful to BAs in planning business change programmes, since they provide useful insights into the stages that the users of changed processes and systems go through, and into the differing ways in which they may need to be supported through changes. In addition, knowledge of these cycles is invaluable to those facilitating workshops (Technique 14), to help ensure that all participants are able and willing to contribute to the event.

The standard representation of the Kolb learning cycle is shown in Figure 7.4.

Figure 7.4 Kolb's learning cycle

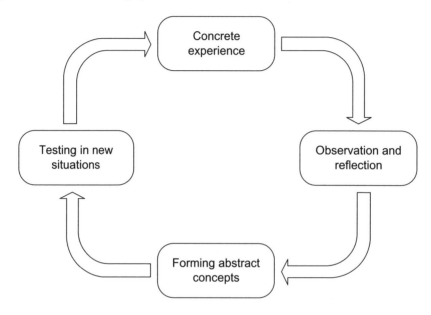

The four stages in Kolb's model are as follows:

Concrete experience: In this stage learners have a new experience: learning to ride a bicycle, say. They push off, start pedalling, go a few metres and fall over.

Observation and reflection: Now learners reflect on the experience they have just had. They wonder why they didn't get further, speculate that maybe their balance wasn't right or they didn't start pedalling early enough, and try to work out what went wrong – and what they could do better next time.

Forming abstract concepts: Based on their reflections, learners now develop a theory about what they are attempting to do, in this case riding a bike. They theorise, for example, that success has something to do with balance, gaining initial impetus and sustaining their velocity long enough to cycle with some stability.

Testing in new situations: Finally, learners work out how they will apply their theories at their next attempt.

All humans go through this cycle in learning something, but we differ in where we like to start. In our description we have started with the concrete experience, but other people prefer to start somewhere else. For example, many people in the IT field like to start by studying their subject, assimilating the theory and planning in advance before they attempt the experience.

Peter Honey and Alan Mumford, in their 'learning styles' (Honey and Mumford 1982), utilise the same concepts but characterise people into four classes corresponding to the stages of the cycle, as shown in Figure 7.5.

Figure 7.5 Honey and Mumford's learning styles

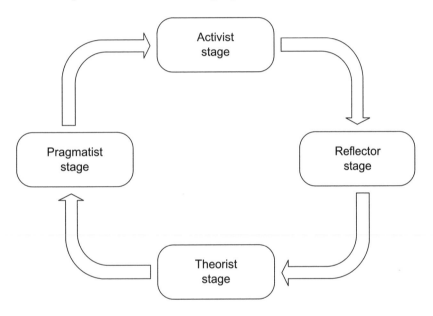

The four personality types identified by Honey and Mumford are:

Activist: Activists jump in to new experiences with gusto and are open-minded and flexible in their approach. They tend to act first and think about the consequences afterwards.

Reflector: Reflectors are cautious and like to collect and analyse data before acting. They reach conclusions slowly.

Theorist: Theorists value rationality and objectivity, and assemble the facts into coherent theories. They are very disciplined in their approach.

Pragmatist: Pragmatists get impatient with endless discussion, and are always looking for practical ways in which ideas can be implemented. They tend to get to the point quickly and act decisively.

As we have said, training courses can be designed to use these concepts in different ways. For example, one approach is to give students an exercise, let them mess it up and then debrief on how it could have been done better – and then do another one. This approach is attractive to Honey and Mumford's activist types – many salespeople are like this – but very off-putting to reflectors and theorists like many IT developers. They prefer to have the theory explained first and then to consolidate that with an exercise.

So what is the relevance of this to planning a business change? Well, as business actors try to masters new skills and systems, they will go through the stages of these cycles and will need support as they do so. The design of the training they receive should reflect an understanding of the cycles, and patience must be shown to the reflectors and theorists if they seem to take longer than their activist colleagues in getting to grips with the new arrangements.

In addition, a BA who is facilitating a workshop to elicit requirements or explore possible solutions needs to keep the learning styles in mind. Techniques such as brainstorming tend to favour the activists, whereas using Post-Its is better for reflectors and theorists. People with a pragmatist bent will tend to grow impatient with long theoretical discussions, and will want to get down to 'brass tacks' and discuss practical issues. If the group contains a mixture of styles, the facilitator will have to use a variety of techniques to avoid alienating some of the participants.

Using the learning cycle

Although the usefulness of the learning cycle is fairly clear, an obvious question that a BA might ask is: 'How do I know what styles I am dealing with?' Honey and Mumford offer questionnaires that, when completed, will indicate people's styles, but trying these on a large user population or prior to staging a workshop is probably not very practical. Over time, however, BAs will develop a 'nose' for the types of people they are working with, and, as we have suggested, people who go into particular occupations tend to exhibit certain learning styles – activist salespeople, reflector or theorist technical specialists and pragmatist engineers, for instance. However, the BA needs to be aware of over-generalising here, since a particular engineer, say, may well not conform to the archetype.

Another practical difficulty is found where a group of people is brought together for a workshop and turns out to contain a mixture of the learning styles. Here, while using techniques like brainstorming will engage the activists, it will alienate the reflectors and theorists. Approaches such as using Post-Its (see Technique 14 for details) allow the latter to think about their answers before recording them but are also suitable for activists.

Technique 70: The conscious competence model

Description of the technique

Unlike the various learning cycle models, which consider people's different attitudes to learning a new skill, this model considers the process of skill acquisition itself. The origins of the model are unclear; as well as classical writers such as Confucius and Socrates, more modern thinkers such as Abraham Maslow have been claimed as its author. Wherever it originated, however, it provides a useful framework for the way people learn and the traumas they may experience whilst doing so.

Figure 7.6 Conscious competence model

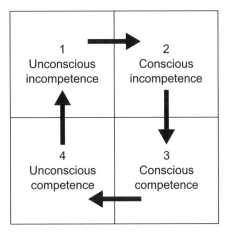

The four stages in the conscious competence model, illustrated in Figure 7.6, are as follows:

1. **Unconscious incompetence:** At this point people do not have a new competence required but they are not aware of the fact, probably because this competence has not formed part of their job before.

2. **Conscious incompetence:** Now people are aware that they are required to have the new competence, but they are also aware that they do not yet possess it. Though they may not admit it, this makes them fearful and worried that they will not have a role in the future. There is a link to the SARAH model here, as, when people realise they lack these new competencies, it leads to shock, anger and rejection.

3. **Conscious competence:** At this point people have received training and are trying to put their new competence into practice. At first this is difficult, and they may have to keep referring to guides and manuals, or consulting with their supervisors, to make sure they are getting it right. Towards the end of this stage people begin to be in the 'acceptance' stage of the SARAH model.

4. **Unconscious competence:** Now the competence is second nature, and people can perform their new duties without conscious effort. On the SARAH model, this is where hope begins to dawn.

Using the conscious competence model

Anyone involved in implementing change needs to be aware of the stages of the learning cycle and provide help, support and mentoring for people to move through the model as quickly as possible.

The starting point is to make people aware of the new competences required when the changed processes and systems are introduced. This must be handled with the utmost sensitivity, or people can be led to feel inadequate and even useless. Apart from the fact that this is not a nice feeling to induce in anyone, it will also tend to stiffen their resistance (either passive or active) to the proposed change.

A careful analysis is also needed of how people are to be transformed from 'consciously incompetent' to 'consciously competent'. Training clearly has a major role to play here, but so do coaching, mentoring and things like lunchtime 'brown bag' sessions to grow their knowledge and understanding. As the 'learning styles' discussed earlier (Technique 69) indicate, effective training needs to be tailored both to the skill levels and also to the personalities involved, and the BAs can have a major influence here as they are the ones with the best knowledge and understanding of the user community.

Even once they reach the conscious competence stage, people cannot be expected to perform to their full potential and deliver optimal performance. This is because they are still having to check things, look things up and seek advice, and productivity is bound to be adversely affected while this is happening. This short-term disruption should have been allowed for, as an impact or risk, when the business case was being constructed.

Even when people have reached unconscious competence there is more for the BAs to do. It is at this point that, in the SARAH model, hope begins to dawn and people begin to have ideas about further improvements to the business processes and systems. Ideally the BAs should be on hand to capture these ideas and to begin to assemble them into packages of enhancements for the future.

BENEFITS MANAGEMENT AND REALISATION

Technique 71: Benefits management
Variants/Aliases
There is some confusion surrounding the terminology of benefits management and realisation. There are, as explained in the introduction to this chapter, two aspects to consider:

- managing the whole project with one eye very firmly on the expected benefits, and in such a way that the chance of achieving these benefits in maximised;

- checking, after the project has been completed, whether the benefits were gained or not, and, if not, what else could yet be done to secure them.

Here we have used the term **benefits management** to refer to the first activity and **benefits realisation** for the second. However, if we look at the leading authors on this topic in the UK, Gerald Bradley (2006) uses the term 'benefits realisation management' to refer to both aspects, whereas John Ward and Elizabeth Daniel (2006) use 'benefits realisation' in the sense of an organisational competence.

Description of the technique

Benefits management is the process of managing a business change project in such a way as to maximise the chance that the business benefits will be achieved. Rather too often in projects, the team is so focused on the project objectives – delivering such-and-such a system on time, in good working order and to budget – that sight is lost of the business objectives that provide its *raison d'être*.

The process of benefits management therefore involves:

- identifying the overall business objective(s) of the project;
- identifying the benefits that will lead to these objectives;
- identifying the business changes that are needed to secure the benefits;
- identifying any enabling changes that will lead to the business changes;
- putting all of this together in the form of a 'benefits map' – in effect, a route-map towards the achievement of the benefits;
- managing the project in accordance with the benefits map.

This is best understood by looking at a benefits map, and one is shown in Figure 7.7.

Figure 7.7 Benefits map

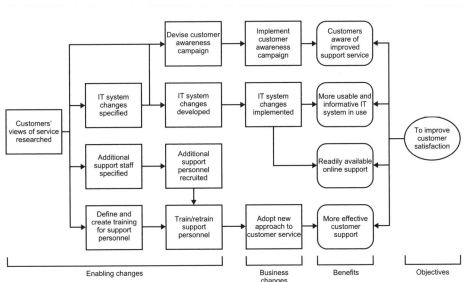

Figure 7.7 represents a project being undertaken by a firm that wants to improve the support it provides to its customers; at the moment, support has

been identified as a major problem and has created a very poor reputation in the marketplace. Based on research among its customers, the company has decided that it needs a new IT system, better-trained support personnel and an advertising campaign to make customers aware of these improvements. There is therefore a series of enabling and business changes that will put these things in place. The final benefits expected to flow from all this are: customers' awareness of the new service, more usable and informative IT systems (for both customers and support staff), online support readily available and a more effective telephone-based customer support team. The overall objective, which is to improve customer satisfaction, depends on these four benefits.

Having identified what work needs to be done to achieve the benefits, that work next needs to be planned for. One approach is to take the required changes shown on the benefits map and to translate them into a bar chart (a Gantt chart), as shown in Figure 7.8, which shows the deadlines by which the various changes and benefits should be attained.

Figure 7.8 Bar chart showing changes and benefits against timeline

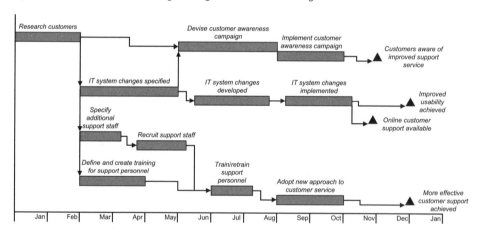

The benefits map and bar chart now provide the basis for a clear plan for the achievement of the benefits, and a complete benefits plan can be developed. This will include the following elements:

Vision: a context for the plan, which can be derived from the business case and/or the project initiation document;

Benefits map(s) and/or bar chart(s):   as shown in Figures 7.7 and 7.8, illustrating the logical dependencies between the benefits and the changes needed to achieve them, and, in the case of the bar chart, when these things should be accomplished;

Measures:	what will be used to measure achievement of the benefits;
Financial analysis:	the payback or DCF/NPV analysis for the programme (see Technique 47, 'Investment appraisal'), again derived from the business case;
Dependencies:	an explanation, if one is required, of the dependencies between the benefits;
Tracking and reporting benefits:	the mechanisms for tracking progress on the achievement of the benefits (and of the changes that lead to them), and a note saying to whom these achievements will be reported (for example, to the project sponsor or steering committee);
Accountabilities and responsibilities:	a summary of the 'owners' of each benefit: these are the individuals who have been tasked with securing the benefits, and they are usually responsible, too, for implementing the changes that lead to them.

Although there is quite a bit of overlap between this plan and the project plan, the focus of the two documents is rather different: the project plan is concerned with the technical issues and activities required to execute the project (and thus to achieve the project objectives); the benefits plan is concerned with the activities required to achieve the benefits (and thus the business objectives).

Benefits management now involves managing the project in accordance with the benefits plan and making sure that all major project decisions – on whether to accept a change in scope, for example – include a consideration of their effect on the possible achievement of project benefits.

Using benefits management
One difficulty with benefits management is that it is a relatively new discipline. Although the concept has been around for some time, the two leading UK texts on the topic only appeared in 2006, and, as a result, there is rather a lot of uncertainty around it. At a corporate level, many organisations have a feeling that something should be done to better manage the achievement of business benefits, but they are often groping towards a method for **how** to do that.

There is also some confusion with related disciplines such as change management, and, it has to be said, the literature does not always help here. Whereas a change manager (if there is one) is responsible for the overall business change, the benefit owners are responsible for specific business benefits. But where does all that leave the project manager, and, more particularly, the programme manager (if there is one)? Part of the problem is that the literature often refers to **roles,** rather than individuals or jobs; and, in practice, there seems to be no reason why on a small project these roles cannot be combined.

Finally, there is a lack of understanding of the role of the benefits owner, and here, we believe, a useful analogy can be drawn with risk management (see Technique 46, 'Risk analysis'). In risk management, whereas the project manager remains responsible for seeing that the risks are managed, it is often the case that other individuals are better placed to take the specific actions that are required in order to manage them. It is similar with benefits management. Whereas the project sponsor, with perhaps the change manager, is responsible for the overall achievement of change, others may be better placed to ensure that the specific individual benefits are managed effectively. And we can identify the benefit owners similarly to risk owners, since they must be named individuals who both understand the importance of the benefits and have the necessary authority to ensure that the required enabling and business changes are made to secure the benefits.

In many cases, therefore, the benefit owners should be the line managers responsible for the areas where the changes are to be made, and it is therefore important that, as part of our stakeholder management, we secure their buy-in to the project and to their responsibilities.

One thing that is important for effective benefits management, however, is that there should be a proper process in place to review the benefits from time to time. The pattern of benefits should be formally reviewed at least at the end of each project stage (as part of the re-evaluation of the business case); and an 'unscheduled' review should be triggered by a significant 'exception situation' arising – such as a change in business strategy, a move by a competitor or the project itself encountering major technical deliveries. By having a review process in place, the organisation ensures that the achievement of business benefits is kept at the forefront of its decision-making as the project proceeds.

Technique 72: Benefits realisation
Variants/Aliases
See the previous technique, 'Benefits management', for a discussion of the often confusing terminology here.

Description of the technique
As we have explained, we have here defined benefits realisation as the set of processes involved in finding out whether the benefits have been achieved – or are likely to be – and taking further actions required if they have not. It also includes the formal review of a project after its completion so as to learn lessons for the selection of future projects. A simple framework for benefits realisation is shown in Figure 7.9.

As Figure 7.9 indicates, the starting point for benefits realisation is the business case, where the benefits were identified. For each of them, evaluation criteria should be developed indicating how it is to be measured; these amount to the 'measures' in the benefits plan described earlier.

As the project proceeds, and particularly after it has been completed, the benefits must be reviewed to see whether they have been achieved or not. If they have not, possible ways of salvaging them should be explored. For example, if we go back to the benefits map in Figure 7.7, one of the expected benefits was a 'more usable and informative IT system in use'. If it is found that the system is not, in fact, being used very much, or very effectively, the reasons might be:

Figure 7.9 Benefits realisation approach

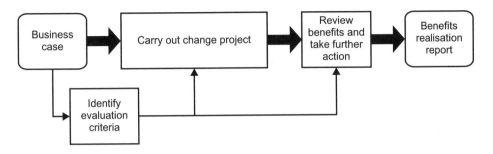

- customers' lack of awareness that they can get support online;
- poor usability of the online support;
- difficulties with the availability of the online support;
- despite training, a lack of competence by the support staff in the use of the system.

Depending on the importance attached to this benefit, actions could be proposed (and costed) to deal with these issues, for example:

- better publicity for the online service to customers;
- work to make the system more user friendly;
- upgrading the servers or communications lines to improve availability;
- further training for the support staff.

Thus, timely benefits realisation reviews can help to save a project that is perceived to be a failure (or not the success that was hoped for).

The other aspect of benefits realisation that is important, however, is that the organisation learns lessons – good and bad – from its past projects. For example, many projects may have been authorised in the past on the basis of vaguely defined 'increases in sales'. By reviewing these projects rigorously and honestly, it might be discovered that there is always a tendency to over claim for these benefits, and that might lead the decision-makers to take similar claims made in the future with a rather large pinch of salt. The reverse can also be true, of course. It may be that various business cases have tentatively claimed 'improved staff satisfaction' as a benefit, but, when assessed, these claims have been found to be conservative and have often been exceeded in practice. The 'bottom line' here is that, over time, the organisation's ability to pick winners, and avoid losers, from the plethora of potential projects it considers is improved.

Using benefits realisation
Having explained and extolled the value in carrying out benefits realisation reviews, we now need to discuss some practical issues associated with them.

One significant issue concerns the timing of the review. Suppose, for example, that a project has been authorised on the basis of a year-on-year sales increase, which starts at 5 per cent in the first year and rises to 50 per cent in year five. Are we really going to wait for five years to see if the project has been a success? And if we do, is it not likely that changes in the business environment will complicate the assessment process? Even if we do wait five years and find that the benefit has not been achieved, it is a bit late to do much about it now. So probably, in this case, we would actually initiate the review after year one, check whether the sales were on the right trajectory to achieve a 50 per cent improvement by year five, and identify any further actions needed to secure that trajectory.

A second issue is the difficulty of disaggregating the effects of multiple projects from one another and from changes in the underlying business situation. For example, if there are five concurrent projects, each aimed at a 10 per cent increase in sales within two years, what do we conclude if the total sales increase after two years is only 30 per cent? That two of the projects have failed? (And, in that case, which two?) That all have fallen short in some way? Or that the business climate has taken a downturn? This is a very real difficulty, and probably one of the reasons why benefits realisation reviews are not always undertaken. The benefits maps can be used to assist in this analysis on the basis that, if the enabling and business changes were successfully introduced, it is a fair bet that so were the benefits. Gerald Bradley's book (2006) has some interesting ideas in this area.

The final issue is to do with organisational culture and politics. It may be that, among the senior management, there is a nasty suspicion that a project has not been successful, but to initiate a benefits realisation review would make this very public and perhaps start a 'witch hunt' to find out what went wrong. In this situation, people being human, it is not surprising if senior managers just do not want to 'lift the stone' and find out the truth. Oddly enough, this may be more of a problem in the private sector, where it is (relatively) easier to 'bury one's mistakes'; in the public sector, bodies like the National Audit Office and parliamentary select committees look into significant projects and uncover shortfalls in them.

REFERENCES

Bennis, W. (1998) *Managing People is Like Herding Cats*. Kogan Page, London.

Bradley, G. (2006) *Benefit Realisation Management: A Practical Guide to Achieving Benefits Through Change*. Gower, Aldershot.

Deal, T.E. and Kennedy, A.A. (1988) *Corporate Cultures: The Rites and Rituals of Corporate Life*. Penguin Books, Harmondsworth.

Handy, C. (1993) *Understanding Organizations*, 4th edition. Penguin Books, Harmondsworth.

Hofstede, G. (1991) *Culture and Organizations: Intercultural Cooperation and its Importance for Survival*. McGraw-Hill International, London.

Honey, P. and Mumford, A. (1982) *Manual of Learning Styles*. Peter Honey Publications.

Johnson, G. and Scholes, K. (1999) *Exploring Corporate Strategy*, 5th edition. Prentice Hall, London.

Lewin, K (1947) Frontiers in group dynamics. *Human Relations*, Vol. 1.

Ward, J. and Daniel, E. (2006) *Benefits Management: Delivering Value from IS and IT Investments*. Wiley, Chichester.

FURTHER READING

Hofstede, G. (2001) *Culture's Consequences: Comparing Values, Behaviors, Institutions and Organizations Across Nations*, 2nd edition. Sage Publications, Beverley Hills, CA.

Where they are tangible, analysts need to be able to work out credible values for them; and where they are intangible, to put the case for them as persuasively as possible.

SWOT (Technique 6)

You could say that business analysis is all about SWOT: helping an organisation to exploit its strengths and overcome its weaknesses, seize opportunities and stave off threats. Don't forget, too, the techniques that feed into SWOT – PESTLE for the external opportunities and threats, and the Resource Audit to uncover strengths and weaknesses.

Prioritisation (Technique 55)

No organisation – however powerful or wealthy – ever has the time, resources or budget to do everything at once, and management is largely a matter of making difficult choices between alternatives. So using a well-defined and understood prioritisation scheme – such as MoSCoW – provides an excellent way of helping managers to make these choices and to deploy the organisation's limited resources in the most cost-effective way.

INDEX

BUSINESS ANALYSIS
SECOND EDITION

James Cadle, Malcolm Eva, Keith Hindle, Debra Paul, Craig Rollaston, Dot Tudor, Donald Yeates

Provides workable skills and techniques, underpinned with academic theory. This practical introductory guide is suitable for those involved with various aspects of business analysis or improving the effectiveness of IT and its alignment with business objectives.

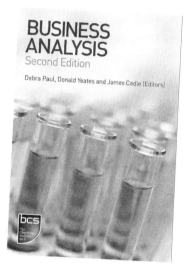

- **New edition of bestselling title**

- **A practical introduction for anyone involved in business analysis, improving efficiency or aligning IT with business objectives**

- **Key areas include: practical business analysis techniques, systems development, process management and resource management**

- **'Great breadth, good depth'**
  (Neil Venn, Seabright Consulting)

AUTHOR INFORMATION
Business Analysis has been written by a team of experts who are practitioners and educators in the business analysis field.

www.bcs.org/books/businessanalysis2

ISBN: 978-1-906124-61-8
Format: Paperback,
             246 x 172, 256pp
Price: £29.95
Published: July 2010

BCS Books, Turpin Distribution, Pegasus Drive, Stratton Business Park, Biggleswade, Bedfordshire, SG18 8TQ, UK
Tel +44 (0)1767 604951 custserv@turpin-distribution.com

A PRAGMATIC GUIDE TO
BUSINESS PROCESS MODELLING
SECOND EDITION

Jon Holt

A practical handbook for carrying out accurate and effective process modelling, drawn from the author's considerable experience in consulting.

- **Bestselling business process modelling title, now in its 2nd edition**

- **Completely revised and expanded to include 5 new chapters covering presentation of process information, a teaching guide, enterprise architecture and more**

AUTHOR INFORMATION
Jon Holt is an award-winning author and public speaker, specialising in all aspects of systems, process and competency modelling. Jon's other work interests include enterprise architecture, standards and education, and he has previously held a variety of positions at universities in the UK and USA. Jon is a Fellow of the IET and BCS.

www.bcs.org/books/processmodelling

ISBN: 978-1-906124-12-0
Format: Paperback, 246 x 172, 248pp
Price: £29.95
Published: July 2009

BCS Books, Turpin Distribution, Pegasus Drive, Stratton Business Park, Biggleswade, Bedfordshire, SG18 8TQ, UK
Tel +44 (0)1767 604951 custserv@turpin-distribution.com

IT-ENABLED
BUSINESS CHANGE
SUCCESSFUL MANAGEMENT

Sharm Manwani

The high profile failure of major IT-related projects in both private and public sectors underlines the need for stringent change management. This book examines the types of business change processes that involve the use of IT, from the reasons organisations change the way they work, to how that change is identified, managed and implemented.

- Guides business and IT leaders through the successful delivery of business change by using information technology

- Content is specifically designed to be accessible to business managers, and detailed enough for use by IT professionals

- Sample questions provided at the end of each chapter allow the reader to test themselves and measure what they have learned

AUTHOR INFORMATION
Dr Sharm Manwani holds an MBA and Doctorate from Henley Management College, where he now lectures in IT-Enabled Business Change. He has held the position of European IT Director at two leading multinationals, leading large-scale international IT-enabled change programmes, supporting mergers, restructuring and business process redesign. Sharm is a Fellow of BCS and has written extensively on business and IT-related issues for a variety of publications including Computing, Computer Business and Computer Weekly.

www.bcs.org/books/businesschange

ISBN:	978-1-902505-91-6
Format:	Paperback, 246 x 172, 160pp
Price:	£24.95
Published:	September 2008

BCS Books, Turpin Distribution, Pegasus Drive, Stratton Business Park, Biggleswade, Bedfordshire, SG18 8TQ, UK
Tel +44 (0)1767 604951 custserv@turpin-distribution.com